Medieval History and Arch

General Editors
JOHN BLAIR   HELENA HAMEROW

Rural Settlements and Society in Anglo-Saxon England

'This is an excellent book, which will rapidly become a benchmark for the subject'

N.J. Higham, *Antiquity*

'An impressively constructed synthesis of the present state of knowledge, readably written, perceptive and wide-ranging'

The University of Leeds

'This is a must-have publication for all Anglo-Saxonists and will be an extremely useful resource for undergraduates and graduate teaching and research'

Tom Pickles, *English Historical Review*

MEDIEVAL HISTORY AND ARCHAEOLOGY

General Editors
John Blair   Helena Hamerow

The volumes in this series bring together archaeological, historical, and visual methods to offer new approaches to aspects of medieval society, economy, and material culture. The series seeks to present and interpret archaeological evidence in ways readily accessible to historians, while providing a historical perspective and context for the material culture of the period.

RECENTLY PUBLISHED IN THIS SERIES

PARKS IN MEDIEVAL ENGLAND
S. A. Mileson

ANGLO-SAXON DEVIANT BURIAL CUSTOMS
Andrew Reynolds

BEYOND THE MEDIEVAL VILLAGE
The Diversification of Landscape Character in Southern Britain
Stephen Rippon

WATERWAYS AND CANAL-BUILDING IN MEDIEVAL ENGLAND
Edited by John Blair

FOOD IN MEDIEVAL ENGLAND
Diet and Nutrition
Edited by C. M. Woolgar, D. Serjeantson, and T. Waldron

GOLD AND GILT, POTS AND PINS
Possessions and People in Medieval Britain
David A. Hinton

THE ICONOGRAPHY OF EARLY ANGLO-SAXON COINAGE
Sixth to Eighth Centuries
Anna Gannon

EARLY MEDIEVAL SETTLEMENTS
The Archaeology of Rural Communities in North-West Europe 400–900
Helena Hamerow

RURAL SETTLEMENTS AND SOCIETY IN ANGLO-SAXON ENGLAND

HELENA HAMEROW

Great Clarendon Street, Oxford, OX2 6DP,
United Kingdom

Oxford University Press is a department of the University of Oxford.
It furthers the University's objective of excellence in research, scholarship,
and education by publishing worldwide. Oxford is a registered trade mark of
Oxford University Press in the UK and in certain other countries

© Helena Hamerow 2012

The moral rights of the author have been asserted

First published 2012
First published in paperback 2014
Impression: 1

All rights reserved. No part of this publication may be reproduced, stored in
a retrieval system, or transmitted, in any form or by any means, without the
prior permission in writing of Oxford University Press, or as expressly permitted
by law, by licence or under terms agreed with the appropriate reprographics
rights organization. Enquiries concerning reproduction outside the scope of the
above should be sent to the Rights Department, Oxford University Press, at the
address above

You must not circulate this work in any other form
and you must impose this same condition on any acquirer

Published in the United States of America by Oxford University Press
198 Madison Avenue, New York, NY 10016, United States of America

British Library Cataloguing in Publication Data

Data available

ISBN 978–0–19–920325–3 (Hbk.)
ISBN 978–0–19–872312–7 (Pbk.)

Links to third party websites are provided by Oxford in good faith and
for information only. Oxford disclaims any responsibility for the materials
contained in any third party website referenced in this work.

For Eric, Max, Anna, and Bee

Contents

List of Figures	viii
List of Abbreviations	x
Preface and Acknowledgements	xi
1. The study of Anglo-Saxon rural settlements	1
2. Anglo-Saxon buildings: form, function, and social space	17
3. Settlement forms and community structures	67
4. The ritualization of domestic life	120
5. Farming systems and settlement forms	144
6. Production, exchange, and the shape of rural communities	163
Bibliography	169
Index	191

List of Figures

1.1	Distribution map showing settlements discussed in the text.	4
2.1	Plan of an earth-fast, posthole building from Mucking, with entrances indicated by arrows.	18
2.2	Building A1 from Cowdery's Down, showing the annexe projecting into a fenced enclosure.	23
2.3	The chronological development of Anglo-Saxon timber buildings.	24
2.4	The superimposed plans of Buildings 2, 3, and 4 from Mucking.	25
2.5	Plan of Building B from Steyning.	29
2.6	Building C10 from Cowdery's Down, showing presumed 'setting out post'.	30
2.7	Building 9150 from Renhold, Water End West.	36
2.8	Late Saxon long halls: A. Cheddar; B. Sulgrave; C. Goltho; D. Bicester.	42
2.9	The plans of Late Saxon long halls, superimposed.	47
2.10	Late Saxon narrow-aisled halls: A. Portchester; B, C. Goltho; D. Raunds Furnells; E. Ketton; F. Faccombe Netherton.	49
2.11	Granaries from Yarnton.	51
2.12	A Mid Saxon barn. Higham Ferrers, Building 2665.	51
2.13	A reconstruction of a *Grubenhaus* as a sunken-floored building.	56
3.1	Schematic plan of the Anglo-Saxon settlement at Mucking, showing broad spatial development.	68
3.2	The Anglo-Saxon settlement at Kilverstone.	72
3.3	The Anglo-Saxon settlement at Cottenham, Phase A.	74
3.4	The Anglo-Saxon settlement at Cottenham, Phase B.	75
3.5	The development of the Anglo-Saxon settlement at Cardinal Park, Godmanchester (one of two alternative sequences).	76
3.6	Schematic plan of the main enclosures at West Fen Road, Ely.	76
3.7	Mid to Late Saxon enclosures at Wolverton Mill.	77
3.8	The development of the Anglo-Saxon settlement at Warmington. Provisional plans.	79
3.9	The latest settlement phase at West Stow.	80
3.10	The late sixth- to late seventh-century phase at Pennyland.	81
3.11	Phased plan of settlement and burials at Gamlingay.	82
3.12	The tenth-century settlement phase at Yarnton.	84
3.13	The Mid Saxon settlement phase at North Elmham.	86
3.14	The Mid Saxon settlement phase at Wicken Bonhunt.	87

List of Figures

3.15	The main settlement zone at Quarrington, showing round and rectangular structures.	92
3.16	Overall plan of Mid Saxon enclosures at Quarrington.	92
3.17	A schematic plan of the settlement at Catholme in relation to field boundaries mapped in 1812.	93
3.18	The Mid Saxon settlement at Yarnton (Phase 2, broadly eighth century).	96
3.19	The Mid Saxon settlement at Yarnton (Phase 3, broadly ninth century).	97
3.20	A comparison of 'Great Hall' complexes at Cowdery's Down (Period 4C), Yeavering (Phase IIIC) and Drayton/Sutton Courtenay.	103
3.21	Symmetrical arrangements of buildings, courtyards, and entrances.	104
3.22	Building D2 at Yeavering, showing position of the deposit of cattle skulls.	107
3.23	Building A4 at Yeavering, showing the position of Grave AX and Post AX.	108
3.24	The Late Saxon settlement at Steyning.	110
3.25	The development of the Late Saxon settlement at Springfield Lyons.	112
3.26	The enclosed settlement at Bramford.	113
3.27	The Mid Saxon settlement at Higham Ferrers, Phase 2b.	114
3.28	Reconstruction of the Mid Saxon settlement at Higham Ferrers.	115
3.29	The Mid Saxon settlement at Higham Ferrers, Phase 2c.	116
3.30	Anglo-Saxon gated entrances.	117
3.31	The Late Saxon settlement at Ketton.	118
3.32	The Late Saxon settlement at Raunds Furnells.	119
4.1	The Anglo-Saxon settlement and burial ground at Bloodmoor Hill.	125
4.2	A placed deposit in a *Grubenhaus* at Horcott (Gloucestershire) consisting of animal bones and an inverted human cranium.	132
4.3	The early medieval settlement at Catholme, Staffordshire.	134
5.1	A reconstruction of the Mid Saxon malting oven at Higham Ferrers.	153
5.2	A reconstruction of the Mid Saxon watermill at Ebbsfleet.	154
5.3	Age profiles for sheep from Brandon (Mid Saxon) and West Stow (early Anglo-Saxon). The age categories, based on tooth wear, are as follows: 1–3 = unworn; 4 = in wear; 5 = full wear; 6 = heavily worn.	158

List of Abbreviations

ASC   *Anglo-Saxon Chronicle*

EHD   D. Whitelock, *English Historical Documents*. Volume I: *c.500–1042*. London: Eyre & Spottiswoode, 1955).

HE   Bede, *Historia Ecclesiastica Gentis Anglorum*, ed. B. Colgrave and R. A. B. Mynors, *Bede's Ecclesiastical History of the English People* (Oxford: Clarendon Press, 1969).

Preface and Acknowledgements

It is remarkable that no major synthesis of the evidence for Anglo-Saxon rural settlements has been attempted since 1976, when Philip Rahtz published his seminal paper on the subject. The reasons for this neglect essentially revolve around two issues: first, the still relatively small number of large-scale settlement excavations, many of which took place in the 1970s and only a few of which have been fully published, a problem discussed further below;[1] and second, the continuing dominance of cemetery studies, especially those relating to the abundant and sometimes dazzling grave goods of the early Anglo-Saxon period, which have absorbed the attentions of generations of archaeologists (Lucy 2000).

Recent years, however, have seen the excavation, often on an impressive scale, of a new generation of Anglo-Saxon settlements. For the first time, we have evidence of sufficient quantity and quality to begin to examine settlements as dynamic social arenas rather than passive agglomerations of archaeological 'features'. Many of these recent excavations have, despite the pressures of 'developer-led' archaeology, embraced current methodologies and have yielded important new information, even if many remain poorly known and much information still awaits publication or lies hidden in archive reports—the so-called 'grey literature' of contract archaeology. There can be no doubt that developer-led archaeology has the potential to revolutionize the study of early medieval settlements, as it has the study of British prehistory (Bradley 2006).[2] These excavations, combined with the results of several major field surveys, enable a much more detailed picture of Anglo-Saxon settlements to be drawn than was possible forty years ago; it is a picture of far greater complexity and diversity than could have been imagined when Rahtz's pioneering survey was published.

The aim of this book is to provide an introduction to the wealth of information yielded by rural settlements and to the enormous contribution that settlement archaeology makes to our understanding of Anglo-Saxon society.[3] I have

---

[1] Indeed, Rahtz described the archaeology of Anglo-Saxon settlements as 'unsatisfactory, incomplete and largely unpublished' (1976, 55).

[2] As Richard Bradley has observed, however, the burgeoning of developer-led archaeology and exponential growth of 'grey literature' has created a situation in England in which it is virtually impossible for researchers to keep track of the results of new excavations: 'It is difficult enough for anyone even to know which are the major projects, let alone to discover what they have achieved' (Bradley 2006, 7). This book makes no claims to having comprehensively trawled this enormous data-set, but it has drawn extensively on unpublished reports made available thanks to the generosity and cooperation of the excavators.

[3] It builds on the author's earlier survey of early medieval settlements on the mainland of north-west Europe, which also briefly considered the evidence for Anglo-Saxon settlements (Hamerow 2002).

not set out to deal separately with the question of settlement patterns—itself the subject of several major recent studies (inter alia Lewis et al. 2001; Williamson 2003; Jones and Page 2006; Rippon 2008)—although the relationship of individual settlements to their fields and the wider landscape is considered. While generalizations are inevitable in a study such as this, I have sought to avoid a 'normative' approach: as will become apparent to readers, variability is the norm when it comes to the settlements of Anglo-Saxon England.

The sources cited in the Bibliography at the end of this volume form only part of the foundation on which this survey rests: the readiness of colleagues and friends to read draft chapters and discuss ideas has been no less important. I have drawn on countless such discussions held at conferences, seminars, and in departmental corridors, and am particularly indebted to Debby Banham, John Blair, Richard Bradley, Ros Faith, Mark Gardiner, and John Newman for so readily sharing their knowledge with me.

Without access to unpublished material, and especially to the 'grey' literature already mentioned, it would have been impossible to obtain an adequate overview of the evidence for Anglo-Saxon settlements. I am grateful to the following individuals and organizations for generously allowing me to cite such material in advance of publication: Pam Crabtree, Jo Caruth, Vicky Crewe, Alan Hardy, Robin Jackson, Kris Poole, Dominic Powlesland, Steve Rippon, Mark Robinson, Clifford Sofield, Gabor Thomas, Steven Upex, Archaeological Research Services, The Cambridgeshire Archaeological Unit, Cotswold Archaeology, John Moore Heritage Services, Northamptonshire Archaeology, Oxford Archaeology, Suffolk County Council Archaeological Service, Thames Valley Archaeological Services, and Worcestershire County Council. I am immensely grateful to John Blair, Chris Gosden, and the anonymous referees, whose comments on the draft of this volume served to improve the finished product in many ways.

The University of Oxford and the British Academy have provided me with essential periods of research leave without which this book would surely have been many more years in the writing. I am also grateful to Molly Boyle, Molly Hester, Julia Schlozman, Nathanial Donohue, Keru Cai, and Devon Sherman from Harvard University who, through the good offices of Mike McCormick, provided invaluable research assistance. The illustrations were prepared by Alison Wilkins, Institute of Archaeology, Oxford.[4]

Warm thanks also go to Christopher Wheeler, Stephanie Ireland, and Dorothy McCarthy at OUP for seeing this volume through to production.

Although having a young family is perhaps not wholly conducive to the writing of books, mine has given me the creative energy I needed to write this one: a final thanks goes to them.

---

[4] Site plans have, wherever possible, been published to the same scale to facilitate comparison.

1

The study of Anglo-Saxon rural settlements

Introduction

In the course of the fifth century, the farms and villas of lowland Britain were replaced by a new, distinctive form of rural settlement comprised entirely of buildings made of timber and other perishable materials and conventionally referred to by archaeologists and historians as 'Anglo-Saxon'.[1] This volume considers the evidence for these settlements from across England and throughout the Anglo-Saxon period, from the fifth to eleventh centuries, and what it reveals about the nature of the communities who built and lived in them, and whose daily lives went almost wholly unrecorded.

This book examines the evidence for rural settlements, yet it must be said at the outset that the distinction between rural and urban in this period is not as clear-cut as might be imagined. The coastal and riverine trading settlements of the seventh to ninth centuries commonly referred to as '*emporia*' or '*wics*' are not considered here; on the other hand, some Late Saxon settlements which were considered to be minor towns by the time of Domesday Book, yet which differed little in terms of buildings, layout, and material culture from farmsteads of the same period, are discussed, albeit briefly, in Chapter 3. Similarly, the difficulties of distinguishing between the settlements of high-status secular households and early monasteries are, in the absence of written evidence, so considerable that they have generated a significant body of literature (summarized by Blair 2005, 205 ff.). While historically attested monastic sites do not, for the most part, feature in this study, the discussion in Chapter 3 of high-status settlements considers several that were probably either themselves monastic, or associated with monasteries.

Most of the evidence for Anglo-Saxon rural settlements is archaeological, and it is this evidence that forms the basis of this study. It must be admitted

---

[1] The use of the term 'Anglo-Saxon' to refer to certain types of buildings, burials, and artefacts has, like most historical labels, been subject to criticism (recently summarized by Carver 2009, 136–40). It is used here to refer both to a chronological period—from around the middle of the fifth century to the late eleventh century—and a characteristic material culture, rather than an ethnically coherent group.

that it lacks somewhat in visual appeal, consisting as it does largely of post-holes, pits, and ditches. Furthermore, most Anglo-Saxon rural settlements are—with some notable exceptions—disappointingly 'clean' in archaeological terms, yielding few finds other than pottery and bone, and many producing precious little even of these (e.g. Millett 1984, 249). Middens and preserved ground surfaces, particularly those associated with buildings, remain rare, although the number of examples is slowly increasing. Preservation of organic materials is often poor, and we have yet to identify and excavate a single water-logged settlement of this period,[2] in marked contrast to settlements on the other side of the North Sea, where some contemporary timber buildings are astonishingly well-preserved, with walls standing more than a metre in height (Hamerow 2002a).[3] These factors may in part explain why relatively little scholarly attention has been devoted to Anglo-Saxon settlements. Yet it is an area of early medieval studies where some of the most significant new discoveries of the past two decades have been made.

Before examining these new findings and their implications, it is important to consider how certain biases in, and limitations of, the archaeological record affect the study of Anglo-Saxon settlements, as they do the settlements of all periods. The geographical distribution of known settlements remains uneven: few have been recognized, for example, in the Mercian heartland of the West Midlands, the north-west of England, and the western counties of Wessex: Wiltshire, Somerset, Dorset, and Devon. Excavated settlements are sparse even in some counties known to have been critically important in the formation of the earliest Anglo-Saxon kingdoms, such as Kent.[4] Counties such as Oxfordshire, Cambridgeshire, Suffolk, and Northamptonshire, on the other hand, have yielded exceptionally large numbers of these settlements (Rahtz 1976, fig. 2.1; Fig. 1.1; see Chapter 6 for a consideration of the relationship between the distribution of Anglo-Saxon settlements and that of Romano-British villas). Despite the uneven spread of sites, research into early medieval settlement has now extended well beyond the traditional focus on the 'champion landscapes' of central England and a comparative approach is not only possible but essential: for the first time, we can consider how—and, less easily, why—rural

---

[2] The chief exception is a small number of watermills, such as the Mid Saxon mill at Tamworth (Staffordshire), where excavation recovered some well-preserved, waterlogged timbers (Rahtz and Meeson 1992; see Chapter 5 for a review of the evidence for watermills).

[3] Potentially waterlogged Anglo-Saxon settlements have been identified, however. Building remains found during the construction of the M3 motorway at Abbots Worthy in the Itchen valley in Hampshire, for example, lay just 30m north of the valley peat deposits and raise the possibility of well-preserved waterlogged settlement remains (Fasham and Whinney 1983).

[4] Significant headway has been made, however, in filling some of these 'blanks'. In 1972, Addyman wrote that 'there is hardly an excavated [Anglo-Saxon] house from the whole of Yorkshire', yet one of the most extensive settlement excavations ever to be undertaken in England began only six years later in the Vale of Pickering (Haughton and Powlesland 1999).

settlements developed in different ways in different regions, not only within Britain, but around the North Sea Zone.

Factors affecting the recognition of Anglo-Saxon settlements clearly come into play when considering their geographical distribution. While there seems to have been a genuine preference in the fifth to seventh centuries for light soils, for example on river terraces, it is also true that settlements of all periods are easier to identify on such soils, particularly on aerial photographs, and that gravel extraction is one of the chief means whereby early Anglo-Saxon (i.e. fifth- to mid seventh-century) settlements in particular come to light (Hamerow 1992; 1999). While aerial photography remains extremely important in identifying early medieval settlements in Britain (for example, on the Yorkshire Wolds; see Stoertz 1997, 58–9), some sites not previously recognized on aerial photographs have been identified through field-walking (i.e. the systematic collection of artefacts from the surface of recently ploughed fields), for example at Chalton, Hampshire (Addyman et al. 1972). Field-walking is, however, of only limited use in identifying Anglo-Saxon settlements due to the friability of much of the pottery of this period, and the use of perishable building materials (Tipper 2004, 19). Geophysical survey (especially magnetometry) also has a role to play, although primarily as a means of defining in greater detail settlements that have already been recognized as cropmarks in aerial photographs (David 1994). While the post-built timber structures that are a major component of many Anglo-Saxon settlements are generally neither discernible on aerial photographs nor susceptible to geophysical prospection, the latter can, under ideal conditions, be used to identify *Grubenhäuser* with some degree of reliability (see Chapter 2; David 1994, 6–7). Serendipity will, however, always have a role to play in the discovery of Anglo-Saxon settlements: the impressive, high-status settlement at Cowdery's Down (Hampshire.) came to light during the investigation of a complex of cropmarks dating to the Bronze Age and Civil War era (Millett 1984).[5]

Most Anglo-Saxon settlements yield few if any closely datable finds and contain little in the way of deep stratigraphy or even inter-cutting features. This presents obvious difficulties when trying to define phases of occupation, and has led in particular to the assumption that settlements were abandoned around the time of their latest datable finds. In some regions, however, seventh- and eighth-century occupation might be all but invisible due to a sharp decline in the use of pottery and the scarcity of the tiny silver coins, commonly known as

---

[5] The use of metal detectors has revealed a form of Anglo-Saxon occupation site that still eludes precise definition, the so-called 'productive sites'. These are sites of Mid Saxon date that have yielded significant quantities of coinage and metal finds, but have, in those few cases where excavation has been possible, produced little or no evidence of buildings. At least some are likely to have been periodic market places (Pestell and Ulmschneider 2003). Other Mid Saxon sites, notably that at Lake End Road, near Dorney (Berkshire), appear to have consisted of little more than dozens of pits of uncertain function (Foreman et al. 2002).

4 *The study of Anglo-Saxon rural settlements*

Fig. 1.1. Distribution map showing settlements discussed in the text.

Key:

1. Barking
2. Barton Court Farm/Barrow Hills
3. Baston (Hall Farm)
4. Bicester
5. Bishopstone
6. Black Bourton
7. Brandon
8. Broome
9. Cadbury-Congresbury
10. Carlton Colville (Bloodmoor Hill)
11. Catholme
12. Chalton
13. Cheddar
14. Collingbourne Ducis
15. Corbridge
16. Cossington
17. Cottam
18. Cottenham
19. Cowdery's Down
20. Dorchester (Allington Avenue and Poundbury)
21. Dorney (Lake End Road)
22. Ebbsfleet
23. Ely (West Fen Road)
24. Eye Kettleby
25. Eynsham/New Wintles Farm
26. Faccombe Netherton
27. Flixborough
28. Flixton
29. Fremington
30. Friars Oak
31. Gamlingay
32. Godmanchester (Cardinal Park)
33. Goltho
34. Hartlepool
35. Higham Ferrers
36. Hoddom
37. Ipswich
38. Jarrow
39. Ketton
40. Lakenheath
41. Market Lavington
42. Mawgan Porth
43. Melford Meadows
44. Milfield
45. Mucking
46. Northampton
47. North Elmham
48. Old Windsor
49. Orton Hall
50. Pennyland
51. Polebrook
52. Portchester
53. Quarrington
54. Raunds/West Cotton
55. Renhold, Water End West
56. Ribblehead (Gauber High Pasture)
57. Riby Cross Roads
58. Rivenhall
59. Romsey
60. Ryall Quarry
61. Shakenoak
62. Simy Folds
63. Spong Hill
64. Springfield Lyons
65. Sprouston
66. Steyning
67. Sulgrave
68. Sutton Courtenay/Drayton
69. Tamworth
70. Thetford (Brandon Road)
71. Thirlings
72. Thwing
73. Upton
74. Warmington
75. Wellington
76. West Heslerton
77. West Stow
78. Wharram Percy
79. Whithorn
80. Wicken Bonhunt
81. Wolverton
82. Wykeham
83. Yarnton
84. Yeavering

sceattas, that circulated in large numbers across much of the south and east of England in this period (Hamerow 1991).

A final difficulty is presented by the dispersed nature of, in particular, early Anglo-Saxon settlements and their lack of obvious focal points or clear 'edges' (see Chapter 3). This means that archaeologists cannot take the same approach to sampling settlements of this period as to a Roman villa, an Iron Age farm, or a later medieval village. Large-scale area excavation—while by no means the best approach to every kind of site—has demonstrated that the significance of the results obtained by excavating one Anglo-Saxon settlement in its entirety, or near entirety, can generally not be equalled by investigating small fragments of three or four settlements, which may (and often do) provide little more than a few more examples of buildings and a few more dots on a distribution map, as Philip Barker recognized over thirty years ago (Barker 1977, 16–20).

Nevertheless, the scale of excavation of Anglo-Saxon settlements has until recently remained relatively small, at least when compared to some excavations in southern Scandinavia, Germany, and the Netherlands, where different, less labour-intensive excavation methods enable large areas to be investigated relatively quickly and cheaply (Hamerow 2002a, 9–10).[6] There are, of course, some notable exceptions: the excavations at Mucking, Essex, remain one of the largest in Britain, at $c.$180,000m^2 (Hamerow 1993), while at Yarnton, Oxfordshire $c.$55,000m^2 of the 15 ha investigated yielded Anglo-Saxon buildings (Hey 2004). Other extensively excavated settlements whose plans have been published in detail are Catholme, Staffordshire, $c.$37,000m^2 (Losco-Bradley and Kinsley 2002), Bloodmoor Hill, Suffolk, $c.$30,000m^2 (Lucy et al. 2009) and Cottenham, Cambridgeshire, with $c.$100,000m^2 (Mortimer 2000). The epic excavations at West Heslerton, Yorkshire have uncovered over 200,000m^2 since work began in 1978 (Powlesland 2003). With the exception of West Heslerton, however, these were all rescue excavations, and while large-scale research projects to study Iron Age/early medieval settlements have been funded in recent years in Denmark, the Netherlands, and Germany,[7] it is unlikely that funding will be available in the foreseeable future for a comparable research excavation of an early medieval settlement in Britain.

Written sources such as charters and place-names have the potential to contribute significantly to our understanding of the character of later Anglo-Saxon settlement and landscape in particular, as work by Hooke, Gelling, and others has shown (Gelling 1984; Hooke 1998; Banham and Faith, forthcoming), yet they shed frustratingly little light on the character of individual settlements. A small number of passing references in Anglo-Saxon histories, laws, and poems do, however, provide tantalizing glimpses of Mid to Late Saxon buildings and settlements, even if these appear merely as a stage-set for the main action. The most famous reference to an Anglo-Saxon building, from

---

[6] It must be said, however, that techniques of archaeological excavation and recording in Britain, while they render large-scale area excavation prohibitively expensive, are arguably better attuned to retrieving bioarchaeological data, recognizing depositional and post-depositional processes, and recording structural detail.

[7] For example: The Settlement and Cultural Landscape Research Programme begun in 1993, funded by the Danish State Research Council for the Humanities; The Central Netherlands Project (Heidinga 1990); the Flögeln project, 'Die Entwicklungsgeschichte einer Siedlungskammer im Elbe-Weser Dreieck seit dem Neolithikum', funded in part by the Deutsche Forschungsgemeinschaft (Zimmermann 1992).

Bede's *Ecclesiastical History*, takes this form, when one of King Edwin's advisors compares a human life to 'the swift flight of a lone sparrow through the banqueting-hall.... Inside there is a comforting fire to warm the room.... This sparrow flies swiftly in through one door of the hall, and out through another' (II.13; Colgrave and Mynors 1969). Even for the eleventh century, however, when Domesday Book offers us 'an unparalleled view of the rural landscape', written sources actually reveal remarkably little about the appearance of individual settlements and how they operated in social and economic terms (Reynolds 2003, 98; see Sawyer 1985).

All sources should, of course, ideally be considered together in order to provide as complete a picture as possible of Anglo-Saxon settlements. Yet, for understanding the character and diversity of individual settlements, archaeology remains our primary, and yet arguably our most under-utilized, resource.

The study of Anglo-Saxon settlements

The first Anglo-Saxon settlement to be recognized as such and subjected to systematic excavation and recording was at Sutton Courtenay, Oxfordshire (then in Berkshire), where E. T. Leeds, then Keeper of the Ashmolean Museum in Oxford, carried out small-scale excavations of buildings in advance of gravel quarrying on and off during the 1920s and 1930s (Leeds 1947). The unpromising circumstances of that excavation proved to be typical of Anglo-Saxon settlement archaeology for decades to come: it was a 'rescue' excavation which uncovered only small areas of the settlement, with poor structural preservation and virtually non-existent organic preservation. Leeds excavated a total of thirty-three buildings which have come to be known by their German name, *Grubenhäuser*, literally 'pit houses' (discussed in Chapter 2).[8] Although he recorded a number of postholes which he believed represented a 'shed' (but which almost certainly formed part of a larger post-built timber building), he assumed that the *Grubenhäuser* were dwellings (Leeds 1947, 84 and fig. 1). A similar assumption was made by the archaeologists Lethbridge and Tebbutt, whose excavations in the 1930s of *Grubenhäuser* at St Neots (Huntingdonshire) led them to envisage conditions of daily life that were, to say the least, rustic:

We have here people living in miserable huts in almost as primitive a condition as can be imagined. They had no regard for cleanliness and were content to throw the remains of a meal into the furthest corner of the hut and leave it there. They were

---

[8] All that generally remains of these buildings is a dug-out hollow and varying numbers of postholes. Their reconstruction and function, which have been much debated, are discussed in Chapter 2. *Grubenhäuser* are alternatively known as 'sunken-featured buildings', or SFBs, a more neutral term coined by Rahtz which does not necessarily imply a sunken floor (as distinct from a cellar) or use as a habitation (Rahtz 1976, 70–3). Neither term is without its drawbacks and detractors. The most recent and substantial work to deal with these buildings argues for a return to *Grubenhaus*, the term adopted here (Tipper 2004, 3).

not nervous about ghosts, since they did not mind having a skeleton sticking out of the wall of one of their huts. Pit 1 shows two distinct layers of occupation, and it is possible that when the hut became too stinking and verminous it was either abandoned for a time or a layer of soil spread over the old floor to make it sweeter.... It is almost certain that the inhabitants were wretchedly poor serfs. (Lethbridge and Tebbutt 1933, 149)

This view of life in Anglo-Saxon villages persisted for decades, and words such as 'squalid' appear widely in descriptions of living conditions (e.g. Moore 1963–6, 412; Page 1970, 150). As recently as 1972 uncertainty remained as to whether *Grubenhäuser* '[constituted] the main or most common *dwelling* in such settlements' (Addyman 1972, 302; author's italics). The first ground-level Anglo-Saxon timber buildings were not recognized until the 1950s, at the royal vill of Yeavering (Northumberland) and at Linford in Essex, subsequently recognized as belonging to the extensive settlement complex at Mucking (Barton 1962; Hope-Taylor 1977; Hamerow 1993).[9] Despite seminal articles published by Radford and Cramp in 1957, which pointed out that more sophisticated Anglo-Saxon timber buildings were sure to be uncovered in due course, it was not until the 1970s that sufficient numbers of this kind of building had been excavated to enable a distinctive type of Anglo-Saxon timber building to be defined.

The 1970s saw a series of landmark publications in settlement studies. The proceedings of the first conference devoted to 'Anglo-Saxon Settlement and Landscape' were published in 1974 and were soon followed by Rahtz's pioneering survey of the evidence for Anglo-Saxon 'Buildings and rural settlement', published together with a Gazetteer of Anglo-Saxon 'domestic settlement sites', a work which is still of enormous value (Rowley 1974; Rahtz 1976). There then appeared, in quick succession, monographs on two Anglo-Saxon royal settlements, at Yeavering (Northumberland) and Cheddar (Somerset) (Hope-Taylor 1977; Rahtz 1979). Indeed, in 1976, Rahtz could truthfully write that 'there are few subjects in which such progress has been made in recent years as Anglo-Saxon settlement' (Rahtz 1976, 51).

Despite this optimistic outlook, the study of Anglo-Saxon settlements stagnated somewhat during the 1980s and early 1990s, when many of the major excavations of the 1960s and 1970s remained unpublished and literature on the subject was largely dominated by detailed analyses of buildings. This flurry of interest in buildings was due at least in part to the publication of the impressive, well preserved, and carefully recorded building plans at Cowdery's Down

---

[9] Although not published until 1977, the excavations at Yeavering took place between 1952 and 1961 and had a great impact on British archaeology. J. W. Moore, in his account of excavations at the Anglo-Saxon settlement at Wykeham, North Yorkshire in 1952, could scarcely contain his excitement: 'latterly has come news that a hall of the type described in Beowulf has at last come to light in this country at Yeavering' (1963–6, 436).

(Millett 1984; James, Marshall, and Millett 1985; Fernie 1991; Huggins 1991; Marshall and Marshall 1991; Marshall and Marshall 1993).

The settlements of the Late Saxon period remained particularly neglected. An edited volume on the subject contained not a single paper dealing with an excavated rural settlement (Hooke 1988). Some of the reasons for and consequences of this neglect have been set out by Andrew Reynolds, who, in his book on *Later Anglo-Saxon England*, has done much to rectify the situation (Reynolds 1999, 112–56; Reynolds 2003, 100). Paradoxically, it was precisely during this period of scholarly neglect that a number of excavations were taking place which were to revolutionize our view of Anglo-Saxon settlements, especially of the Mid Saxon period (i.e. mid seventh to mid ninth centuries), including those at Brandon (Suffolk), Flixborough (Lincolnshire), West Heslerton, Riby Cross Roads (Lincolnshire), and Pennyland (Buckinghamshire) (Carr et al. 1988; Loveluck 2007; Haughton and Powlesland 2001; Steedman 1995; Williams 1993).

Thanks largely to these and other excavations, there has been a strong revival of interest in the subject and several attempts at overview, in some cases resulting from studies of particular settlements, such as Mucking, West Heslerton, and Flixborough (Powlesland 1997; Loveluck 2001; Hamerow 2002a; Reynolds 2003; Tipper 2004). It is, nevertheless, disheartening that undergraduate reading lists on the subject of Anglo-Saxon settlements remain dominated by a handful of sites excavated over thirty years ago, and that so few works of synthesis have been attempted. This must be due in part to the fact that the number of Anglo-Saxon settlements of which we can confidently say that at least half has been excavated remains small, indeed tiny in comparison to the number of extensively excavated cemeteries, which still form the basis of our understanding of Anglo-Saxon communities of the fifth to seventh centuries (Lucy 2000). Yet work over the past twenty years has generated a mass of new data pertaining to Anglo-Saxon settlements of all periods, most of it from excavations. Indeed, as already noted in the Preface to this volume, the developer-funded excavations that have dominated the last two decades have the potential to revolutionize the study of Anglo-Saxon England. This new evidence makes it possible to address a range of fundamental questions for the first time, such as: how large and how organized were Anglo-Saxon settlements and how did this change through time? What was the impact of towns and monasteries on the economy and social lives of rural producers? What was the scale and efficiency of landed production in the Mid to Late Saxon periods? What does the changing relationship between settlements and burials reveal about wider changes in Anglo-Saxon society? To what extent do the origins of planned medieval villages of tofts and crofts lie in the Anglo-Saxon period? These questions will be considered in later chapters, but it is first necessary to address a problem that has intrigued and vexed generations of historians and archaeologists, namely the relationship of early Anglo-Saxon settlements to late Romano-British farms and villas.

Anglo-Saxon settlements in a post-Roman landscape

The nature of post-Roman settlements was already the subject of considerable debate in England in the nineteenth century. In 1883, F. Seebohm, in his book *The English Village Community*, asserted that the origins of the English village lay in the Romano-British period; some years later, F. W. Maitland argued precisely the opposite, namely that 'we are compelled to say that our true villages…are not Celtic, are not Roman, but are very purely and typically German' (Maitland 1897, 222). Scholarship has of course come a long way since the 1890s, yet in recent years the relationship of Anglo-Saxon settlements to the late Roman landscape has again been the subject of vigorous debate. Indeed, interest in the cultural origins of the landscape is almost as ideologically charged in Britain today as it was over a century ago (Higham 1992; Hamerow 1997). Fundamental questions still exist regarding the continuity of the late Roman countryside—its fields, roads, and land units (e.g. Barnwell 1996; Draper 2004)—but it is the fate of individual Romano-British farms and villas that is particularly relevant to understanding the origins and nature of early Anglo-Saxon communities. A recent survey has identified some 28,000 rural settlements of the Romano-British period in England, and it is clear that, apart from a few upland areas, most of the countryside was dotted with farms in this period; in some regions, it must have been difficult to avoid earlier settlement sites (Taylor 2007). In the words of Jones and Page (2006, 31), early Anglo-Saxon settlements operated 'within an inherited landscape which already possessed structure and form from earlier periods, and offered opportunities or imposed limitations'.

In contrast to Iberia and Gaul, where late Roman settlement patterns survived to a considerable extent, there is a general perception that Britain rapidly 'went native' once it ceased to be part of the Roman Empire in the early fifth century (Esmonde Cleary 1989; Higham 1992, 77 ff.). Certainly most archaeologists today would describe southern and eastern Britain in the first half of the fifth century not as 'Anglo-Saxon' but as 'post-Roman' in recognition of the very limited quantity and extent of distinctively 'Anglo-Saxon' material culture that can be firmly dated to this period. Furthermore, a number of Romano-British cemeteries and settlements (both rural and urban) appear to have continued in use during that century, even if the material culture associated with them is less obviously 'Roman' and in some cases all but invisible to the archaeologist. Indeed, it is even possible that in some parts of Britain it was relatively common in the fifth century to find villas that were still occupied: as Higham has pointed out, we cannot 'date the physical decay of a hard-core of Roman villas other than to argue for this occurring at some point *after* the final cessation of the flow of easily dated and Romanised goods onto the site, early in the fifth century' (Higham 1994, 229).

Evidence of continuity is easier to find the further west one looks. The large, late Roman cemetery at Cannington in Somerset continued in use at least until the seventh century (Rahtz, Hirst, and Wright 2000), while the Romano-British roadside settlement at Shepton Mallet near the Wiltshire/Somerset border has produced three burials (one with hobnails at the feet) that have been radiocarbon dated to the sixth and seventh centuries (Leech and Evans 2001, 45 and 288). The cemetery at Wasperton, in Warwickshire, too, remained in apparently continuous use throughout the fourth to seventh centuries (Carver et al. 2009). It may be that if radiocarbon dating were to be used more widely in late Romano-British cemeteries—which are generally simply assumed to have gone out of use around or before AD 410—more evidence of continuity would be found, although the nature of the radiocarbon curve for the fifth century makes it difficult to date material from this period with precision. Indeed, three late Romano-British burial grounds in the Upper Thames Valley, at Shakenoak (Oxfordshire), Tubney Wood (Oxfordshire), and Horcott Quarry (Gloucestershire), have all recently produced radiocarbon dates indicating that 'late Roman' mortuary practices continued at these sites through the fifth and into the sixth century (Simmonds et al. 2011, 117–21).[10]

Where the inhabitants of lowland Britain were living in the fifth century is thus far from clear. Indeed, were one to take the archaeological evidence for British settlements at face value, it would be difficult not to conclude that Freeman's infamous assertion that the Britons 'had been as nearly extirpated as a nation can be' was not far off the mark (Freeman 1888, 74). Their settlements have stubbornly resisted efforts to find them and researchers have been forced to conclude that, at least in the south and east, they are—in archaeological terms—effectively invisible. In the south-west of England, however, a small number of post-Roman British settlements have been identified. The most extensively investigated of these was identified at Poundbury, Dorset (Green and Davies 1987).[11] Here, a fifth- to sixth-century settlement complex consisting of a number of irregular timber buildings set within ditched enclosures was established on the site of a late Roman cemetery, elements of which—notably several mausolea—conditioned the layout of the settlement.

But what of southern and eastern England, where indigenous settlements are invisible but early Anglo-Saxon settlements—i.e. those comprised of *Grubenhäuser* and rectangular, earth-fast timber buildings, whose occupants used a material culture largely derived from the continental mainland—were relatively numerous by the beginning of the sixth century? Of the hundreds that have

---

[10] An apparent example of such continuity at the Late Roman cemetery at Queenford Farm, Oxfordshire, has recently been shown to conform to the conventional pattern after all: radiocarbon dates of five Romano-British burials, which had originally indicated that the cemetery continued in use well into the fifth century and beyond, have now been re-analysed using Bayesian techniques. The cemetery can now be seen to have gone out of use in the first half of the fifth century, to be succeeded by an 'Anglo-Saxon' cemetery founded around the same time at nearby Berinsfield (Chambers 1988; Hills and O'Connell 2009).

[11] At Fordington, Dorchester, also in Dorset, an undated post-Roman settlement was identified immediately overlying Late Roman occupation (Davis et al.1986).

been identified,[12] only a small minority lay immediately adjacent to, or on top of, late Romano-British farms and villas.[13]

Barton Court Farm in Oxfordshire is a good example of such a site, in part because it illustrates how difficult they are to interpret (Miles 1986). Here, a small Romano-British farm or villa that was probably established in the second half of the first century AD reached its peak in the late fourth century. In the fifth century, a coin hoard was deposited in one of the buildings; probably in the same century, several *Grubenhäuser* were constructed outside of, but adjacent to, the villa's main ditched enclosure, parts of which contained early Anglo-Saxon pottery deep within its fills (Miles 1986, 18).[14] In the mid to late sixth century, a few Anglo-Saxon graves were placed within the, by now derelict, Romano-British buildings. The material cultures of the two phases—the latest Roman and the earliest Anglo-Saxon—are radically different, despite the absence of any significant chronological gap separating them. What was the relationship between the occupants of the villa and the people who built the *Grubenhäuser*? Does Barton Court Farm represent continuity of population, or merely contiguity of occupation? The answer continues to elude us, although some continuity of population seems most likely; put another way, complete discontinuity in such circumstances is inherently unlikely.

Evidence for continuity of a rather different kind comes from the Romano-British farmstead at Orton Hall Farm, near Peterborough in the Nene valley, where the latest Romano-British pottery is likely to have continued in use into the fifth century (MacKreth 1996).[15] A distinctive type of bone comb indicates that objects from the other side of the North Sea were also in use on the site in the first half of that century, while a mortarium sherd apparently manufactured in an 'Anglo-Saxon' fabric points to some form of interaction between the two traditions. At some point in the early Anglo-Saxon period, a rectangular earthfast timber building of a type widely found on Anglo-Saxon settlements, as well as a probable *Grubenhaus*, pits, a nine-post granary, and a ditched enclosure, were constructed. The arrangement of these features within the main yard of the Romano-British farmstead and their relationship to some of its structures

---

[12] In 1976, Philip Rahtz published a gazetteer of some 210 settlements, although this included towns. This number has grown very considerably.

[13] Many more settlements, however, lie on land that was clearly once part of a Romano-British estate. It is not uncommon, for example, to find large quantities of relatively 'fresh' Romano-British pottery and objects in early Anglo-Saxon settlements, and in a growing number of cases analysis has revealed that this material must have been deliberately collected (e.g. Going, in Hamerow 1993).

[14] The maintenance and use of Roman ditched enclosures is itself unusual in early Anglo-Saxon settlements (Miles 1986, fig. 4).

[15] The excavator of Orton Hall Farm gives an excellent account of the enormous stratigraphic complexities involved in recognizing Anglo-Saxon occupation on a Late Roman site (MacKreth 1996, 27–8).

suggest that the occupants—who used Anglo-Saxon pottery—either maintained or took over the farmstead in more or less full working order (MacKreth 1996, 27, 237). At the very least, many of the Anglo-Saxon features 'only make sense if Roman structures were still standing' (ibid. 27). At Orton Hall Farm, then, a relatively strong case can be made for continuity of occupation—and of population—despite, as elsewhere, a radical and precipitate change in material culture.[16]

At the Romano-British villa at Rivenhall in Essex, a sequence comparable to Orton Hall has been proposed (Rodwell and Rodwell 1985). The villa's aisled barn had Anglo-Saxon pottery on the surface of its gravelled floor (ibid. 65). Just outside the west wall of this building, and possibly associated with it, was a well or waterhole containing sherds of Anglo-Saxon pottery and a glass cone beaker, probably imported from the Continent (ibid. 69). Adjacent to one of the main villa buildings, Building 2, were over 200 sherds of Anglo-Saxon pottery as well as traces of a poorly preserved timber building (Building 5) of presumed early Anglo-Saxon date. The western end of this building is argued to have abutted the eastern wall of Building 2, leading to the suggestion that Building 2 was at least 'not a...collapsing ruin' at the time the earliest Anglo-Saxon structures and artefacts were in use, and indeed that Building 5 could even be regarded as an addition to Building 2 (ibid. 70 ff.). As at Orton Hall Farm, a pottery sherd Roman in form but Anglo-Saxon in fabric was identified (ibid. 74). The excavator concludes that the evidence provides no grounds for assuming a change of ownership, or 'that "Germanic" artefacts were the successors of "Roman" artefacts in strict chronological terms' (ibid. 74). This suggestion of course has enormous implications for our understanding of the Roman–Saxon transition. Nevertheless, the artefactual and stratigraphic basis for this argument has been subject to criticism, and it must be concluded that the case for continuity at Rivenhall remains open (Millett 1988).

A number of other Romano-British villas have produced evidence of what has conventionally been called 'squatter occupation', although this is now generally regarded not as representing the re-use of abandoned sites, but rather the final phase of their occupation (see below). Although in fact quite varied, these sites share certain characteristics, including the adoption of ephemeral, perishable building materials, some re-use of building materials from derelict villa buildings, and the adoption, at least to a limited extent, of 'Anglo-Saxon' material culture. Perhaps most significantly in the context of the current discussion, these post-Roman sequences invariably appear to have been short-lived. Thus

---

[16] Another possible example of a similar sequence comes from the villa at Darenth (Kent), where an Anglo-Saxon timber building was found set within the central area of the villa, while two *Grubenhäuser* lay some 20m to the south of the main complex; two hand-made sherds of 'Anglo-Saxon' type pottery were also found on the floor of one of the villa's rooms. The excavations were less extensive than at Orton Hall Farm, however, and the relationship of the Anglo-Saxon structures to the 'ultimate' Romano-British phase is far less clear (Philp 1973, 150; Philp 1984).

at Frocester (Gloucestershire), a stone-built house with a walled courtyard reached a 'peak of prosperity' in the later fourth century, before burning down (Price 2000). Post-Roman structures included a timber building that incorporated a platform of stone, clay, and gravel and is described by the excavator as being 'of some pretension' (ibid. 113–15). Its date is uncertain, although an ox skull found on the earlier of two floor layers was radiocarbon dated to between AD 540 and 649,[17] and Anglo-Saxon pottery was found in 'the occupation or abandonment deposit above the building' (ibid. 115). The villa building at Little Oakley, Essex was dismantled at some point in the fourth or fifth century, 'and the rubble was used to make platforms, probably for timber buildings.... These rubble rafts contained handmade grass-tempered [i.e. Anglo-Saxon] body sherds' (Barford 2002, xiii). These sites and others all display short-lived post-Roman sequences rather than 'continuity' per se. There is therefore currently little reason to doubt that, by the mid fifth century, Romano-British villas 'as aristocratic foci for the expenditure of surplus extracted from rural producers' had ceased to be (Halsall 2007, 357–8).

It has been argued that the kind of evidence just described does not represent the abandonment of the villas by their owners and subsequent reoccupation by impoverished 'squatters', but rather the continuing occupation of these sites by the same families, who nevertheless adopted very different building styles and lifestyles, abandoning a Roman aesthetic which had become 'socially irrelevant' (Lewit 2003, 268). It is unlikely, however, that the abandonment of buildings made of mortared stone and roof tiles was entirely a matter of cultural choice. As Bryan Ward-Perkins has pointed out, without a complex, coin-based economy, specialist production, and sophisticated transport networks, the marketing of building materials such as roof tiles (along with wheel-thrown pottery and other mass-produced, durable consumer goods) would simply have become impossible (2005, 123–37). Regardless of whether these changes were driven primarily by socio-political shifts or by a lack of available building materials and workforces, immediately post-Roman sites such as those at Orton Hall Farm, Frocester, and Little Oakley bear little resemblance to early Anglo-Saxon settlements such as Mucking and West Heslerton (see below).[18]

While sequences such as that seen at Orton Hall Farm remain extremely rare, there is some evidence for the *re-use* of villa sites in the Anglo-Saxon period, following a period of abandonment. The villa at Shakenoak, for example, was almost certainly occupied into the fifth century, but the bulk of the Anglo-Saxon artefacts contained in the villa's boundary ditch are of seventh- and eighth-century date (Brodribb et al. 1978, 205–10;

---

[17] This has more recently been recalibrated, giving a date at 95% probability of 430–660 cal AD (Reynolds 2006, 136).

[18] A recent multi-disciplinary study of the region around Avebury, in Wiltshire, has concluded that there, 'the Roman legacy...is very limited overall and likely to be virtually non-existent in terms of the survival of individual estates into the middle ages and beyond' (Reynolds 2005, 180).

and 1968, 96–101; 1972, 74–7).[19] A Roman farmstead at Ryall Quarry (Worcestershire), apparently abandoned around the mid third century, attracted six *Grubenhäuser* dating to between the mid sixth and mid seventh centuries, to judge from radiocarbon dates (Barber and Watts 2006). The villa at Whittington (Gloucestershire), which was built in the fourth century and occupied into the fifth century, produced several Mid Saxon dress pins and hooked tags from post-Roman levels (O'Neill 1952, 77 and fig. 13). As John Blair first suggested in 1994, such re-use may relate to a wider phenomenon of 'created continuity' in which ancient monuments were appropriated in an attempt to bolster the position of new landowners (Bradley 1987; Blair 1994, 33–4). It should not, however, be assumed that it reflects an invisible undercurrent of continuous occupation (cf. Higham 1992, 113).

Two very different case studies illustrate, not the continued use of late Romano-British building complexes, but a much more common phenomenon, namely the establishment of early Anglo-Saxon settlements on Romano-British farmland. At Mucking, an extensive Anglo-Saxon settlement complex was established on derelict Romano-British farmland on a gravel terrace overlooking the Thames estuary in the first half of the fifth century (Hamerow 1993). The excavations yielded not only two Anglo-Saxon cemeteries and over 200 Anglo-Saxon buildings, but also a Romano-British farmstead dating to the first and second centuries and four Romano-British cemeteries. The latest burials in these cemeteries are likely to post-date AD 350 (Going 1993 and pers. comm.). There may, therefore, have been only a relatively short chronological gap between the latest Romano-British burials and the establishment of the Anglo-Saxon cemeteries. The latter were, nevertheless, founded on new sites, entirely—and presumably deliberately—separate from the Roman cemeteries. It is clear, furthermore, that a series of ditched enclosures relating to a Romano-British farmstead had been allowed to silt up by the middle decades of the fifth century (ibid.).[20]

In the north of England, in the Vale of Pickering (North Yorkshire), lies the site of West Heslerton, the largest early medieval settlement excavation to take place in Britain in the last thirty years (Haughton and Powlesland 1999; Powlesland 2003). The results have yet to be fully published, but the excavator has already offered tantalizing glimpses of an interpretation that is radically different from the one put forward above (Powlesland 1997). The settlement site at West Heslerton covered some 20 ha and was occupied—apparently continuously—from the late fourth century until at least the late eighth century.

---

[19] Graves previously thought also to be of Mid Saxon date, which carefully follow the alignment of the ruined villa buildings, have, however, recently been radiocarbon dated to between the mid fifth and mid sixth centuries (Broadribb et al. 1973, 33–4 and figs. 16–17; Simmonds et al. 2011).

[20] The early Anglo-Saxon occupation at Lakenheath (Suffolk) also overlies a Romano-British settlement which survived at least into the late fourth century, yet 'where the Roman and Saxon settlements occupy the same space, there are significant deposits of worked, buried soils which…can be seen to be lying between the Roman and Saxon features' (Caruth 2005).

The excavator has suggested that even in the fifth century, the settlement was large and not merely organized, but planned; indeed he has described it as 'a proto-type village or even proto-type town' (Powlesland 1997, 110; this is considered in greater detail in Chapter 3). Aerial photographs show other extensive settlement complexes in the Vale of Pickering, leading him to suggest that the area was densely populated throughout the fourth to sixth centuries. This runs counter to the generally accepted view, based on both written and archaeological sources, that there was a marked decline of population at the end of the Roman period in many, probably most, regions of Britain. What is more, there is evidence at West Heslerton for Anglo-Saxon re-use or possibly even maintenance of Romano-British enclosures (Powlesland 1997). A Romano-British religious complex with stone structures interpreted as shrines lies to the south of the Anglo-Saxon settlement, and it has been suggested that this complex also remained in use into the early Anglo-Saxon period (ibid.). It is perhaps best not to draw firm conclusions on the basis of interim statements, but it is already clear that West Heslerton will change the way we think about the post-Roman landscape of northern England.

There are, of course, other examples of Anglo-Saxon settlements overlying, or adjacent to, late Romano-British farms and villas. These are nevertheless in the minority. Furthermore, in each case—including West Heslerton—the architecture, settlement layout, and material culture associated with the latest Romano-British phases and the earliest Anglo-Saxon phases are radically different in almost every respect, as we shall see in the following chapters.

This brings us to one of the most contentious issues in the archaeology of this period, namely the extent to which people and ideas from the European mainland were responsible for the distinctive character of early Anglo-Saxon settlements. There has been a tendency since the 1990s to downplay interpretations that present the archaeology of this period as essentially 'intrusive', and to see the radical changes in material culture instead as the result of internal developments (e.g. Lucy 2000). But it is possible both to accept that the number of immigrants was, overall, relatively small *and* to recognize that there were dramatic discontinuities in material culture, the economy, and social relations. As Wickham has argued, 'it seems inescapable to link this collapse with the withdrawal of the Roman state' (Wickham 2005, 309). There is a growing consensus that Germanic immigration—on whatever scale—was the result, not the cause, of the demise of Roman Britain and, furthermore, that the distribution of early Anglo-Saxon settlements and burials broadly mirrors that of Romano-British rural settlement—at least of villas—rather than marking the progress of a mass migration (cf. Halsall 2005, 2007). It is clear that, as elite wealth and hence demand collapsed in the early fifth century, housing underwent a rapid and complete transformation, seen in the shift to smaller, simpler structures built of timber; the form that housing ultimately took during the fifth and sixth centuries, however, was largely derived from the other side of the North Sea, as we shall see in Chapter 2.

2

Anglo-Saxon buildings: form, function, and social space

The study of the Anglo-Saxon house[1]

In 1958, in the first major survey of the evidence for the Anglo-Saxon house, Ralegh Radford predicted that evidence for timber farmhouses built of earth-fast posts, similar to those that had recently been excavated in Westphalia, would be found in England were large-scale area excavation to be adopted (1958, 28; Winkelmann 1958).[2] Sutton Courtenay served him as an illustration of 'what must have been lost by the excavator's inability to carry out work on an adequate scale' (ibid. 29). Within a few years of his prediction, the remains of Anglo-Saxon timber buildings were indeed recognized in England. These, however, were smaller and less complex than the longhouses which were, from the Iron Age to the Migration Period, the main type of farmhouse found in the continental North Sea regions, in which byre and living area lay under one roof, supported on rows of massive internal posts (Hamerow 2002a, 14–26). The 'Anglo-Saxon house' in contrast averaged only 8–10 metres in length and 4–5 metres in width, lacked a byre, and supported the weight of the roof on the walls (e.g. Fig. 2.1).[3] A further forty years of excavation has underscored the impressive scale and complexity of Continental longhouses (which can reach over 60m in length and contain five or more rooms: ibid.), while confirming

---

[1] Elements of this chapter are based on Hamerow 1999.

[2] At the time when Radford wrote his article, the great halls of the Northumbrian royal vill at Yeavering had already been uncovered, but no ordinary Anglo-Saxon houses had yet been published, although the building at Linford, Essex had been excavated in 1955 (see Chapter 1; Barton 1962).

[3] The term 'house' is used here to refer to the type of rectangular, earth-fast timber building widely found on Anglo-Saxon settlements, while recognizing that not all such buildings necessarily served as dwellings (see below). John Hines has pointed out that the term 'hall', which is widely used by archaeologists to refer to these buildings, should be restricted to the large buildings described in the literature of the period which are associated with assembly, cult activities, and political leaders, and seen in the archaeological record only at a few high-status sites (see below). There is no evidence that ordinary houses were referred to as 'halls', or that they served the same range of functions (J. Hines, pers. comm.).

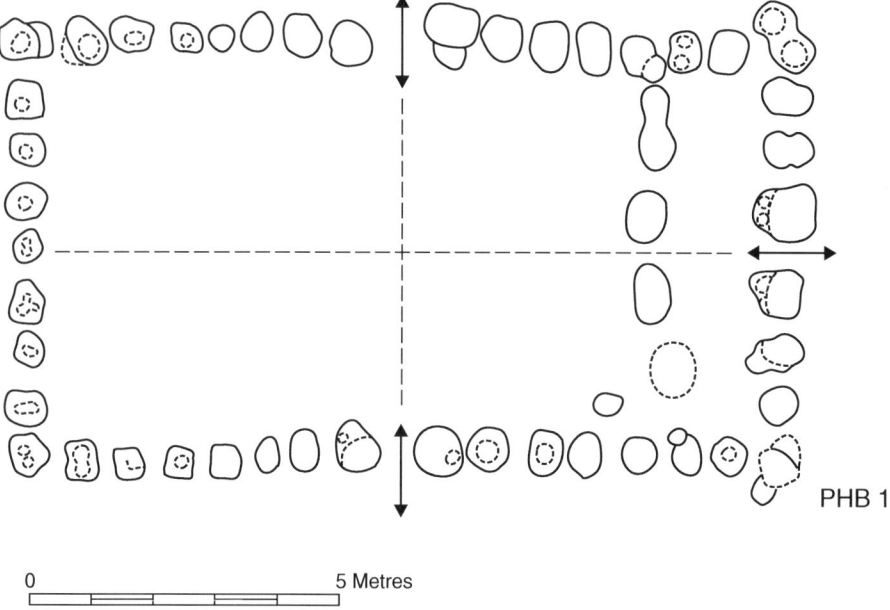

Fig. 2.1. Plan of an earth-fast, posthole building from Mucking, with entrances indicated by arrows (after Hamerow 1993).

the impression that the Anglo-Saxon house—at least in the fifth and sixth centuries—was small and simple in comparison. The progress made in the fifty years since Radford described the study of the Anglo-Saxon house as 'one of the most intractable problems in the whole range of early medieval studies' (1958, 27) has been impressive, yet key issues regarding its construction and function remain unresolved.

Origins of the Anglo-Saxon timber building tradition

The origins of the timber building tradition seen in early Anglo-Saxon England have generated considerable discussion which itself mirrors a wider debate regarding the cultural affinities of early Anglo-Saxon material culture. Indeed, the primary objective of many published attempts at reconstruction has been to discern whether particular features and constructional techniques are Romano-British or Germanic in origin.

In his 1976 overview of the subject, Rahtz asserted that the buildings seen at West Stow and Mucking had late Roman origins (1976, 56), echoing a view previously expressed by Addyman (1972, 274). Dixon pursued this line of argument to its logical conclusion in an article entitled 'How Saxon is the Saxon House?', suggesting that, in view of the marked differences between the buildings found in southern Britain during the fifth to seventh centuries and contemporary examples on the European mainland—in particular the absence of the longhouse in England—the predecessor of the Anglo-Saxon house was most likely to have been Romano-British (1982). His article raised important questions and reflected a wider mood of dissatisfaction among British archaeologists in the 1970s and 1980s with the use of migration as a sweeping explanation for the changes in material culture apparent in lowland Britain in the fifth and sixth centuries (Hamerow 1997). The introduction of a possible Romano-Saxon hybrid into the debate, however, merely left archaeologists with a more complex—but still unresolved—dilemma, as aptly summarized by Marshall and Marshall:

> [The Anglo-Saxon house] appears to bear little resemblance either to earlier Romano-British or to Continental models.... The hybrid Anglo-Saxon style seems to appear full-blown with no examples of development from the two potentially ancestral traditions.... The consensus... was that the Anglo-Saxon building style was predominantly home grown. (Marshall and Marshall 1991, 29)

Attempts to resolve this paradox have tended to concentrate on particular constructional techniques and on the overall 'shape' of the buildings (James et al. 1985; Marshall and Marshall 1991; Marshall and Marshall 1993; Zimmermann 1988). The extent to which the basic form of the Anglo-Saxon house reflected or ignored wider architectural trends has, however, until recently received little detailed attention.[4]

Before considering whether Anglo-Saxon buildings reflect wider European developments, it is important to stress that, despite the apparent absence of the longhouse in England,[5] the number of Continental examples of byre-less buildings of the kind found in England is growing and they can no longer be described as rare (James et al. 1985, 199; Hamerow 1999, fig. 2). Continental archaeologists, furthermore, no longer dismiss these as 'sheds' and 'outhouses' (Dixon 1982, 278); instead they regard them as 'short houses', as at Wijster in the Dutch province of Drenthe (whose Type BII buildings provide close parallels for buildings at West Stow, Suffolk; Van Es 1967, 74 ff.; West 1986, 112), or Vorbasse and Nørre Snede in central Jutland, where small houses interpreted as living quarters and possibly workshops (some with no, or only one pair of, internal roof-supporting posts) were nearly as common as longhouses in the fifth and sixth centuries (Hansen 1987, 180, figs. 7.8, 7.10, 7.11). The need to look to a late Romano-British timber building tradition (which itself has left relatively little trace) to explain the basic form of the early Anglo-Saxon house is thus unnecessary and the parallels remain inconclusive (Hamerow 1999, 170).

---

[4] James et al. 1985 forms a notable exception.
[5] A possible longhouse has, however, recently been identified at Eye, Suffolk (J. Newman and J. Tipper, pers. comm.).

The use of a 'two-square module' has been identified by James, Marshall, and Millett in the layout of some Romano-British buildings and more than half of Anglo-Saxon buildings (1985).[6] The two-square module and its variants can also be applied to Continental buildings (ibid. 203), although Marshall and Marshall suggest that this was 'a tradition adopted from the Romans on the Continent' which was then 'assimilated into a Romano-British tradition of building' (1993, 395). Its use, however, was not confined to former Imperial territory, although examples from beyond the frontier are rare and mostly found in the Netherlands (Tummuscheit 1995, 113). In fact, the layout of at least some Anglo-Saxon buildings compares more closely with buildings on the Continent than has generally been appreciated. Metrical analysis of buildings has revealed a high degree of dimensional coherence around the North Sea littoral, including Anglo-Saxon England (Zimmermann 1988). Zimmermann's comparison of the ground plans of a number of Continental buildings with English examples reveals a striking correspondence in terms of the placement of walls, entrances, pairs of roof-supporting posts, and subdivisions (Zimmermann 1988). This suggests widespread and long-lived correlations between templates or modules used in the layout of buildings throughout these regions from the Iron Age to the Middle Ages. This dimensional regularity implies a conservative building tradition as well as a considerable degree of contact.[7]

There is, then, considerable evidence for Continental precursors of the Anglo-Saxon 'wall-post' house appearing alongside longhouses, and for the adoption in much of Anglo-Saxon England of building templates in use on the European mainland. Furthermore, Tummuscheit has shown that the percentage of Continental buildings without rows of internal roof supports and without byres increased in the fifth and sixth centuries (Zimmermann 1988, 472 and 1992, 139; Tummuscheit 1995, 111–15, Karte 4),[8] while during the same period the length of longhouses decreased markedly in much of the North Sea coastal zone (cf. Zimmermann 1992, 139; Hvass 1983, 131).

---

[6] This refers to rectangular buildings laid out as two equal squares, usually to either side of centrally positioned doorways.

[7] Herschend has, furthermore, noted a remarkable parallel for the unusual layout of the large building C12 at Cowdery's Down (Herschend 1998, fig. 3). House XV from Wijster (NL), dated to the later phases of the settlement, is in effect the living-room end of a longhouse, with four sets of paired wall posts as well as four pairs of inner roof-supporting posts and opposing central doorways. In the eastern gable end (where the byre would normally be located), a further entrance leads into a small room from which the main body of the building could be entered. At the west end is another, somewhat larger room. While their construction techniques differ, the layouts of Wijster XV and Cowdery's Down C12 are strikingly similar. This particular layout is, however, rare both on the Continent and in England, although many longhouses had a third entrance sited in the eastern gable end (e.g. Flögeln Houses 15, 42, 43, 44, 64, 55, 98, 111, etc. Zimmermann 1992), as did some English buildings (see below).

[8] The percentage is highest in the Netherlands (Tummuscheit 1995). In a typology of Dutch house types proposed by Waterbolk, the Anglo-Saxon house most closely resembles Type Odoorn A, dated c.550–650 (Waterbolk 1982, 106). West Stow Building 2, for example, makes similar use of double posts (West 1986, 111, fig. 10).

Anglo-Saxon timber buildings should be considered against the background of these wider developments around the North Sea that suggest that the 'typical' early Anglo-Saxon house is related to a long-lived building tradition found across much of north-west Europe. This is not to deny the likelihood that Anglo-Saxon buildings were influenced in various ways by indigenous traditions. Certain features appearing in the later sixth or seventh centuries—such as double-plank construction and annexes at the gable ends of buildings—are, furthermore, distinctively 'English', though both are comparatively rare (see below, James et al. 1985, 205). Other features once believed to be Romano-British in origin, such as post-in-trench construction (Rahtz 1976, 85), are now considered unlikely to have been common in Late Roman Britain (James et al. 1985, 203).

Two explanations for the absence of the longhouse in England and the origins of the Anglo-Saxon house are generally posited. The first, as expressed by James, Marshall, and Millett, is that 'Germanic immigrants [adopted] British buildings...but still used their own constructional techniques developed...to imitate the fine stone buildings of early times' (1985, 206). The close links between the Anglo-Saxon house and Continental buildings in regions well beyond the Imperial frontier appear to rule this out. The alternative explanation, namely that the 'idea' of the Anglo-Saxon house was imported from the Continent, even if many of its occupants were descendants of the Romano-British population seeking to emulate the politically ascendant Germanic elite, is more plausible (ibid.).[9] There is, of course, no reason to assume that timber buildings in Northumbria or the West Midlands would have developed along exactly the same lines as those in the south and east of England, although buildings have been identified in Northumberland that would not look out of place in East Anglia or Essex (e.g. Thirlings Buildings G, H, and I; O'Brien and Miket 1991). The absence of the longhouse in England seems likely, therefore, to be the result of the combined impact of migration and acculturation, and of changes in the composition and economy of the household. The fact that the *Grubenhaus* is found throughout early Anglo-Saxon England in a form apparently unchanged from the European mainland, as discussed later in this chapter, strongly suggests that the reason for the absence of the longhouse has little to do with ethnic identity. The construction of a longhouse and associated buildings as seen in the enclosed, ancestral farmstead complexes of north-west Europe was a social act as much as a technical one; it required access not only to substantial quantities of material capital (i.e. timber[10]) but also

---

[9] The milder English climate has also been put forward as a possible explanation for the lack of longhouses, but Bede notes in his *Ecclesiastical History* that in the mild climate of Ireland 'there is no need to store hay in summer for winter use or to build stables for beasts', implying that in eighth-century Northumbria, at least, it was necessary to do both (see below; *HE* I.i).

[10] The raw materials required to reconstruct Building A from the settlement at Thirlings (Northumberland), which measured 12m x 6m, included: *c.*30 tons of green, fifty- to sixty-year-old oak, 'substantial quantities' of willow, hazel, and birch for the wattle panelling, *c.*25 tons of clay, straw, and water, seventy ash poles, 1,800 bundles of reed, and 125 bundles of sedge (Mills 1999, 70).

to considerable social capital in the form of reciprocal labour obligations, perhaps extending across several communities.[11] Social capital in this form may have been difficult to accumulate during the social, economic, and political upheavals of the fifth and sixth centuries.

Form and chronological development: an overview

The large numbers and excellent preservation of excavated buildings from the Late Roman Iron Age and early medieval period along the Continental North Sea coast have enabled detailed typological studies to be undertaken (e.g. van Es 1967; Zimmermann 1988; Waterbolk 1991; reviewed in Hamerow 2002a, 14–26). No comparable typological sequence exists, however, for Anglo-Saxon timber buildings.[12] In his seminal study of 1972, Addyman felt it was simply too soon to classify such buildings, of which few examples were as yet known, although he was the first to recognize the general trend from individual post construction to post-in-trench, and occasionally sill-beam, construction in the Mid and Late Saxon periods (1972, 304). More than three decades later, however, it is hard to blame the absence of a building typology on a lack of examples. There have been several attempts to reconstruct the superstructure of Anglo-Saxon buildings, yet while these help us assess their visual impact and the resources required in their construction, they bring us no closer to understanding how and why architectural forms changed over time (e.g. Addyman 1964; Addyman et al. 1972; Millett 1984; O'Brien and Miket 1991). The difficulty of dating such buildings must be partly to blame for the absence of a clear architectural typology for Anglo-Saxon England, while the irregularity and incompleteness of many ground plans make them difficult to 'read'.

These difficulties notwithstanding, two studies undertaken by Marshall and Marshall point to certain trends (1991; 1993). Their work suggests that fifth-century buildings adhered most closely in layout to the two-square module and its variants. They were, furthermore, uniformly small (i.e. less than 12m in length), aligned east–west, and built using timbers set into individual postholes. The sixth century saw somewhat greater variation in the length and proportions of buildings. The use of foundation trenches was introduced towards the end of that century, as were annexes at one or both gable ends (Fig. 2.2); the latter, however, were quite rare and had largely gone out of use by the eighth century (though see below, n. 31). The first exceptionally large buildings (i.e. with floor

---

[11] By social or symbolic capital I follow Bourdieu's definition of the obligation and prestige that is accumulated, sometimes over generations, by means of services rendered and gifts bestowed (Bourdieu 1990).

[12] A comparison of British excavation reports such as those for Cowdery's Down and West Stow, in which each building receives detailed description, with German, Dutch, and Danish reports, which frequently discuss buildings according to type rather than individually, reflects the difficulty of classifying Anglo-Saxon buildings and the consequent tendency to see each as unique (e.g. Millett 1984; West 1986).

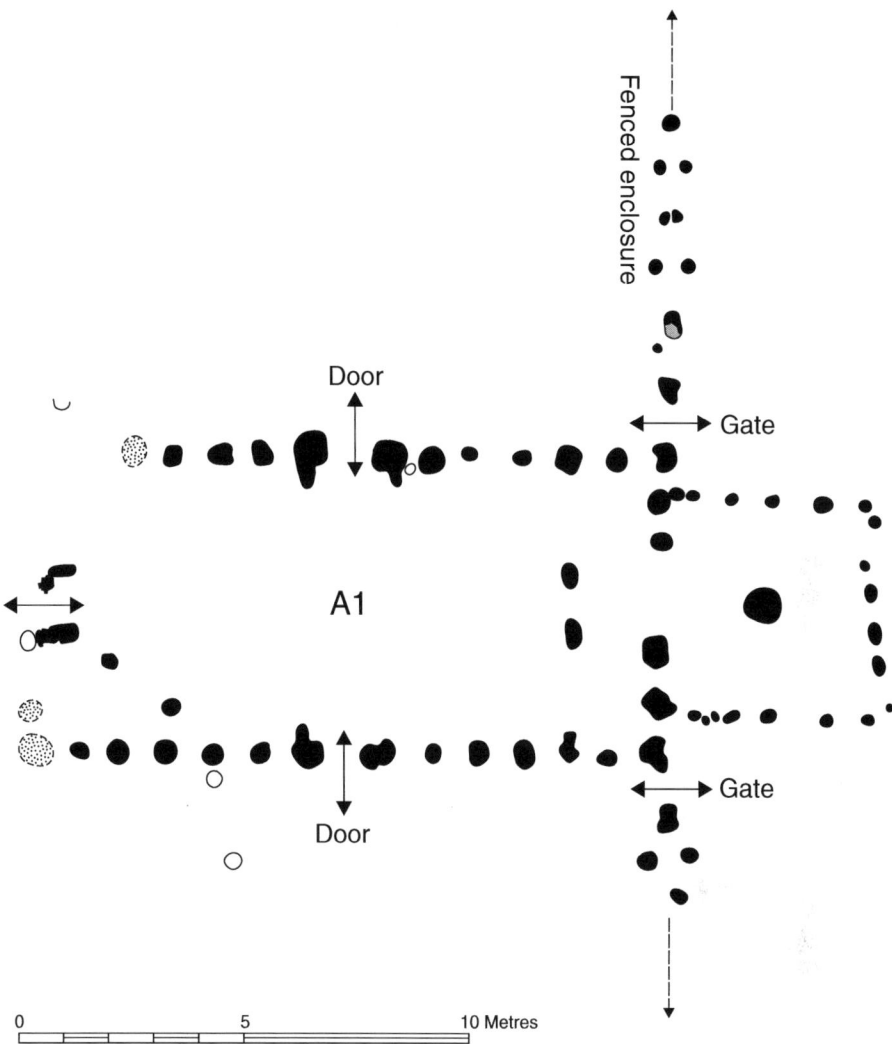

Fig. 2.2. Building A1 from Cowdery's Down, showing the annexe projecting into a fenced enclosure (after Millett and James 1984).

areas greater than 100 m²) appeared c.600. Very small buildings (i.e. less than 6m in length) also became more common in the seventh century. Roughly half of buildings were now constructed using foundation trenches and, for the first time, a significant proportion, roughly one-third, were aligned north–south.[13]

---

[13] In northern Germany, the Netherlands, and southern/central Denmark, residential buildings (indeed nearly all buildings) were almost invariably aligned east–west during the fifth to seventh centuries. From the eighth century, however, it is not uncommon to find buildings, especially barns and sheds, aligned north–south.

24   *Buildings: form, function, and social space*

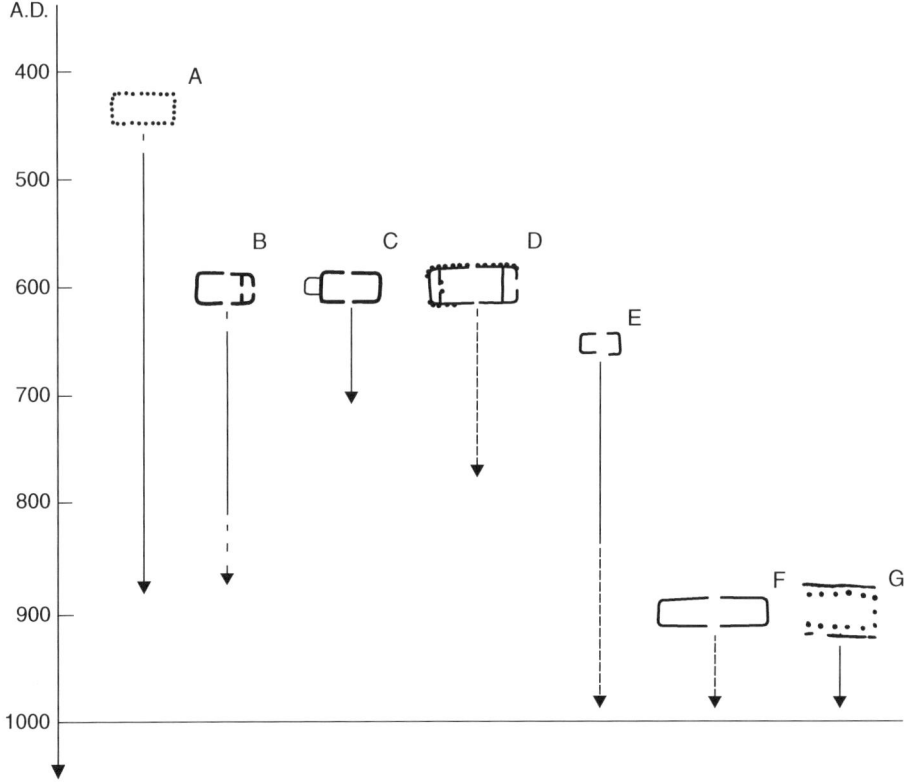

Fig. 2.3. The chronological development of Anglo-Saxon timber buildings.

By the eighth and ninth centuries, foundation trenches were used in more than 75 per cent of buildings and the two-square module had ceased to predominate as a wider range of proportions came into use. Indeed, the Late Saxon period is marked by a diversification of building forms and constructional techniques generally, as will be seen shortly. By the tenth century, building with continuous foundation trenches was 'becoming obsolete' (Gardiner 1990, 242).[14] Instead there was a trend towards buildings with load-bearing side walls, and shallower (or even non-existent) end-wall trenches; around the beginning of the eleventh century, there appears in some cases to have been a return to the use of posts set into individual postholes, as at North Elmham (Norfolk) (Wade-Martins 1980, fig. 131; Gardiner 1990, 242). Despite the difficulties of dating such buildings closely, a tentative attempt to depict this development in diagrammatic form is shown in Fig. 2.3.

---

[14] The use of post-in-trench construction using discontinuous trenches, however, persisted into the twelfth century and possibly even into the thirteenth (M. Gardiner, pers. comm.).

Building the Anglo-Saxon house

Standardized ground plans

A number of studies have sought to identify a system of standard lengths used in Anglo-Saxon buildings and to establish whether such a system, if it existed, had Roman or Germanic roots (e.g. Fernie 1986 and 1991; Bettess 1991; Huggins 1991). While a preference for lengths using multiples of 3.5m and 5.0m has been suggested (the latter possibly relating to the medieval 5.03m rod, first attested in the thirteenth century: Fernie 1991, 2), no conclusive archaeological evidence has been published for the widespread use of standard lengths (for example, an Anglo-Saxon 'foot') in buildings of the fifth to seventh centuries, with the royal vill at Yeavering forming the notable exception (Marshall and Marshall 1991, 37, 42). An unpublished study by Tummuscheit does, however, identify remarkable correspondences not only in the dimensions of buildings, but also in the positioning and width of entrances and internal subdivisions, both between buildings in the same settlement (e.g. Fig. 2.4) and between different settlements, correspondences that only become fully apparent when the plans of these buildings are superimposed (Tummuscheit 1995, Abb. 66, 94, 95). This reveals a striking degree of standardization between the ground plans of some early Anglo-Saxon buildings. Such standardization, however, is only apparent for a relatively small proportion of fifth- to seventh-century buildings.

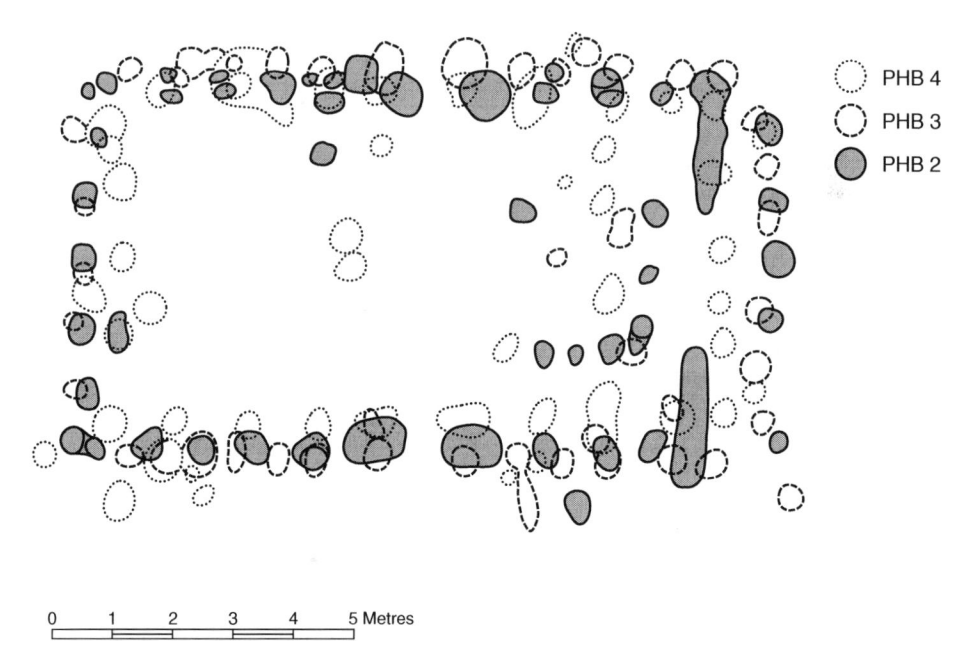

Fig. 2.4. The superimposed plans of Buildings 2, 3, and 4 from Mucking (redrawn from Tummuscheit 1995).

The majority survive only as irregular, often poorly defined agglomerations of postholes. The buildings with clearly defined, standardized ground plans tend, furthermore, to be somewhat larger than those with irregular plans. Dixon has argued that irregular ground plans reflect the use of irregular timbers, asymmetrically arranged rather than paired, and evidently not making use of tie beams (2002, 93). Conversely, the well-defined, regular, standardized buildings would have required access to relatively straight timbers.

Late Saxon diversification

Early medieval building sequences seen in the Netherlands, north-west Germany, and southern Scandinavia all reflect a general trend away from the longhouse, with its internal roof-supporting posts and attached byre, to an open hall in which the interior space was free of load-bearing posts and from which livestock was largely or entirely excluded. The end result, which emerged by the eighth century in the Netherlands and northern Germany and somewhat later in southern Scandinavia, was the 'Warendorf' or 'Odoorn C' house; this was a single-span building with straight or slightly bowed long walls and external raking timbers, which presumably countered the downward and outward thrust of the rafters (Reichmann 1982, 170; Heidinga 1987, 49; Näsman 1987, 461; Herschend 1989). Variations of this type of house appeared all along the North Sea coast and Denmark, and Waterbolk has suggested that the trading centre at Dorestad, near the mouth of the Rhine, played an important role in the spread of this building type, which, as Heidinga has observed, transcended 'the political and cultural vicissitudes of the moment' (Waterbolk 1999; Heidinga 1987, 54). Yet, curiously, the 'Warendorf type' house has not yet been found in Anglo-Saxon England.[15] While similarities between ninth- and tenth-century timber buildings in London and Hedeby hint at links across the North Sea, at least between towns (D. Goodburn, pers. comm. 1997), the far-reaching influence of the 'Dorestad house' does not appear to have been felt in the Anglo-Saxon countryside.

Instead, the relative uniformity of early Anglo-Saxon ground plans appears to have broken down in the eighth and ninth centuries to be replaced by a less coherent, more diverse picture. Indeed, it even remains unclear to what extent these later buildings actually derive from the earlier timber building tradition described above. It must be recognized at the outset, however, that comparatively

---

[15] A small number of 'bow-sided' buildings have been identified in England (Addyman 1972, 300; Huggins 1991; Rahtz 1976, 88; Richards 2000, 301). Yet the most commonly cited examples (e.g. at Goltho, Cheddar, Buckden, St Neots, and North Elmham) differ markedly from the 'Odoorn C' type and it is debatable whether they are truly bow-sided buildings. The 'long halls' at Cheddar, Bicester, Goltho, and Sulgrave (Fig. 2.8) may be better regarded as 'angle-sided' (Gardiner, forthcoming). While three of the buildings at *Hamwic* have been published as having slightly bowed walls (Structures 1, 15, and 29) the ground plans are too incomplete and irregular to establish this with any certainty (Andrews 1997, 50).

few eighth- to eleventh-century building plans have yet been published. The picture is further clouded by the fact that a high proportion of those buildings that have been published derive from high-status settlements, both secular and monastic, as will become apparent in the discussion that follows. Despite these biases in the archaeological record, it is clear that timber buildings of the eighth to eleventh centuries displayed a greater variety of constructional techniques and forms than those of the preceding centuries.

Constructional techniques

Apart from churches and a handful of late, high-status buildings, timber construction—mostly using oak—continued to dominate during the Mid and Late Saxon periods. Post-in-trench and plank-in-trench foundations came increasingly into use from around 600 onwards, enabling the construction of larger, and especially, wider, buildings, with a variety of wall constructions, including both vertical and horizontal planking (Addyman 1972; Marshall and Marshall 1993).[16] By the eighth century, foundation trenches were more common than individual posthole construction, although the latter continued in use. Within these broad trends, however, considerable variability is apparent, even within contemporary buildings in the same settlement. Thus two tenth-century buildings at Steyning (Sussex)—potentially contemporary and nearly identical in size—were built using quite different techniques, one with planks set end to end, the other with squared timbers (Fig. 2.5, Gardiner 1993, 28–32). At the seventh- to tenth-century settlement at Flixborough (Lincolnshire), some buildings had paired posts (implying the use of tie-beams), while others had irregularly spaced posts; some made use of base plates at ground level, others below ground level; still others were built partly or entirely using post-in-trench construction (Darrah 2007). It is notable that the only completely trench-built building (Building 7) was dated to the tenth century and had nearly twice the floor area of earlier buildings on the site (Loveluck 2001). The correlation between foundation type and building dimensions is far from absolute, however. Thus while post-in-trench and plank-in-trench buildings display greater variation in width, they are not invariably wider than posthole structures (Marshall and Marshall 1991, 36). Different types of foundations were sometimes even combined within the same building. At the settlement of Catholme (Staffordshire), for example, five buildings combined individual posthole and post-in-trench construction (Losco-Bradley and Kinsley 2002, 86).[17]

---

[16] This discussion is restricted to buildings with earth-fast foundations; by definition, those without earth-fast foundations are unlikely to leave any archaeological trace, although their existence, certainly by the later Saxon period, is not in doubt. A building identified as a kitchen and dated to the mid ninth century at Goltho, for example, had no earth-fast foundations, but was recognized by its well-preserved clay floor (Beresford 1987, 59).
[17] These, however, display no consistency: in Building AS45, the northern half of the building was of posthole construction, the southern half post-in-trench; in Building AS41, the long walls were post-in-

In short, it remains unclear why one form of foundation was chosen over another. One theory is that some constructional techniques—the use of sill-beams or stave-built walls for example—were more prestigious than others because they made more lavish use of timber and were more labour-intensive (Scull 1991, 55).[18] It is notable in several cases that one wall of a building was more carefully built than the others. Thus, at Steyning, the southern wall of Building A made 'extravagant use of planks clearly exceeding the number required purely for structural purposes', in contrast to the northern wall, which contained fewer posts. The excavator goes on to suggest that this may have been 'the equivalent of close studding used in later medieval buildings…to display the status and wealth of the owner' (Gardiner 1993, 32). At least one building (Building 2666) at the Mid Saxon estate centre excavated at Higham Ferrers (Northamptonshire) appeared to possess a 'façade' in which foundation trenches and postholes on the south-eastern ('front') of the building were more substantial in both plan and section than those along the 'back' (Hardy et al. 2007, 40).

A recent study suggests that at least some Late Saxon posthole buildings were erected as a series of trusses laid out and pre-assembled on the ground, then raised and positioned into postholes ('transverse assembly'; Gardiner and Murray, forthcoming).[19] The evidence from some buildings with foundation trenches suggests an alternative method of assembly. The foundation trenches of Structure D at the Late Saxon settlement at Bishopstone (Sussex) indicated that greater care had been taken to cut the inner face of the trench, which was vertical, whereas the outer face was sloping and irregular (Gardiner and Murray, forthcoming). A similar phenomenon has been observed at a number of other Late Saxon settlements, for example at Springfield Lyons (Essex), where the foundation trench of Building 18 had in places 'a vertical edge on its inner side and a moderately sloping edge on the outer' (Tyler and Major 2005, 136). Gardiner argues that this points to 'longitudinal assembly', in which the side and long walls were pre-assembled and the sloping outer edge of the trench used to slide these sections of wall into place, while the vertical face of the inner edge would help to align the sections (Gardiner 2011; Thomas 2010, 189).[20] While this technique emerged most clearly after 900, there are hints that it was also being used in the

---

trench, while the gable ends were postholes; AS35 had one long wall with a trench foundation and one of postholes, and so on.

[18] The best examples of stave construction in this period include the 'long hall' at Goltho and the water-mill at Tamworth, Staffordshire (Beresford 1985; Rahtz and Meeson 1992).

[19] Hope-Taylor, in his report on Yeavering, was the first to suggest that an element of 'prefabrication' was involved in the construction of Anglo-Saxon timber buildings (1977, 137).

[20] Not all foundation trench buildings were constructed in this way, however. The foundations of Building 1 at Polebrook (Northamptonshire) were cut into the cornbrash, with the timber posts 'set against the steep outer face of the bedding trench with cornbrash packing behind and on the inside of the structure' (Upex 2002, plate 5).

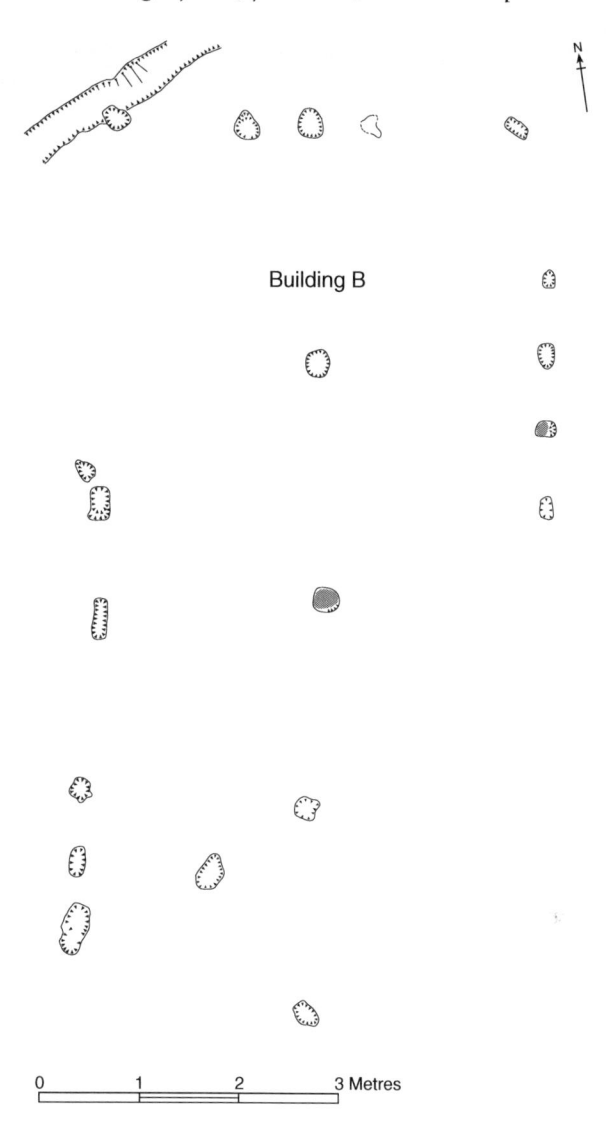

Fig. 2.5. Plan of Building B from Steyning (after Gardiner 1993).

construction of earlier, probably seventh-century, buildings (Hamerow, Hayden, and Hey 2008; Millett 1984, fig. 57; Hinchcliffe 1986, fig. 5, sections 2, 3). Further indications of longitudinal assembly may be found at Cowdery's Down: the alignment of the walls in Structure C8 differs slightly on either side of the central doorway of the northern long wall, suggesting the use of separate 'panels' on either side of the doorway, while the corners of Structure B4 comprise two posts, suggesting that the end walls and the long walls had been prefabricated separately and then raised and joined together

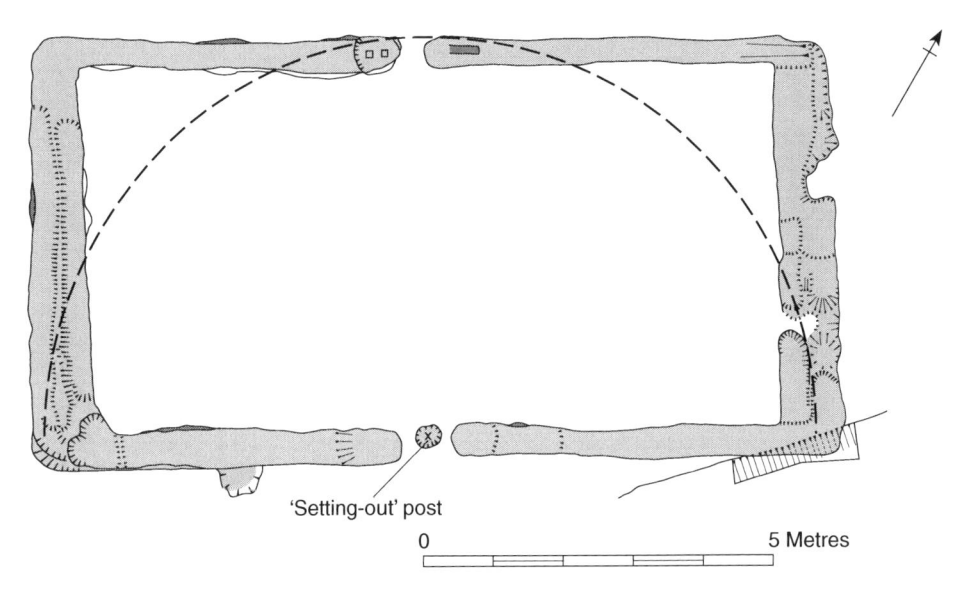

Fig. 2.6. Building C10 from Cowdery's Down, showing presumed 'setting out post' (redrawn from Millett and James 1984).

(Millett 1984, figs. 37, 39). This feature, too, is seen in later buildings, such as Building S10 at Portchester (Cunliffe 1976, fig. 19).[21]

It may even be possible to discern the Anglo-Saxon surveyor at work. A Late Saxon building at Middle Harling contained a posthole in the middle of one of the long walls (Rogerson 1995, fig. 14), argued by Gardiner to represent the position of a setting-out post, used to lay out the building symmetrically (Gardiner and Murray, forthcoming). Postholes located in the centrally positioned doorways of the long walls of Cowdery's Down Structures C9, C10, and possibly C12 appear to have served a similar function (Fig. 2.6; Millett 1984, figs. 40, 41, 45).

These various assembly methods suggest that the carpentry techniques of the Mid and Late Saxon periods were rather more advanced than has generally been supposed. Vernacular building specialists have traditionally held that the true mortise and tenon joint—without which it is impossible to create a structure which is sufficiently rigid to be raised in this way—was absent in Anglo-Saxon England (Darrah 2007). Dixon, for example, has suggested that it may 'even be impossible satisfactorily to erect a prefabricated timber structure...in postholes', arguing that posthole buildings therefore had to be assembled without pre-cut joints, which had instead to be made '*in situ* against a standing post'; an extremely tricky business (2002, 91). While this debate cannot be definitively resolved on the basis of the data currently available, the evidence presented above, and the discovery in London of a waterlogged tenth-century

---

[21] I am very grateful to Mark Gardiner for discussing this evidence with me.

structural timber believed to be a top-plate with cut mortises and, presumably, loose tenons (Hill and Woodger 1999, 29–35), suggest that traditional views of pre-Conquest timber building techniques have tended to underestimate their sophistication.[22]

Regional variation

In his seminal paper on the Anglo-Saxon house, Addyman noted that it would be surprising 'if the combined effects of environment, differing resources and varying inherited tradition had not produced wide regional variations' (1972, 304). Yet it is precisely the geographical uniformity of building traditions across much of England during the fifth to seventh centuries that is so remarkable.[23] This includes regions of northern England, where earth-fast timber buildings identical to those found in the south are increasingly being recognized, notably at Thirlings (Northumberland), Quarrington (Lincolnshire), but above all at West Heslerton (O'Brien and Miket 1991; Powlesland 1997; Taylor 2003b).

By the Later Saxon period however, just as building layouts and constructional methods diversified, regional variation became more marked. Several studies have identified distinctive building types in northern, especially upland, parts of England, although the number of buildings that can be firmly dated to this period remains small. King has recently echoed Morris in observing that 'so little [is] known of the post-Roman building tradition in upland Britain, that identifying subsequent innovations [is] made more difficult' (King 2004). This is arguably an understatement, and his conclusion that, despite the limited data-set, what we see in the upland regions is 'a house which undertakes in stone and timber what elsewhere...was an earthfast timber form', is debatable (ibid. 340). Despite the adoption of the *Grubenhaus* as far north-west as Fremington, Cumbria (Oliver et al. 1996), building techniques generally diverged quite markedly from those of southern and eastern England. The chief difference is the apparent absence in northern England of earth-fast footings after c.800 and the construction instead of essentially 'self-supporting' buildings. Gardiner, who has carried out a survey of these buildings, sees the use of stone and gravel footings—introduced in the eighth century, for example at Flixborough and Hartlepool (Cleveland)—as a milestone after which 'various methods were used...to try to increase the longevity of the timbers, either by raising

---

[22] In a loose mortise and tenon, the elements remain joined primarily through gravity, and are not sufficiently close fitting to prevent much structural movement, e.g. a 'tusk tenon', in which the mortise was cut all the way through the timber, and the tenon slotted through, so that it projected out the other side (Gardiner, pers. comm.). There is general agreement that tight-fitting mortise and tenon joints that locked the elements together were probably not in use before the twelfth century.

[23] Marshall and Marshall's 1993 study does, however, hint at some subtle regional variation even within this early period and it should be remembered that there may have been regional variation in the superstructures of buildings that cannot be detected archaeologically.

them above the ground, or by protecting them in other ways from moisture' (Daniels 1989, 175 and fig. 26; Loveluck 2001, 85 and fig. 5.6; Gardiner 2004, 345). At Hartlepool, buildings with stone footings were in some cases direct replacements for earlier earth-fast structures. This is particularly striking in the case of Building XX, which had originally been built using post-in-trench construction: 'The posts were removed and the trench backfilled; the trench then had limestone slabs laid on the top of it. It must be concluded that the superstructure was cut off at ground level and stone footings inserted beneath the existing superstructure' (Daniels 1989, 177).[24]

A whole range of buildings dating from the eighth to eleventh centuries have now been recognized which made use of stone or gravel footings. While some of these come from upland regions, for example at Whithorn (Dumfries and Galloway) (Hill 1997), those from Flixborough, Whitby, and Hartlepool demonstrate that this building method was not restricted to these regions. All these settlements were, however, either monastic or had strong monastic connections. Gardiner has argued that by increasing the longevity of these buildings through the use of stone footings, their powerful inhabitants sought to '[project] an image of the permanence of sacred or secular power' (Gardiner 2004, 351). The changing social requirements of buildings, and in particular the desire to establish certain buildings and settlements as quasi-permanent features in the landscape, clearly had an impact upon the 'life-cycle' of buildings, as will be considered in further detail later in this chapter.

Regrettably few 'ordinary' farmsteads of the eighth to tenth centuries in north-western England have been identified and still fewer excavated. The two best-known settlements from the upland regions, Simy Folds in County Durham and Ribblehead in Yorkshire, suggest that it may be possible to detect a shared upland building tradition characterized by certain features, notably rectangular buildings with stone walls comprising facing stones and rubble interiors, internal wall benches, and rounded corners (Richards 2000, 299–300; Coggins 2004). To what extent such buildings should be attributed to Scandinavian influence, however, remains a matter of some debate (summarized in Richards 2000). Insofar as these buildings can be dated, they appear too early to be the result of Scandinavian settlement, and the Scandinavian analogies are in any case unconvincing; in the absence of any clear understanding of local building traditions during the seventh and eighth centuries, it seems unwise to regard these buildings as 'Anglo-Scandinavian' in any meaningful sense.

Further east, there is somewhat better evidence for the development of local timber building traditions in the Mid to Late Saxon period. The settlement at Cottam, on the Yorkshire Wolds, has been convincingly interpreted as of ordinary status, despite its having yielded a relatively large quantity of early

---

[24] Whether this replacement occurred bit by bit as elements of the building rotted and were replaced, or in a single operation as suggested by the excavator, cannot be determined.

medieval metalwork (Richards 1999). Two partially uncovered post-built rectangular structures, dated broadly to between the eighth and early ninth centuries, are essentially identical to earlier Anglo-Saxon traditions elsewhere, while the fragmentary Building 3, tentatively dated to the mid ninth century, appears to have employed post-in-trench construction. While excavation at Cottam was on a comparatively limited scale, the absence of stone or gravel footings at West Heslerton, where several buildings thought to date to the eighth century have been uncovered, may suggest that such foundations were indeed restricted to sites of special status (Powlesland, pers. comm.).

In the south-western counties of Wessex, a number of distinctive post-Roman settlements are known. The settlement at Poundbury in Dorset and the reoccupied Iron Age hillforts at South Cadbury and Cadbury-Congresbury in Somerset and Crickley Hill in Gloucestershire all point to the existence in these regions of timber buildings between the fifth and seventh centuries; their ground plans are irregular, but not invariably insubstantial: a building at South Cadbury may have measured some 19m x 10m, with a subdivision at the eastern end and two aisles (Alcock 1982; Dixon 1988). It would appear that, despite in some cases adopting an 'Anglo-Saxon' burial rite from the seventh century onwards, post-Roman communities in Somerset and Dorset nevertheless continued to reject the Anglo-Saxon timber building tradition (Eagles 1994).

In Devon and Cornwall a distinctive building tradition is apparent even in the Late Saxon period, by which time the region was at least nominally under Anglo-Saxon rule. Groups of buildings excavated at Mawgan Porth, near the north Cornish coast, occupied between the mid ninth and mid eleventh centuries, provide some of the clearest evidence of this tradition (Bruce-Mitford 1997). Three rectangular 'courtyard' houses were excavated, each with a byre at one end and several smaller rooms around the other sides of the yard. The walls were made up of stone facing filled with a mixture of broken-up slate and earth.

The life-cycle of the Anglo-Saxon house

Detailed analysis of the evidence for the repair, rebuilding, extension, and modification of prehistoric buildings has been used by archaeologists to reconstruct the 'cultural biographies' of individual dwellings, following Kopytoff, who argued that objects, like people, can be said to have a 'social life' (1986; see also Ingold 2000, 187–8). Gerritsen, for example, has pointed to the fact that the remains of Bronze Age and Iron Age houses in the southern Netherlands rarely display signs of repair or rebuilding and has argued that they must therefore have been abandoned after only one phase of occupation (1999, 79). While the recognition that farmsteads of this period regularly shifted location is not new, it has conventionally been assumed to be the result of economic and ecological factors, above all farming methods. Gerritsen and others have argued, however, that social and cultural factors should also be taken into account and have noted that links exist in many pre-industrial societies between the life-cycles of houses and their occupants (ibid. 81; Brück 1999). Indeed, the fact that we know of at least one Anglo-Saxon building which was named and thus to some extent anthropomorphized—the Great Hall of Heorot in *Beowulf*—suggests that this approach has some merit when considering buildings of this period (Hines 2011, 28).

Early Anglo-Saxon timber buildings generally display little evidence of substantial repair or renewal. Of the nine reasonably complete ground plans of posthole buildings at Mucking, for example, none produced unambiguous evidence of repair or remodelling, although some double posts could arguably be interpreted as such (Hamerow 1993). Of the seven such buildings at West Stow, only Hall 2 produced evidence interpreted by the excavator as potentially representing a repair (West 1986, 11). Exceptions can of course be found: at Broome (Norfolk), inter-cutting postholes in one of the seven buildings excavated suggested that damaged or rotten posts had been replaced (Robertson 2003). Nevertheless, of some twenty posthole buildings excavated at Eye Kettleby (Leicestershire), none appears to have produced clear evidence of repair or remodelling (Finn, forthcoming).

The relative scarcity of evidence for repair and rebuilding suggests that the majority of early Anglo-Saxon buildings—at least those not destroyed by fire—were abandoned while still habitable and either dismantled or left to decay *in situ*. This is not as unlikely as it may at first appear. Brück has argued that the majority of Middle Bronze Age settlements in southern England were 'single generational' and cites a number of ethnographic analogies in support of her thesis (1999). She goes on to suggest that a house with a lifespan of twenty to forty years might have been 'established upon marriage, occupied throughout the life of the head of the household and his or her spouse, and abandoned upon their deaths' (ibid. 149).

The earliest evidence for significant rebuilding and repair of Anglo-Saxon buildings comes from Cowdery's Down and Yeavering, both occupied primarily during the first half of the seventh century. At Cowdery's Down, two of the four buildings in phase B—Structures B4 and B6—were entirely replaced by others erected on the same 'footprint', while in the next phase Structure C10 was shortened by rebuilding the end walls (Millett 1984, 213). At least seven buildings appear to have burned down, a fate that must have befallen many structures of this period. A similar process is apparent at Yeavering, where many of the major buildings underwent several phases of rebuilding (Hope-Taylor 1977).

In the Mid Saxon period, evidence for repairs and the complete rebuilding of structures on the same spot is easier to find. Richard Darrah has estimated, based on evidence from Flixborough for the use of oak roundwood 0.20–0.25m in diameter, that repairs would have been needed after a period of approximately twenty years, with major rebuilding required after around forty years. Detailed analysis of the buildings as well as dendro-chronological evidence from western Denmark suggests a lifespan of between twenty-five and fifty years for the Flixborough buildings (Loveluck 2007, 50; Darrah 2007).[25] Several buildings of the mid-eighth- to ninth-century phases at Flixborough showed signs of repair and/or of repeated rebuilding. Thus Building 21 was replaced on the same spot by Building 15, while others showed signs of at least partial rebuilding. Other examples include Building 2665 at Higham Ferrers, which appears to have been a rebuild of Building 2664 (Hardy et al. 2007). Evidence of such rebuilds or extensive repairs is not restricted to settlements of obviously high status, however. At the Mid to Late Saxon settlement at Catholme (Staffordshire), at least five structures were dismantled and rebuilt on the same spot, sometimes several times (Losco-Bradley and Kinsley 2002, 87). The main timber building of the eighth- to ninth-century settlement phase at Yarnton (Oxfordshire), Building 3620, was partly rebuilt at least once and probably twice; an annexe appears to have been added to the southern end of the building during the last phase of occupation.[26] The building had on at least one occasion been affected by fire (Hey 2004, 139 and fig. 7.3).

Evidence for such modification and repair is also relatively common in Late Saxon settlements, despite the small number of extensively excavated sites. Excavations at Renhold, Water End West (Bedfordshire) revealed the well-preserved ground plans of five timber buildings dating between the tenth to twelfth centuries. The only building to be completely excavated had been modified in a number of ways (Timby et al. 2007). The eastern (gable) end entrance to Building 9150—a substantial foundation trench structure measuring some 19m x 7m—replaced an earlier, wider entrance; the trenches themselves had been re-cut and posts cut into the slots are also thought to relate to repairs (Fig. 2.7). Posts at the southern and northern (long wall) entrances had also been replaced several times. Similarly, Building Z at North Elmham—a settlement associated with an important ecclesiastical centre—was divided into two rooms by an internal partition; the presumed door posts associated with an opening in this partition had been replaced two or three times (Wade-Martins 1980, 61). Buildings S and U at the same site had been modified by the addition of extensions and a porch (ibid. 57, 139). At the Late Saxon farmstead and probable estate centre at Springfield Lyons (Essex), Buildings 1, 1a,

---

[25] Brück notes, following Wainright, that figures derived by the Forest Projects Research Laboratory suggest a longer lifespan for posts made of oak heartwood, namely *c.*15 years for every 50mm of diameter; thus a 250mm earth-fast post would survive for 75 years (Brück 1999, 149). Darrah points out, however, that roundwood of the thickness seen at Flixborough would be considerably less durable.

[26] What appears to have been a very similar single-annexed structure, radiocarbon-dated to the late seventh or eighth century, was found at Shapwick (Somerset), substantially extending the known geographical range of such buildings westward (Gerrard 2007, 405 ff; I am grateful to John Blair for drawing my attention to this example).

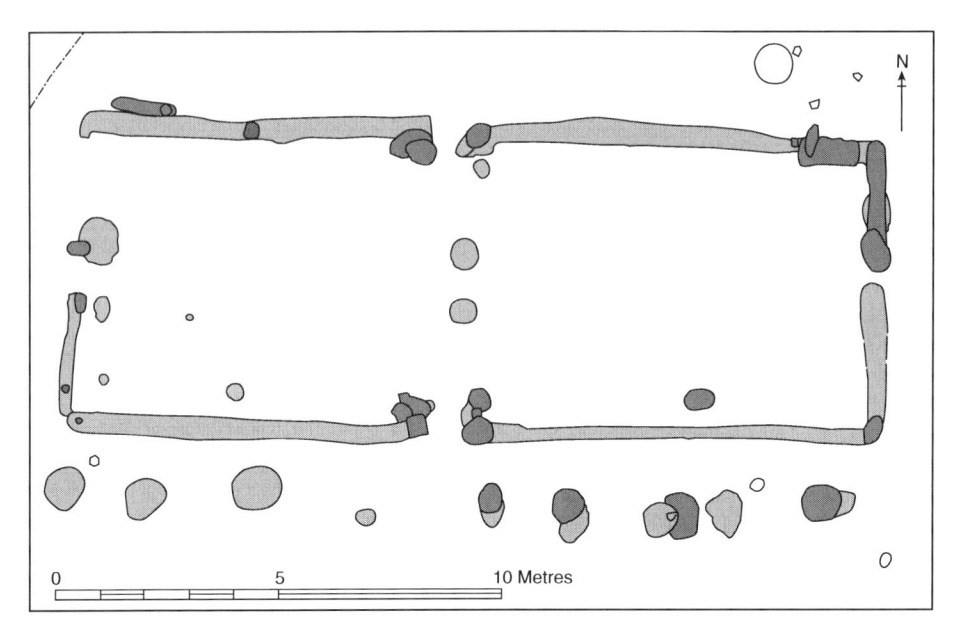

Fig. 2.7. Building 9150 from Renhold, Water End West (after Timby et al. 2007).

4, and 11 appear to represent two, and possibly three, phases of rebuilding on the same plot (Tyler and Major 2005, 131). At Bishopstone, the dense rectilinear pattern of structures indicates that the positions of the main buildings were 'maintained over successive building generations' (Thomas 2005). It is, however, at Goltho that the repeated repair and rebuilding of structures, in several cases on the same foundations, can be seen most strikingly across an entire settlement. Here, up to five superimposed building phases were discernible for structures identified as 'halls', kitchens, 'bowers', and 'weaving sheds' (Beresford 1987). While it may be argued that the need to remain within an enclosed space contributed to this tendency to rebuild on the same 'footprint', this alone is insufficient to explain it.

As already noted, the introduction of stone and gravel footings in high-status buildings in northern England has been linked with a new interest in extending the longevity of important buildings. This appears to be supported by the evidence for the repair and rebuilding of certain timber buildings whose lifecycles—despite their organic and perishable nature—could thereby span several human generations, and thus embody and evoke links with the ancestors.[27] It seems likely that there was a connection between this desire to create long-term

[27] As already noted, it is difficult to be certain how long earth-fast buildings could have remained in use without substantial repairs to their foundations, although two posthole buildings in Northumberland have recently produced a series of radiocarbon dates suggesting they would have stood for perhaps 60–70 years during the fifth and sixth centuries (Johnson and Waddington 2009).

relationships with a place and the growing importance of landholding and inheritance, along with an increasing emphasis on the production and extraction of agrarian surpluses, something explored further in Chapter 5. In his work on the southern Netherlands, Gerritsen observed that, from the Middle Iron Age onwards, an increased emphasis on semi-permanent settlements was accompanied by the abandonment of communal, long-lived cemeteries and their replacement by short-lived, dispersed burial grounds and the burial of certain individuals within settlements themselves (1999). As we will see in Chapter 4, this offers a striking parallel for Anglo-Saxon England.

Form, function and the configuration of internal space

In the 1990s, traditional approaches to excavated buildings which involved 'obsessive' recording of architectural detail and physical features as an end in itself came under severe criticism from researchers concerned that archaeologists 'were somehow missing the point in their substitution of description for understanding' (Parker Pearson and Richards 1994, xi). The recognition, derived from ethnographic studies, that dwellings in particular can 'embody complex cosmological schemes' and important symbolisms led to a desire to re-create the experience of being inside these long-gone buildings (ibid.). While archaeologists studying the early medieval period in England have perhaps been somewhat slower than others in recognizing the potential of this approach, it is also the case that the building remains from this period are singularly uninformative, lacking as they do durable building materials, floor levels, or evidence of internal layout or household activities; indeed it is not even possible to be sure that all of the buildings often referred to as 'houses' were in fact dwellings, rather than, say, barns.[28] These considerable obstacles notwithstanding, a consideration of the internal layout of Anglo-Saxon buildings can enrich our understanding of these structures, even if much must remain speculative.

Entrances, subdivisions, and the hearth

In contrast to the study of the Continental longhouse, little has been written about the functions of Anglo-Saxon timber buildings (e.g. Waterbolk 1991; Zimmermann 1992). Apart from the rare instances where a hearth is preserved, indicating use as a dwelling, any discussion of function must remain largely speculative. Nevertheless, even in the absence of surviving floor levels, the positioning of entrances, internal subdivisions, and occasionally hearths is suggestive of a considerable degree of formality in the layout of internal space, a

---

[28] This is in contrast to Ireland, where the well-preserved remains of early medieval houses coupled with exceptionally rich textual evidence have enabled archaeologists to undertake detailed analyses of the configuration of social space within early medieval dwellings (O'Sullivan 2008).

layout which underwent significant modification between the fifth and eleventh centuries.

The great majority of timber buildings of the fifth to seventh centuries consisted, as far as can be determined, of one room. Marshall and Marshall have calculated that around one quarter produced evidence of an internal subdivision, usually at the eastern end, forming a small compartment, usually between 1.5 and 2.0 metres wide (1993; Fig. 2.1).[29] These buildings were almost invariably entered through opposing doorways positioned approximately centrally within the long walls. Evidence for a third doorway in one of the gable walls (and, very rarely, a fourth) is less common and mostly confined to larger than average buildings. Of nineteen buildings with compartments identified in this study[30], at least twelve could be entered from the outside by means of a doorway leading directly into the compartment, as well from inside the building; as the location of entrances is not always obvious, particularly in the case of post-built structures, it may be that even more had an external entrance. These compartments should not, therefore, be regarded as 'inner' chambers. It is notable that most, and potentially all, of these buildings are likely to date to the late sixth or seventh century.

Another development of the period around AD 600 is the appearance of a small number of buildings with one or two annexes at the gable ends (Fig. 2.2).[31] Unlike the compartments discussed above, these annexes could only be entered from within the building (with the apparent exception of the building at Brandon: Carr et al. 1988, 374). In some cases, the annexes could be shown to have been secondary and of a different—usually lighter—type of construction from the rest of the building, although there is no way of knowing how much time had elapsed between the construction of the main building and the annexe (e.g. Polebrook Building 2, Yeavering B1, and Thirlings C; Hope-Taylor 1977, 73; O'Brien and Miket 1991, 65; Upex 2002).[32]

---

[29] As James, Marshall, and Millett note, however, postholes relating to internal subdivisions are generally shallower than the main wall posts and thus are more prone to erosion; it is therefore possible that a higher proportion of buildings were originally subdivided (1985, 188). They also note three examples, from Yeavering and Cowdery's Down, where the partitions were positioned close to the axis of the transverse doors, rather than in one end (ibid. 190).

[30] This is substantially fewer than the number identified by Marshall and Marshall in their study. I have, however, confined myself to the clearest, most uncontentious examples. These come from the following sites: Cowdery's Down, Thirlings, Yeavering, Mucking, West Stow, Polebrook, and Chalton.

[31] The latest datable examples of annexed halls of this kind come from Brandon and Northampton, both of which are likely to date to the eighth century (Carr et al. 1988, 374; Williams et al. 1985). Building 3620 from Yarnton (Oxon.) is arguably an annexed building, although the annexe was only added in the third, presumed ninth-century, phase of construction and it is debatable whether this should be regarded as belonging to the same tradition as earlier annexed structures (Hey 2004, 109, 145–6 and fig. 7.6).

[32] In addition to the excavated examples discussed here, annexed buildings have also been identified in aerial photographs, notably at Cowage Farm, Wiltshire and Sprouston, Roxburghshire (Hinchcliffe 1986; Smith 1984).

The construction of annexes and subdivisions appears to have been restricted to larger than average buildings, yet their function remains obscure.[33] In several cases, annexes and compartments contained evidence of internal partitions and other features. The compartments in Buildings C9 and C13 at Cowdery's Down had been subdivided to form two smaller rooms, while Building A1 at Chalton had been divided into three more or less equally sized rooms. James, Marshall and Millett (1985, 190) have drawn attention to two buildings with square annexes—Cowdery's Down A1 and Thirlings C—which contained a central post or feature.[34] They draw a convincing analogy with the small square structures at Yeavering and New Wintles Farm (Oxfordshire), subsequently argued by Blair to have served a cultic function, and indeed conjectured by him to represent a kind of 'domestic shrine' (ibid. 190; Blair 1995, 19, fig. 11). Others have seen a connection with a group of early Anglo-Saxon churches with narthex, nave, and chancel, suggesting that annexes may therefore be a marker of high status (Dixon 2002, 96). While a strong case can be made for regarding Building B1 at Yeavering—surrounded as it is by conversion-period burials—and the annexed buildings at Brandon and Northampton as having served a religious function (Hope-Taylor 1977; Carr et al. 1988; Blair 1996), other examples such as those at Cowdery's Down should not be assumed to have had religious or cultic associations (James, Marshall, and Millett 1985, 190).

While the precise function of annexes and compartments cannot be determined and may well have varied, the following general observations can be made. They are restricted to larger than average buildings. In almost all cases, the entranceways into/out of compartments were axially aligned with the gable entrance (or entrances). This would have facilitated procession through the building and inter-visibility, most strikingly in the case of the two axially aligned Buildings A1 and A2 at Chalton. There, 'the posts of the four doors in this area were sufficiently well aligned for it to have been possible for someone standing in the main room of A1 to have seen into the main room of A2 when all four doors were open' (Addyman et al. 1972, 19–20). A notable exception to this rule is found at Yeavering, where a 'purposeful asymmetry' is apparent in several buildings that had been partitioned (Hope-Taylor 1977, 91). In buildings C2, C3, and A3, entrances in the gable ends and the partitions were deliberately staggered (Hope-Taylor 1977, figs. 17, 38). Offset doorways were also apparent in annexed buildings such as C4 and B1 (ibid., figs. 33, 39). Quite what the purpose behind this asymmetry was is far from clear, although the obvious effect would have been to impede inter-visibility along the longitudinal axis of the building.

---

[33] All but one of the nineteen buildings with compartments identified here exceeded 10m in length.
[34] It is possible, however, that the feature inside Thirlings C pre-dated the annexe (O'Brien and Miket 1991, 67).

In a few instances, buildings with compartments and annexes were articulated with enclosures. In the case of the Chalton buildings A1 and AZ1, the compartments led directly into enclosures by means of a doorway in the gable wall, providing 'private access' (Addyman and Leigh 1973, 14 and fig. 3). In contrast, the annexes of Cowdery's Down A1 and Yeavering A1(b) and A3(a) projected into enclosures, yet did not provide entry into them (Hope-Taylor 1977; Millett 1984, 201–3). In the case of Cowdery's Down A1, entrance into the enclosure was via two entrances immediately adjacent to the corners of the building (Fig. 2.2).

The building traditions of the fifth to seventh centuries thus placed considerable emphasis on regularity, formality, even symmetry, characteristics which were particularly marked in larger and arguably more important buildings. This emphasis on regularity is also apparent in later prehistory, and Brück has argued that the symmetrical arrangement of Bronze Age houses 'could have been drawn on to create dimensions of opposition or complementarity in the use of space on either side of the axis' (Brück 1999, 155). While one can only speculate on how social relationships may have been played out within the formalized space of the early Anglo-Saxon house, it is not uncommon to find in the ethnographic record examples of houses that are organized 'in accordance with a set of homologous oppositions' such as front and back, light and dark, or male and female, as famously set out by Bourdieu in his study of the Kabyle house (Bourdieu 1990).[35]

How did the layout of buildings change in the later Saxon period? In their 1991 study, Marshall and Marshall demonstrated not only that the first very large buildings appeared towards the end of the sixth century, but also that there was a general increase in the mean size of Anglo-Saxon timber buildings over time, with buildings using foundation trenches tending to be larger than those built using individual postholes (1991, 42). One might expect, therefore, to see an increase in the use of subdivisions in the Late Saxon period, yet this does not appear to be the case (Marshall and Marshall 1993, 380). Where subdivisions have been identified, their placement varied. Building 9150 at Renhold, Water End West, contained an internal partition which divided it into two roughly equally sized rooms (Fig. 2.7), whereas Buildings S and Z1 at North Elmham, Building S13 at Portchester, and Building 3 at Springfield Lyons contained a large room with an external doorway and somewhat smaller

---

[35] It seems highly likely that the formal arrangement of vessels, furniture, and other items on the floor and hung on the walls of the seventh-century princely chamber grave excavated at Prittlewell, Essex was intended to evoke the formal layout of a Great Hall (MoLAS 2004; Hines 2011). Indeed, Hines has argued that the seventh century marked a period when domestic symbolism in Anglo-Saxon funerary rites became particularly marked, expressed not only in chamber graves, but also in bed burials (Hines 2011). Close links with the Frankish world, with its furniture-packed chamber graves and house-shaped coffins, must have contributed to this development (Hamerow 2002a, 40–2). Such burials, therefore, point to the existence of explicit analogies between 'the cosmos and the life beyond' on the one hand and domestic life as lived in the house on the other (Hines 2011, 27).

'inner' room (Cunliffe 1976, fig. 22; Wade-Martins 1980, 57 and figs. 78, 84; Tyler and Major 2005, fig. 72).

The proportions and layouts of later Saxon buildings suggest, furthermore, that by the ninth century, regularity and formality were less important than during the fifth to seventh centuries (though see the discussion of 'long halls', below). This impression is strengthened when the placement of entrances and, therefore, systems for entering and leaving buildings, are considered. During the fifth to seventh centuries, the placement of doorways was remarkably consistent: as already noted, opposing doors were almost invariably centrally positioned in the long walls, with a third entrance occasionally found in the eastern gable wall. Tummuscheit has shown that even the width of the entrance 'zone' was relatively standardized (1995).

In Mid to Late Saxon buildings, however, both the number and placement of entrances varied considerably, although it is not uncommon to find buildings with two opposed doorways positioned centrally in the long walls, following the earlier tradition (e.g. Portchester Building S11; Cunliffe 1976, fig. 290). Some buildings apparently had only a single doorway, such as Hartlepool Buildings VIII, X, XIV and North Elmham, Buildings Z and U (Daniels 1989; Wade-Martins 1980, figs. 84, 120);[36] a few had entrances in gable walls only (e.g. Cheddar West Hall; Rahtz 1979, fig. 50); still others had two entrances in the same wall, suggesting some form of internal partitioning, even where little or no trace of this remains, as in the Long Hall at the royal settlement at Cheddar, Building 1185 at Chapel Street, Bicester (Oxfordshire), and Building 3 at Springfield Lyons (Rahtz 1979, fig. 30; Harding and Andrews 2002; Tyler and Major 2005, fig. 72). Such internal partitioning did survive, however, in the Long Hall at Goltho. A partition divided the interior into a large, eastern room containing a hearth, a smaller western 'antechamber' and a still smaller annexe. The hearth room—the floor of which had been raised in the eastern half by about half a metre to form a 'dais'—could be entered from the outside by means of a narrow doorway in the eastern gable wall, while much wider opposing doors in the long walls led into the 'antechamber'. The annexe, like its earlier counterparts, could only be reached from inside the building.

Some later Saxon buildings contained both narrow and wide entrances. Thus the long hall at Cheddar contained, in addition to two opposed entrances centrally positioned in the long walls, a third doorway in the northern end of its eastern long wall measuring just over half the width of the central, presumably main, entrances (Rahtz 1979, fig. 30). A comparable arrangement is apparent in Building 18 at Springfield Lyons, where the width of the two opposing entrances in the western and eastern long walls varied considerably (Tyler and

---

[36] The Hartlepool buildings are exceptionally small and there may be a correlation between the size of the building and the number of entrances. Champion has also noted that the smallest buildings at Chalton tended to have only one doorway (Daniels 1989; Champion 1977, 364).

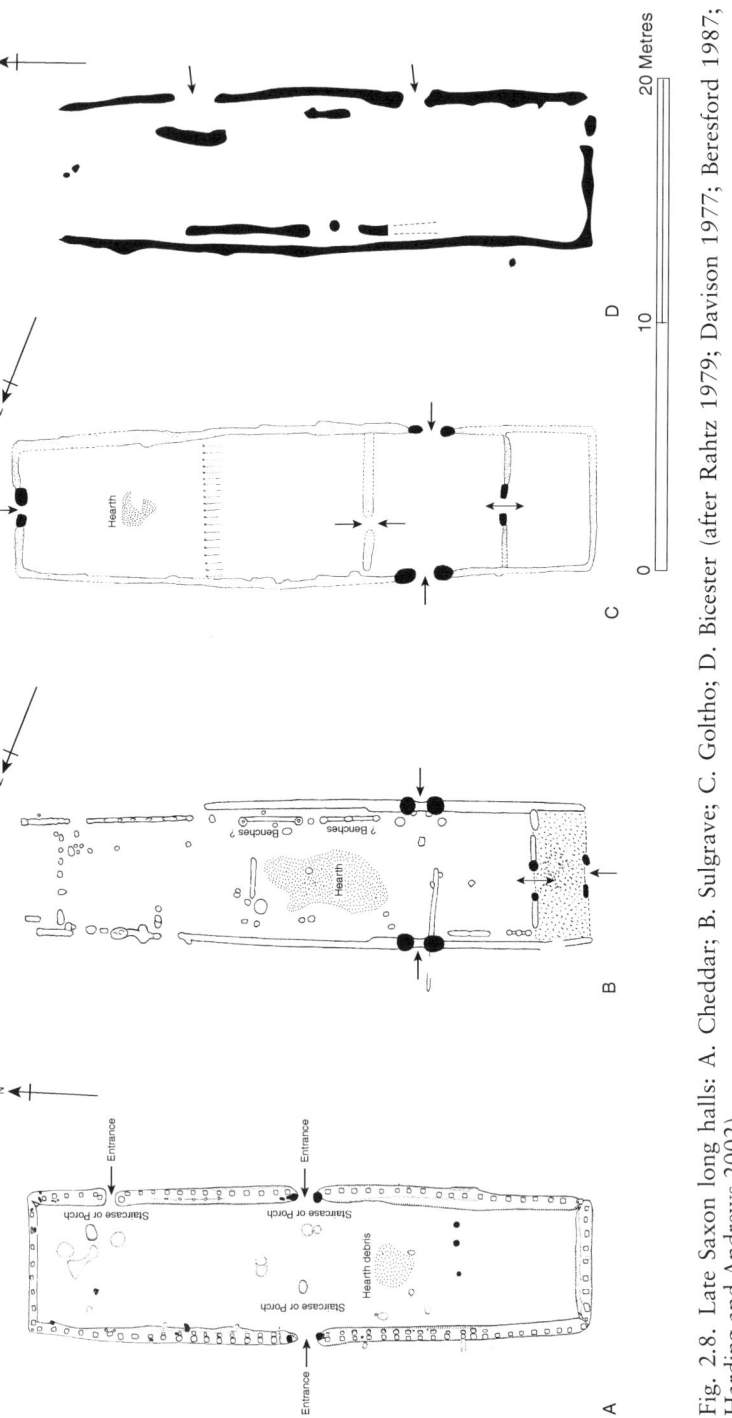

Fig. 2.8. Late Saxon long halls: A. Cheddar; B. Sulgrave; C. Goltho; D. Bicester (after Rahtz 1979; Davison 1977; Beresford 1987; Harding and Andrews 2002).

Major 2005, fig. 82). Building 9150 at Renhold, Water End West contained two opposing, central entrances, each around 1m wide, as well as a 3m-wide entrance in the western gable wall, and another 0.60m-wide doorway in the eastern gable wall (Fig. 2.7; Timby et al. 2007). At Faccombe Netherton (Hampshire) and Renhold, Water End West, doorways into Buildings 3 and 9150 respectively were modified to make them narrower, or indeed to block them off entirely (Fairbrother 1990, fig. 4.7 and p. 95).

While the placement and width of entrances displayed greater variation in the Late Saxon period, their importance throughout the period is apparent in the use of large doorposts, pointing to the use of massive doors in some buildings (e.g. Mucking PHB 1, 2, and 3: Hamerow 1993, fig. 54), as well as the evidence for the frequent repair and replacement of these posts. Thus, at North Elmham, one of the doorposts marking the entranceway between the two rooms in Building S had been replaced two or even three times, as had the posts in the northern and southern doorways of Building 9150 at Renhold, Water End West (Fig. 2.7; Wade-Martins 1980, 61). Doorways appear to have been given ritual emphasis in Building A2 at Yeavering, which contained the horn of a sheep or goat in a doorpost in the southern wall, while the 'teeth of ox and boar were identified in the door-pits of the eastern and western partitions'; the gable-end doorways in C4(a) also displayed signs of elaboration (Hope-Taylor 1977, 53, fig. 39).[37]

The written sources of the period suggest that the hearth possessed considerable symbolic importance in Anglo-Saxon England. In addition to the famous passage in Bede's *Ecclesiastical History* mentioned in the previous chapter, are two legal clauses in which the hearth is used to represent an entire house or property. In the late seventh-century laws of King Ine of Wessex (*EHD* 32, 61), the hearth stands for the whole house in the calculation of tax: 'Church-scot is to be paid from the haulm ['stubble', referring to fields from which the harvest had been gathered] and the hearth where one resides at midwinter.' In the eleventh-century laws of Cnut, an individual described as *heorðfæst*, or seated at a hearth, was one who owned his own property (Whitelock 1955, *EHD* 20a; Dölling 1958, 52). Archaeologically, the presence of a hearth in a building has generally been taken to indicate its use as a dwelling, yet very few examples of *in situ* hearths have been identified in Anglo-Saxon buildings. The lack of preserved floor surfaces—which have almost invariably been ploughed or otherwise eroded away—is undoubtedly largely responsible for this.[38] At

---

[37] See Chapter 4 for a consideration of burials at entrances at Yeavering and elsewhere. A rare, waterlogged tenth-century oak building along the waterfront at Bull Wharf in the City of London had door jambs made of ash—a tree which was believed to have magical properties—raising the intriguing possibility that, in the Late Saxon period too, doorways were sometimes accorded ritual significance (D. Goodburn, pers. comm.).

[38] The lack of preserved floor levels is demonstrably responsible, at least in part, for the scarcity of hearths in Continental longhouses: only twelve of the more than 150 examples at the poorly preserved settlement of Flögeln-Eekhöltjen yielded traces of hearths; in contrast, nearly every longhouse at the

Flixborough, for example, where ground surfaces were comparatively well preserved, a relatively high proportion of buildings produced evidence for hearths (Loveluck 2007). Some archaeologists have argued that at least some buildings originally had raised timber floors, which would also help account for the lack of hearths. At Polebrook, for example, despite clear evidence of entranceways, the lack of any sign of wear on the cornbrash floor suggests that it was covered in some way (Upex 2005). Raised planked floors have also been suggested for at least some of the buildings at Cowdery's Down (Millett 1984, 240–1). The use of floorboards at ground-floor level, however, is virtually unknown in the earliest surviving vernacular buildings, making their widespread use during the Anglo-Saxon period—either in earth-fast timber buildings or in *Grubenhäuser* (see below)—less likely.[39]

Four of the timber buildings from West Stow—Halls 1, 2, 3, and 5—produced evidence for internal hearths. While the hearths found in Hall 5 (a poorly defined agglomeration of postholes which appears to represent several buildings or phases of building) were made up of Roman tile, the evidence in the other buildings consisted only of patches of burnt sand or clay. Yet the fact that all three were positioned in the middle of the building at almost precisely the same distance from the western gable wall and, in Halls 1 and 2, just offset from the entrances, greatly strengthens the likelihood that these burnt areas did indeed mark the position of a hearth (Tummuscheit 1995, Abb. 11). A hearth in Building C at Eye Kettleby also lay approximately 4 metres from one end of the building, but in this case it had been positioned against one of the long walls. The two wall posts adjacent to it were large, and stones had been placed between the posts and the hearth, 'presumably to fireproof the posts at, and below, ground level' (Finn, forthcoming). At least one other building also had an area of earth discoloured by heat close to the line of one long wall. Two other relatively early examples come from Yeavering Buildings D3—which had two presumably contemporary hearths and was identified by the excavator as a kitchen—and D4 (Hope-Taylor 1977, fig. 48). Building D3 was unusual in having not only two hearths but also a sunken floor, despite being constructed of earth-fast timber posts. The hearth in D4 was identified on the basis of a 'circular patch of reddened clay' overlying the original floor level, lying more or less centrally within the room to the west of the central corridor formed by the opposing entrances, not unlike the West Stow examples (ibid. 117 and fig. 53). Several *in situ* hearths—also mostly sited along the central axis of the building—have been found in Mid and Late Saxon buildings, such as Springfield Lyons Building 3, Faccombe Netherton Buildings 3 and 9, North Elmham Building Z, and Portchester Building S13 (Cunliffe 1976,

---

contemporary, waterlogged settlement a few miles away at Feddersen Wierde, had a hearth (Zimmermann 1992, 147; Haarnagel 1979).

[39] I am grateful to Mark Gardiner for this observation.

fig. 22; Wade-Martins 1980, fig. 84; Fairbrother 1990, figs. 4.7, 4.16; Tyler and Major 2005, fig. 72).[40]

Before considering the functions of Anglo-Saxon buildings, it is important to note that the variety of building techniques used in the late Saxon period was accompanied by a diversification of building forms. While rectangular buildings still predominated, square forms were also built (for example, Buildings L, J, and P at North Elmham, Buildings 2 and 20 at Springfield Lyons: Wade-Martins 1980, figs. 122, 123, 132, 143; Tyler and Major 2005, 128–9, 139). At Springfield Lyons, a small, square building, measuring approximately 4m x 5.4m (Building 1) with unusually deep foundation trenches has tentatively been identified as a free-standing tower associated with Building 1A, and a similar interpretation might apply to the square structure just to the north of a timber building at Bishops Waltham (Hampshire) (Tyler and Major 2005, 193; Lewis 1985). The base of what may have been another tower of similar dimensions, but stone-built and dating to the eleventh century, was excavated at Portchester, which had been one of the defended sites of the Burghal Hidage and was by this time presumably a manorial centre (Cunliffe 1976, 60).[41] A small number of cellared buildings—long recognized in urban contexts such as York and London—have also been identified on rural sites, notably at Bishopstone, where the remains of such a building was almost certainly the base of another tower (Thomas 2009). There is other evidence—although it is neither direct nor unproblematic—to suggest that some Late Saxon buildings possessed an upper storey, as in the case of the Long Hall at Cheddar (Rahtz 1979, 100–3). The existence in Late Saxon England of high-status buildings with upper storeys appears, as Reynolds has noted, to be confirmed by images on the Bayeux Tapestry and an entry in the *Anglo-Saxon Chronicle* (Reynolds 1999, 125).[42]

Function

Anglo-Saxon laws and other sources appear to indicate that, by the tenth century at least, food preparation, storage, stabling of animals, etc. were sited in separate buildings, as was the case elsewhere in the North Sea Zone (Hamerow 2002a, 20–1); yet, although each of these structures is mentioned by name, their physical appearance is nowhere described (Dölling 1958, 55–8).

---

[40] The remains of a hearth were also found in the long hall at Cheddar, although these have been interpreted as having fallen from a collapsed upper floor (Rahtz 1979, fig. 31).

[41] Despite the apparent relationship between the tower (S18) and an adjacent building (S13) (see Reynolds 1999, 127 and fig. 49), which appears to mirror that between Buildings 2 and 20 at Springfield Lyons, the second phase of the tower, at least, was in fact constructed after the building was no longer standing (Cunliffe 1976, 51, 60).

[42] *ASC* s.a. 978. 'In this year the leading councillors of England fell down from an upper storey [*in uno solario*] at Calne...'. There has been some debate about whether the Bayeux Tapestry's depiction of buildings is entirely realistic, or based ultimately on Late Antique models (Hart 1999, but see also Williams 1992).

Recent work by Gardiner on the eleventh-century text known as *Gerefa*, which contains instructions for the reeve on the management of the lord's farm, suggests that references to, for example, a kitchen, could just as well refer to an area or room within the house as to a separate building (Gardiner 2006).[43] List B of *Gerefa*—one of two lists of tools needed for the farm— appears to group them according to where they are kept in the farmstead, i.e. the kitchen, the dairy, granary, buttery, barn, bake- or brewhouse. Gardiner further notes that this grouping accords well with what is known of the way in which space was organized in later medieval farmsteads of *c*.1300. The evidence from Renhold, Water End West could point to such an arrangement. The quantities of food waste recovered from the fills of foundation trenches in Building 9150, especially from the western half of the building, and the deposition of cooking waste and oven fragments in a pit some 3 metres from the building, suggest the concentration of food preparation in certain areas, despite the lack (as far as we can see) of a purpose-built kitchen (Timby et al. 2007, 169, 172).

Influenced by written sources, archaeologists have sometimes—perhaps too readily—assigned specific functions to excavated buildings. While it may indeed be the case that the decision to build a rectangular, square, or L-shaped building was essentially governed by its intended use, identifying the functions of excavated buildings remains for the most part highly problematic. Nevertheless, convincing examples of halls, kitchens, bakehouses, barns, and even latrines have all been identified in the archaeological record.

Halls
In their 1985 paper, James, Marshall, and Millett identified a group of settlements containing mostly large buildings, that is, with a floor area measuring more than around 100m². These large, obviously communal, buildings may not unreasonably be identified as the halls (OE *healle*) referred to in Anglo-Saxon literature, which are distinguished in written sources from ordinary houses (OE *hus*) and appear as exceptional, one-roomed structures with the 'high seat' of the lord, a hearth, and benches for his followers where, in Rosemary Cramp's words, 'all public business such as the reception and feasting of visitors [took] place' (Cramp 1957, 71; Dölling 1958, 52). The highly formalized and symmetrical layouts of the largest buildings from the late sixth- and seventh-century settlements at Yeavering and Cowdery's Down have already been commented upon. Four tenth-century examples of so-called 'long halls' excavated at Sulgrave (Northamptonshire), Goltho, Chapel Street, Bicester, and Cheddar display strikingly close similarities in plan (Fig. 2.9), reflecting a

---

[43] As Harvey has demonstrated, however, *Gerefa* is essentially a literary work and not a practical manual; in Gardiner's words, the text 'is more the product of the scriptorium than the farmyard' (Harvey 1993; Gardiner 2006, 260).

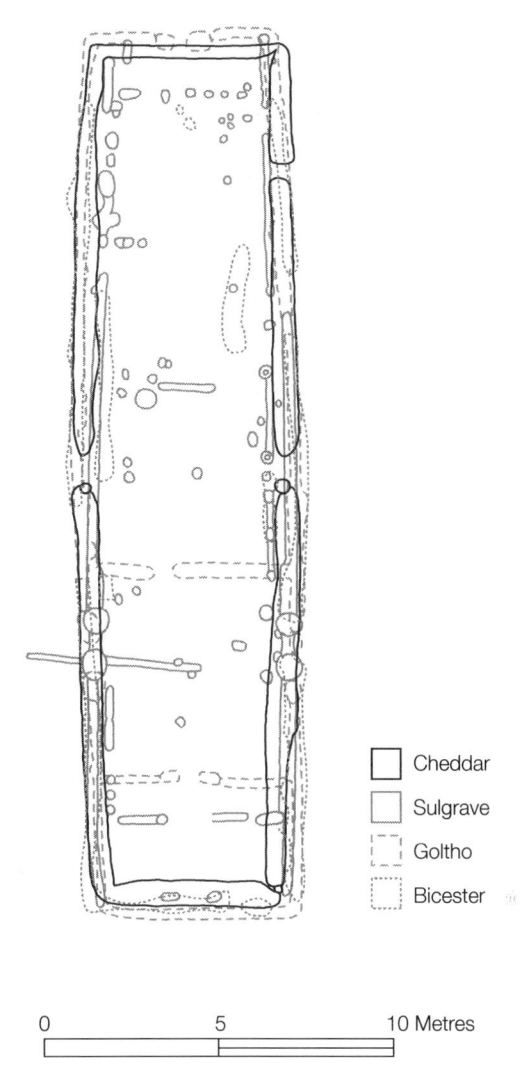

Fig. 2.9. The plans of Late Saxon long halls, superimposed.

continuing interest in standardized layout and measurement.[44] It is interesting to consider in this connection a passage in the Boldon Book, a twelfth-century estate record of the services of the tenants of the Bishop of Durham, which specifies that, in anticipation of the Bishop's visit, the villeins of Bishop Auckland were to build for him a 'Great Hall in the forest, 60 feet long and 16 feet broad within the posts', dimensions remarkably close to those of the late Saxon

---

[44] Despite being somewhat shorter, the 'eastern timber hall' at Raunds Furnells displays essentially the same form as these 'long halls' (Audouy and Chapman 2009, fig. 5.14).

'long halls' (Rees 1963, 162).[45] It is notable, however, that the positioning of doorways and hearths varied to a surprising degree between the four buildings and the internal arrangement of space would, therefore, have been quite different in each. Despite their elongated proportions and the fact that they are slightly wider in the middle than at the ends, the long halls appear to be related to the earlier building tradition seen at Yeavering, Northampton, and Cowdery's Down (as James, Marshall, and Millett noted in relation to Cheddar (1985, fig. 14)). Internal postholes and slots along one long wall of the Sulgrave and Bicester halls may relate to furniture or benches. As at Goltho, the Sulgrave hall contained three rooms. To the west of the main hearth room, it contained a 'service room', identified as such on the basis of the quantity of animal bone and pottery it contained. Beyond this was an open 'porch' with a cobbled floor (Davison 1977).

Another tenth-century development saw a distinct break with this earlier tradition, with the appearance in a number of high-status settlements of 'narrow-aisled' halls, in which the longevity of roof-carrying posts was increased by placing them inside the building, while the relatively light external walls could be easily repaired or replaced (Fig. 2.10; Gardiner 2004; Thomas 2010, 189–90). Such buildings, which would have been technically demanding to design and build, may represent 'an evolutionary link between pre-Conquest aisled buildings as excavated and the earliest standing vernacular buildings of later medieval England' (Thomas 2010, 190; Gardiner, forthcoming). This period also saw the use of stone in apparently secular buildings for the first time, albeit only in buildings of high status (Cunliffe 1976, 41–3; Boddington 1996, fig. 3; Meadows, forthcoming; Beresford 1987, fig. 60; Fairbrother 1990, fig. 4.5).[46] The fact that Anglo-Saxon elites, in contrast to their Frankish counterparts, continued to build their halls in wood rather than stone almost certainly reflects a deep-seated Germanic ideology, reflected in the use of the word *timber* to refer to 'building'; it may also relate to the link between the life-cycles of dwellings made of perishable materials and those of their inhabitants (Shapland, forthcoming).

Kitchens and bakehouses
While buildings containing ovens can reasonably be identified as detached kitchens or bakehouses, examples of such buildings are extremely rare in the archaeological record. Building AM at North Elmham, dated to the Mid Saxon period, appears to have housed a series of three ovoid, clay-lined ovens, although their contemporaneity with the building could not be conclusively demonstrated.[47] The main part of the building was nearly square,

---

[45] I am grateful to James Campbell for drawing this to my attention.
[46] Potentially secular stone buildings have been found at Sulgrave, Faccombe Netherton, and Portchester (Davison 1977, 112–13; Fairbrother 1990, 85–7; Cunliffe 1976, 60). The debate about the status of the Anglo-Saxon stone 'hall' at Northampton is a good illustration, however, of the difficulties involved in distinguishing secular from religious structures in this period (Blair 1996).
[47] Building AM cut an earlier oven which may indicate the presence on the same spot of an earlier bakehouse (Wade-Martins 1980, 69, fig. 87).

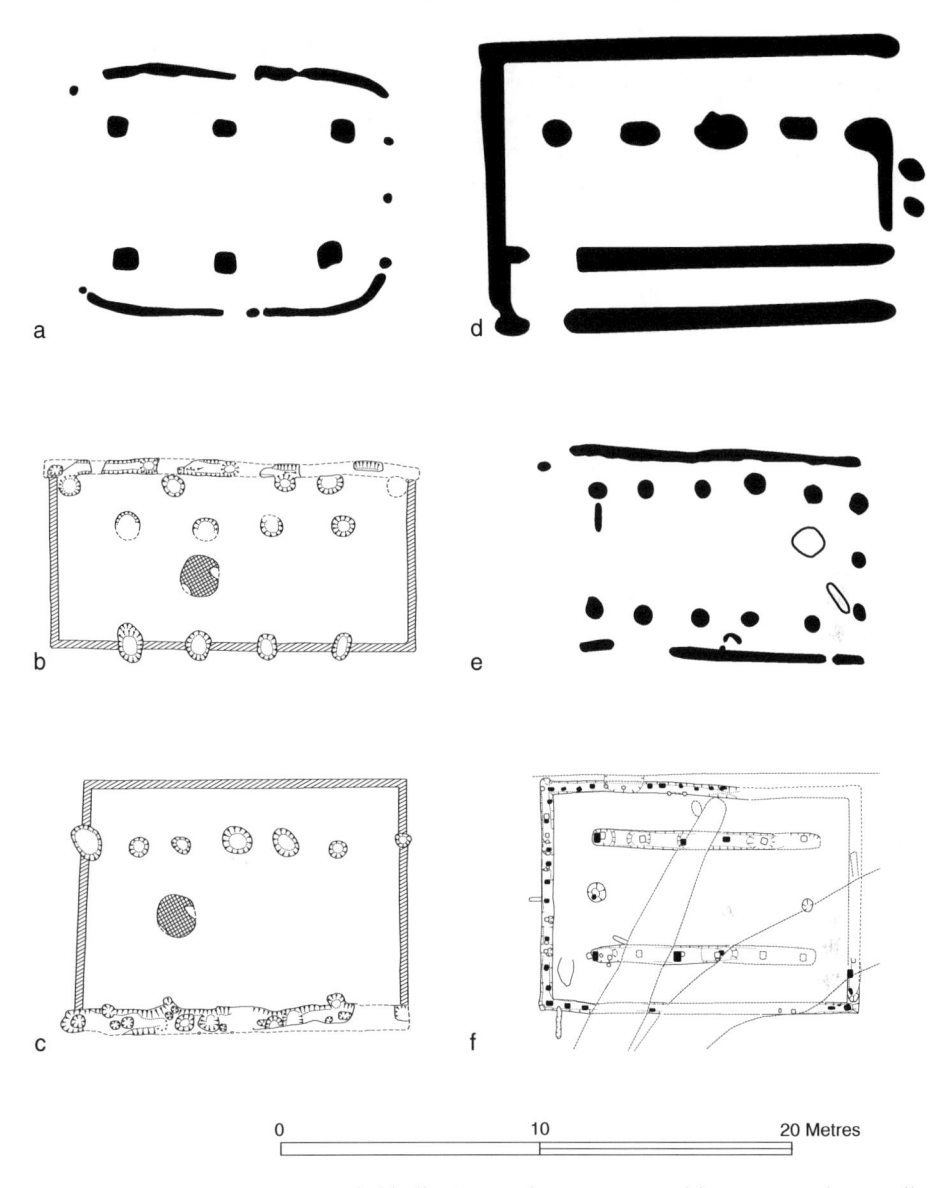

Fig. 2.10. Late Saxon narrow-aisled halls: A. Portchester; B, C. Goltho; D. Raunds Furnells; E. Ketton; F. Faccombe Netherton (after Cunliffe 1976; Beresford 1987; Boddington 1990; Meadows forthcoming; Fairbrother 1990).

measuring around 5.4m x 6.0m, with a small extension added to the south side. Building S11 at Portchester, which measured *c.*5.8m x 8.5m and dated to the ninth or tenth century, contained a rectangular oven (which replaced an earlier, poorly preserved oven) constructed mainly of re-used Roman tiles and limestone lumps set in clay (Cunliffe 1976, 29–32; Wade-Martins 1980, 69–73). A series of five kitchens were identified at Goltho. The earliest of these, built c.850, measured around 6.3m x 3.9m, and had a thick clay floor and central oven (Beresford 1987, 59). The floor of one of the later kitchens was 'covered with pottery, bone, and fragments of burnt daub emanating from the oven', while outside were 'numerous deposits of midden emanating from the kitchen' (ibid. 83). Regrettably, no botanical remains were published from the site despite the good state of preservation of several of the kitchens, at least one of which is recorded as having contained a malting oven (ibid. 69). Building 16 at Springfield Lyons has also been tentatively identified as a kitchen, based on the range of plant remains recovered in the vicinity (Tyler and Major 2005, 193) while two small, square structures—Buildings 2 and 20—were also interpreted as detached kitchens, on analogy with Goltho (ibid.). A two-roomed post-built structure axially aligned with the long hall at Sulgrave which contained a hearth and soak-away may also have served as a kitchen, although, like most of the examples just cited, this identification must remain tentative in the absence of further evidence. Finally, building D3 at Yeavering—already mentioned on account of its two hearths—was associated with a 'working hollow' lying immediately to the north and a pit complex immediately to the west; the fills of both the pits and working hollow contained a large quantity of bone fragments, mostly cattle long bones, which had been chopped and split (Hope-Taylor 1977, 103–6). The hearths, together with the evidence for butchery, led the excavator to describe D3 as a 'kitchen'. While it is very likely to have been connected with food preparation and ritual consumption, its early date and position within a remarkable cultic complex—including the 'temple' D2 and a prehistoric stone circle which acted as a focus for burials in the Anglo-Saxon period—emphasize its uniqueness.

Barns and granaries
The scarcity of grain storage facilities on Anglo-Saxon, and indeed most later medieval, settlements is in marked contrast to the situation in Iron Age and Roman Britain and has long puzzled archaeologists. It is perhaps reasonable to assume, based on evidence from contemporary settlements in the Netherlands and Germany, that unthreshed grain was stored in the rafters of houses, in *Grubenhäuser* (see below) and/or in ricks (which would leave no archaeological trace), and then threshed as the need arose (Powlesland 1997; Hamerow 2002a, 22–38). Large deposits of cereals associated with a few Anglo-Saxon buildings—such as the charred oats found in the postholes of Building 6 at Springfield Lyons and Structure 1200 at Chapel Street, Bicester—are suggestive of grain storage (Pelling 2002, 170; Tyler and Major 2005, 195). While a few convincing examples of Anglo-Saxon granaries have been published—for example at Pennyland (Buckinghamshire), Orton Hall Farm, Yarnton, and Wicken Bonhunt (Essex)—build-

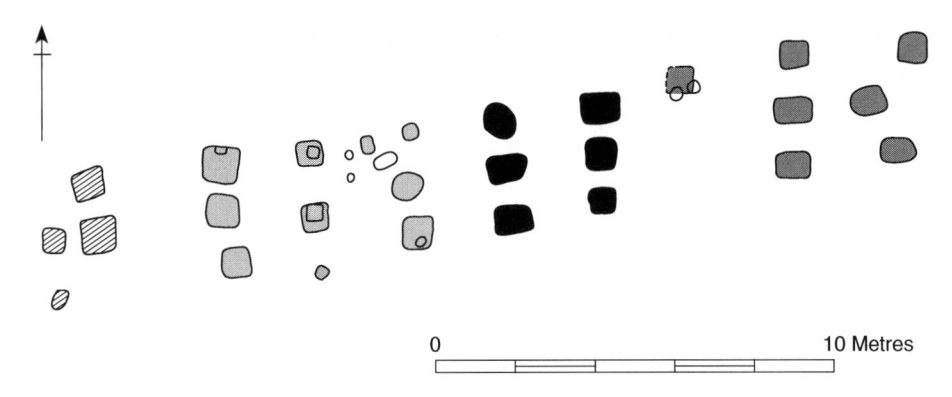

Fig. 2.11. Granaries from Yarnton (after Hey 2004).

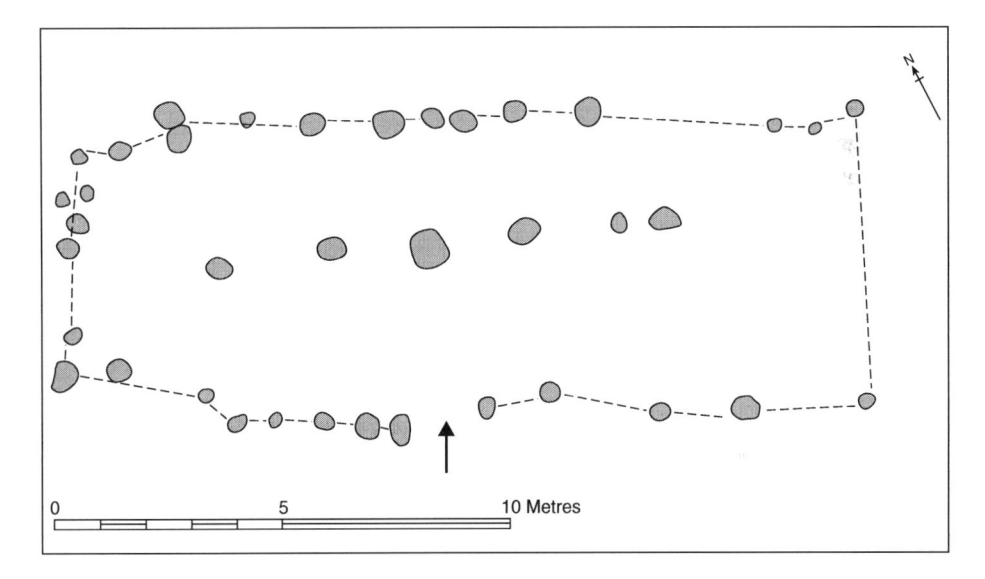

Fig. 2.12. A Mid Saxon barn. Higham Ferrers, Building 2665 (redrawn from Hardy et al. 2007).

ings which can reasonably be interpreted as barns are extremely rare (Fig. 2.11; Wade 1980, 98; Williams 1993, 82; MacKreth 1996, 89–90; Hey 2004, 124–5, figs. 6.22–23). Two of the most convincing examples were excavated at Higham Ferrers. Building 2664 and its successor, Building 2665, were elongated, rectangular post-built structures, *c*.6m x 15m, with a central line of roof-supporting posts running along the length of the building (Fig. 2.12). Similarities with early medieval barns excavated in the Netherlands, together with a 'high concentration of cereal remains from one of the postholes' of Building 2665, support the interpretation of these buildings as barns (Hamerow 2002a, fig. 2.15; Hardy et al. 2007). In fact, however, most Anglo-Saxon settlements included a variety of structures and sheds that could have served as storage facilities.[48]

Latrines

A number of distinctive structures identified as latrines have also been identified in Late Saxon settlements, in most cases adjacent to major buildings. At Bishopstone, an apsidal-ended structure enclosing a central cesspit has been interpreted as a latrine, as have rectangular structures at Eynsham Abbey, North Elmham—Building O, immediately outside Building P—and Faccombe Netherton, where the latrine lay adjacent to a building identified as the 'hall'. A similar structure outside the western entrance to the West Hall at Cheddar may also have served as a latrine (Rahtz 1979, 156–7; Wade-Martins 1980, 142–5; Fairbrother 1990, 65 and fig. 4.18; Hardy et al. 2003, 486, fig. 3.16; Thomas 2010 195). At Goltho, a long, narrow cesspit was housed in a building that appears to have been attached to a corner of a large building identified by the excavator as a 'bower'; two other cesspits may originally have been housed in similar structures (Beresford 1987, 57, 68, 79, fig. 68).[49]

It will not have escaped the reader's notice that nearly all the buildings which have yielded evidence of a specific function (excluding those which merely contained a hearth) date to the Mid and, especially, Late Saxon periods and that most if not all come from settlements regarded as high status. We undoubtedly suffer from a lack of excavated 'ordinary' settlements of the Late Saxon period (a problem considered in more detail in Chapter 3), which itself introduces a danger of circularity into any argument about status. It is not unreasonable to suggest, however, based on current evidence, that the construction of special-purpose buildings was a marker of high status in Late Saxon England. Reynolds has drawn attention to the 'growth of manorial-type settlements during the tenth and eleventh centuries' and the increase in excavated buildings identified as the residences of *thegns*, the highest-ranking social group in Anglo-Saxon England, and provides a helpful survey of written sources relating to such settlements (1999, 57–63, 123–4). Of particular relevance to this discussion is one of the most oft-cited texts on the subject of status, an early eleventh-century document known as the *Geþyncðo* (or the 'promotion law'), which famously states that in order to rise to the rank of *thegn*, a *ceorl* (a free peasant landholder) must first possess, amongst other things, a *burh*-gate and a bell

---

[48] A building provisionally identified as a Mid Saxon threshing barn has also recently been excavated at Lyminge (G. Thomas, pers. comm. 2011).
[49] Thirteen green-stained pits—some associated with postholes—were found at Catholme. Some of these could have been latrines, although none contained cess and other functions are possible (Losco-Bradley and Kinsley 2002, 36–40).

(Whitelock 1955, 432).[50] A later version of this text specifies a 'bell house' (which has been argued to suggest a tower, although this cannot be assumed), and adds a church and kitchen to the list (Reynolds 1999, 60).

Earth-fast timber buildings: concluding thoughts

The preceding discussion has inevitably focused on those kinds of structures for which we have the best evidence—namely, rectangular, earth-fast timber buildings. But we should not forget that there is evidence—albeit scanty and as yet poorly understood—for other kinds of timber buildings in Anglo-Saxon England, such as those with sill-beam foundations and roundhouses. At Quarrington, three circular, post-built buildings, each measuring some 6 metres in diameter, were eventually replaced by rectangular posthole structures of the kind normally associated with settlements of this period, while at Yeavering, a roundhouse 'curiously reminiscent of the...native settlements of the region' was found on the site formerly occupied by Building D3 (Hope-Taylor 1977, 105; Taylor 2003b). We should not be surprised by the persistence of roundhouses into the post-Roman period in light of Bede's description in his *Life of St Cuthbert* of the structure built by the saint on the island of Farne as 'almost round in plan, measuring about four or five poles from wall to wall', although in this case, with walls made of unworked stone and turf and a dug-out floor (Bede, *VSC* XVII).

Grubenhäuser

Introduction

Grubenhäuser are by far the most numerous type of Anglo-Saxon building to be identified archaeologically and, unlike their earth-fast counterparts, their Continental pedigree has never been seriously questioned (Hamerow 2002a, 31–5). Despite this, they remain poorly understood. As noted in Chapter 1, the fact that they comprise a large, sunken hollow, usually associated with a variable number of postholes, means that the great majority of finds from early Anglo-Saxon settlements tend to come from these structures. Indeed, settlements with few or no *Grubenhäuser* generally produce little in the way of finds or pottery. Analyses of these buildings therefore centre on three closely related issues: their reconstruction, their function, and the extent to which finds contained within their fills reflect their date and the activities carried out in and around them.

Despite their ubiquity, no comprehensive study of Anglo-Saxon *Grubenhäuser* had been undertaken until a recent monograph by Jess Tipper devoted

---

[50] Although Whitelock translates *burhgeat* as 'castle gate', Williams has pointed out that, in this context, the term refers to a defensible manor house, not a fortified administrative centre (Williams 1992).

entirely to the study of these enigmatic structures (Tipper 2004). They are described by him as follows:

The *Grubenhaus* is a building type in which a pit forms the central component.... They are typically sub-rectangular in shape, measuring c 3 x 4m in area x c 0.3–0.5m in depth with sides sloping down to a roughly flat base. There are often two post-holes along the short walls of the pit, often referred to as the gable post-holes, although the number of post-holes varies from zero to six, including additional post-holes in the four corners of the pit. These post-holes presumably took the supports for the superstructure. Internal structural evidence other than the post-holes is rare. (Tipper 2004, 1)

Tipper's study is based primarily on a data-set of over 400 buildings from West Stow, Mucking, and West Heslerton—and the results of his analyses enable several long-standing questions about these structures to be answered. Nevertheless, even after such detailed study, the superstructure and function of these buildings remain matters of conjecture. The following discussion summarizes some of Tipper's main findings with regard to certain structural and typological aspects of *Grubenhäuser* before considering the implications of his findings for their reconstruction and function.

The widely varying proportions of *Grubenhäuser* to earth-fast timber buildings seen on different settlements has long been assumed to relate to underlying geology; settlements sited, for example, on chalk are less likely to contain large numbers of *Grubenhäuser* than those on soft subsoils. Tipper's study broadly confirms this. Nevertheless, their distribution across the very large area excavated at West Heslerton, which contained within it variable underlying geology, suggested that 'geology played a prominent, but not determining, role in the distribution of structural types across the site' (ibid. 24).

The size of *Grubenhäuser* also varies widely, although Tipper's study reveals 'a strong central tendency for *c.* 4 x 3 m' (ibid. 64 and tables 18, 19). It has been recognized for some time that the seventh century saw the appearance of larger *Grubenhäuser*, i.e. measuring around five or more metres in length (Hamerow 1993, 11). Although his study appears to confirm this, Tipper argues that, 'in the absence of other dating evidence, it should not be assumed that other large *Grubenhäuser* are necessarily seventh-century or later' (Tipper 2004, 66). Nevertheless, while it cannot be assumed that *Grubenhäuser* smaller than 5 metres in length are fifth- or sixth-century in date, there are no examples known to the writer or cited by Tipper of larger *Grubenhäuser* which can be firmly dated earlier than the seventh century.

The widely varying depth of these structures has also puzzled archaeologists: neighbouring structures on the same site can have markedly different depths, from just a few centimetres to around a metre. Tipper's study demonstrates that there is no correlation between floor area and depth and observes that depth is therefore likely to relate to function. This, as will be seen later, has implications for the reconstruction of these buildings (ibid. 65–6).

A final typological conundrum is why some *Grubenhäuser* had two posts, while others had four or six. Tipper's study establishes that while the number of posts is not related to chronology, there is regional patterning: while buildings with two posts are the most common overall, those with six posts are largely restricted to East Anglia and the south-east of England (ibid. 68–70). This corresponds well with the evidence for regional traditions seen elsewhere in the North Sea Zone (Hamerow 2002a, 31).

Reconstruction: sunken or suspended floors?

Traditionally, *Grubenhäuser* have been seen as modest, sunken-floored structures which were ancillary to earth-fast, ground-level dwellings. They have usually been reconstructed, based on a range of historic and ethnographic analogies, with a sunken floor and with a roof, supported by two ridge-posts, extending more or less to the ground to form a tent-like structure (Fig. 2.13); such a building would require a minimum of labour and materials and would be relatively short-lived in comparison to earth-fast timber buildings (West 1986, 116). Stanley West, based on evidence uncovered during his excavations at West Stow, was the first archaeologist to argue that the sunken hollow had in fact been covered by a planked floor which rested on joists laid on the ground surface beyond the edges of the pit as well as on a central joist, half-lapped to the ridge-posts (West Stow Environmental Archaeology Group 1974; West 1969). The evidence from West Stow on which this interpretation was based consisted primarily of the following (West 1986, 116–21):

1. Oak timbers interpreted as floor and wall planks had been preserved in two buildings that had been destroyed by fire.
2. None of the pits displayed evidence of entrances.
3. None of the pits displayed signs of wear on the bottom of the hollow or erosion of the sides, despite having been dug into soft, sandy subsoil, nor evidence of revetments.
4. Many of the pits had very restricted floor areas, making them impractical as workrooms.
5. The fine, homogenous nature of the lowest, 'primary' fill was suggestive of debris that had filtered through spaces between floorboards.
6. Clay hearths in the upper fills of several *Grubenhäuser* overlapped the edge of the sunken hollow, suggesting that they had rested on a suspended floor, while two articulated dog skeletons in SFB 16 were thought to be the remains of animals that had crawled into the space under the suspended floor. (West 1986, 23)

The *Grubenhäuser* from West Stow were thus reconstructed as substantial buildings, whose superstructure differed little in size and appearance from

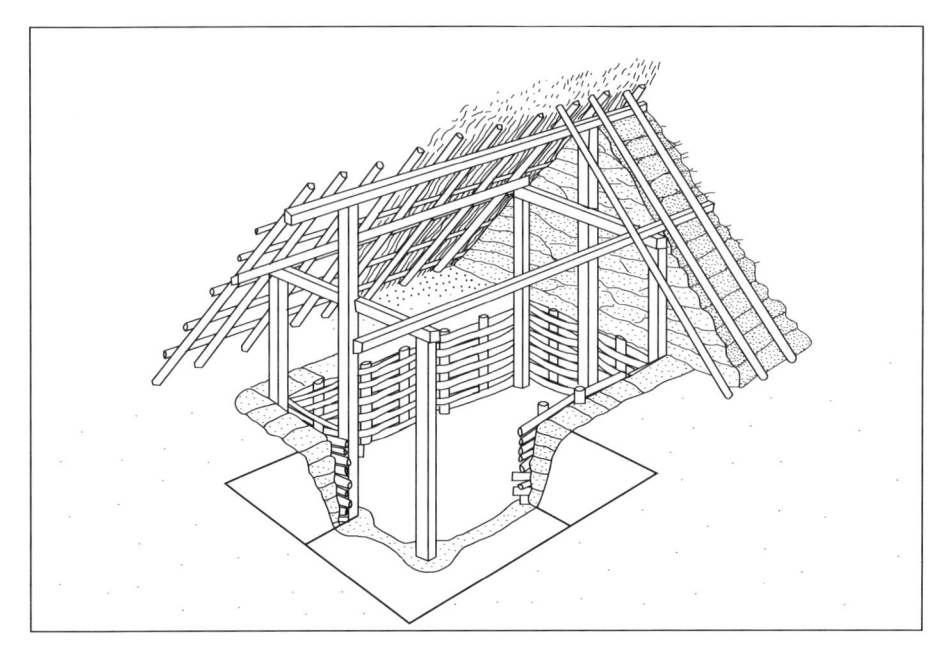

Fig. 2.13. A reconstruction of a *Grubenhaus* as a sunken-floored building (after Heidinga and Offenburg 1992).

earth-fast timber buildings. They were, nevertheless, interpreted in the final publication as secondary structures, which formed 'satellites' around earth-fast dwellings. It was argued that the most likely function of the sub-floor space was to improve air circulation, thus prolonging the life of the main structural timbers; storage was seen as another possible use.

This alternative reconstruction obviously has enormous implications for how early Anglo-Saxon settlements are interpreted. West acknowledged that, while his model resolved certain problems of interpretation, it also created others, and that one could not assume that all *Grubenhäuser* had suspended floors (1986, 120). Ever since West put forward this alternative reconstruction, the question of whether *Grubenhäuser* were in fact sunken-*floored* structures, or whether instead a planked floor was laid over the hollow, has dominated discussion of these buildings.

In his 2004 study, Tipper points out that some of the evidence used to support the 'sunken-floored' model does not withstand close scrutiny (2004, 74–93). He has identified several categories of evidence that are particularly problematic, broadly corresponding with West's original observations:

1. The relative rarity of evidence for wooden revetments lining the edges of the hollow and the fact that even hollows without revetments generally show little evidence of erosion, suggest the presence of suspended floors.

2. The restricted floor area in small *Grubenhäuser* and those with sloping sides would have made them 'impractical as a living or working space' (ibid. 74).

3. The evidence for planked floors and walls is central to the argument in favour of suspended floors (ibid. 79). In fact, of the small number of excavated *Grubenhäuser* that had been destroyed by fire, most have produced evidence for planked floors, although debate remains about whether these were originally suspended across the pit, or lying on its base (ibid. 86).

4. The lack of evidence for entrances into the sunken hollows—which could be up to about 1 metre deep—implies the use of suspended floors (ibid. 83).

5. Some of the published evidence for wear on the base of the pit and occupation levels on the base of the hollow is suspect, although Tipper accepts that 'a small number had trampled central hollows' (ibid. 92). The majority of *Grubenhäuser* do not display such evidence and the base of many of the pits was too irregular to have served as an effective floor surface. A micromorphological study of deposits overlying the base of a *Grubenhaus* at Bloodmoor Hill (Suffolk) suggests that these were the result of natural processes, not human occupation (ibid. 84).[51]

6. A few pits conforming roughly to the size and shape of *Grubenhäuser* have been interpreted as *Grubenhäuser* without gable posts (ibid. 72–4). Tipper argues that gable posts (which are often relatively shallow) were not essential to the stability of the building and were effectively scaffolding for a superstructure which was 'self-supporting with the main weight of the roof borne on wall-posts of load-bearing turf walls around the outside of the pit' (ibid. 93). Tipper acknowledges, however, that evidence from a small but significant number of *Grubenhäuser* for the repair and replacement of gable posts[52] militates against this interpretation (ibid. 72).

7. Stakeholes in the base of the pit (as distinct from revetments around the edges) have been identified in many *Grubenhäuser* and on a variety of subsoils. It is difficult to imagine what function such arrangements of stakes could have served beneath a suspended floor. Tipper believes, however, that virtually all represent rodent or root disturbance 'mistaken as stakeholes by excavators with preconceptions of what a typical *Grubenhaus* should look like' (ibid. 88).

8. Hearths. Having re-examined the evidence for hearths in *Grubenhäuser*, Tipper concludes that no unequivocal examples which were contemporary

---

[51] A similar study of a *Grubenhaus* at Sherborne House, Lechlade (Gloc.) suggests that the lowest fill represents backfill of the hollow with soils from the surrounding area, i.e. it represents re-deposited material rather than an occupation layer (Bateman et al. 2003).

[52] An example may be seen at Botolphs (Sussex), where the gable posts of one *Grubenhaus* 'were replaced during the use of the building', despite the shallowness of both the pit and the postholes (Gardiner 1990, 226 and fig. 7).

with the buildings' original use could be identified. The burnt clay deposits at West Stow, interpreted by the excavator as the remains of hearths that rested on suspended floors, are reinterpreted as relating to the re-use of partly backfilled hollows (ibid. 89–92).

Tipper concludes that the suspended-floor model 'fits more easily with most of the archaeological evidence' while admitting that 'aspects of this interpretation are also problematical' (ibid. 93). It should be recognized that, while his study has exposed as flawed some of the evidence used to argue for the existence of sunken floors, it has not identified any direct, unequivocal evidence for suspended floors, although such evidence by its very nature would be extremely elusive.

The argument in favour of the suspended-floor model thus rests mostly on the scarcity of evidence for entrances, for wear on the floor, for occupation layers,[53] and for lining of the sides of the pit in most structures (although there is some evidence for all of these), as well as the restricted and/or uneven floors of many of the structures. All of these objections, however, assume that these buildings were occupied. As will shortly be seen, there is growing evidence that one of their main uses was for storage, in which case one would not necessarily expect to find doorways, wear, or occupation layers.

The plausibility of the 'suspended-floor' model is, furthermore, equally open to scrutiny. While some stakeholes may have been misidentified, others clearly have not. The excavators of several *Grubenhäuser* at Riverdene, Hampshire, for example, identified and excavated numerous stakeholes on the base of several of the pits; the area outside the structures was carefully examined to ensure that these were not the result of natural disturbance, but 'no similar features were seen outside the [*Grubenhaus*]' (Hall-Torrance and Weaver 2003, 80).[54] The marked variability in the depth of these buildings almost certainly does relate to function, but if the pit served merely as an air-space, this variability becomes more difficult to explain. It is striking that most of the *Grubenhäuser* which burned down produced evidence of planked flooring, yet it should be recalled that the laying of a timber floor is an expensive undertaking, requiring substantial amounts of labour and materials. Planked ground floors are, furthermore, absent in the earliest surviving vernacular buildings of the late twelfth and early thirteenth centuries (Walker 1999). It would be remarkable, therefore,

---

[53] A more convincing example of an occupation layer comes from Ryall Quarry (Worcestershire), where 'a thin gritty silt deposit' directly overlying the base of the pit of SFB 4 is interpreted as having formed during the building's use, a theory supported by the remarkably consistent radiocarbon dates of cal AD 595–660, 540–670, and 560–660 (at 95.4% confidence) produced by charcoal fragments (deriving from two different species) recovered from this layer (Barber and Watts 2006).

[54] Other features in the base of some *Grubenhäuser* also seem inconsistent with the use of a suspended floor, such as the evenly formed ramp at one end of a large *Grubenhaus* excavated at Hurst Park, East Molesey, Surrey (Andrews 1996). A *Grubenhaus* excavated at Wharram Percy not only produced evidence of a hearth (see below), stakeholes, a 'trampled chalk surface', and a wattle revetment, but had been partly dug into an earlier Roman ditch, the fill of which 'had become trampled to form a hard compacted surface' (Milne and Richards 1992, 20, 82).

if the majority of buildings in early Anglo-Saxon England possessed such floors. In some cases, furthermore, the pits of *Grubenhäuser* have been re-cut or modified, which would require a planked floor to be taken up and replaced; indeed it is difficult to see why a sub-floor space would need to be expanded or modified in this way.

A few *Grubenhäuser* have, furthermore, produced clear evidence of clay floors on the base of the hollow. Building C1 at Yeavering produced not only exceptionally well preserved evidence of planked revetments and walls, but also of 'a floor of well-prepared clay' that 'rested on clean, undisturbed natural sand' (Hope-Taylor 1977, 90–1 and plates 56–8). Building D3 also had a sunken floor covered with clay, although its construction in many ways resembles that of a posthole building more closely than it does a *Grubenhaus*, making this building highly unusual (see the discussion of such 'hybrids' below). The exceptionally large *Grubenhaus* excavated at Upton (Northamptonshire) is recorded as having had a 'made up floor' covering at least part of the base, and three buildings at Marlow Car Park, Canterbury, are also recorded as having had clay floors (Jackson et al. 1969, 206–10; Blockley et al. 1995; Tipper 2004, 84).

Finally, a few *Grubenhäuser* have been found with rows of clay loomweights resting on the base of the hollow, generally interpreted as having fallen from upright, warp-weighted looms (Rahtz 1976, fig. 2.12). The question of whether these buildings were actually used for weaving is considered below; of relevance here is how such rows could have survived intact if the loom and/or loomweights had collapsed into the hollow along with a planked floor.

In the absence of decisive new evidence, the debate about the superstructure of *Grubenhäuser* continues to rely heavily on issues of plausibility; there is persuasive, if indirect, evidence in support of both models. It is likely that the buildings that have been grouped together under the label of *Grubenhäuser* in fact displayed more than one kind of superstructure, something that was already recognized in the West Stow report (West 1986, 116–21). While there can be little doubt that the 'sunken-floored' model has sometimes been uncritically adopted, 'suspended floors' have also at times been too readily proposed for features which in fact produced little evidence to support either model, perhaps in a revisionist desire to counter the traditional view of these buildings as 'unsophisticated and low-cost structures' (Tipper 2004, 78).

If we are to believe that most *Grubenhäuser* possessed suspended planked floors and would therefore have resembled and been as large as many of the earth-fast timber buildings discussed in the preceding section, then this has enormous implications for their function. They would, for example, represent at least as great an expenditure of labour and materials as most earth-fast buildings. Far from being ancillary structures—the conventional interpretation, adopted by both West and Tipper (West 1986; Tipper 2004, 184)—they would need to be regarded as equivalent to, if not of higher status than, earth-fast buildings, as Rahtz was the first to recognize (1976, 79). Other evidence for the function of these structures must first be considered before returning to this problem.

Formation processes and function

Central to Tipper's re-evaluation is a detailed analysis of the processes involved in the formation of *Grubenhaus* fills in order to establish whether the artefacts they contain reflect the date and function of these buildings—an assumption often made but rarely tested. As already noted, the sides of most *Grubenhaus* pits display little evidence of erosion, indicating that, once the structures were abandoned, the pits were rapidly backfilled, a theory which finds strong support in experimental work carried out at West Stow (Tipper 2004, 104–5). This may seem encouraging to those who hope to find clues to the buildings' uses amongst the finds they contain, but Tipper's investigation suggests that the process by which the pits filled up was anything but straightforward.

Many *Grubenhäuser* contain so-called 'tripartite' fills. The conventional interpretation of such fills is that the lowest layer, which is often dark and humic, represents an 'occupation deposit', argued by West to have accumulated beneath a suspended floor during the use of the building. In other cases, the fills overlying the bases of *Grubenhäuser* have been interpreted as the remains of collapsed turf walls and roofs. The middle fill is usually characterized as representing 'rubbish deposits, surface dumps, [or] spoil from the excavation of later *Grubenhäuser*', i.e. secondary deposits (Tipper 2004, 107). The upper fill is usually interpreted as having formed as the lower fills compacted, creating a hollow that 'gradually silted up with material from the surrounding ground surface, acting as an artefact trap for surface rubbish, although dumps of material might also have been deposited' (ibid.).

Based on a small number of micromorphological studies and re-evaluation of original site records, Tipper concludes that the West Stow fills and other supposed occupation layers were in every case actually secondary. He believes, furthermore, that the discovery in a few buildings of cross-joining sherds (i.e. joining pieces of the same vessel) between lower, middle, and upper fills suggests that even *Grubenhäuser* with tripartite fills must have been 'backfilled in a single phase or, at least, that the material derived from a single source' (ibid). This apparently contradictory evidence is hard to explain, and Tipper accepts that 'further research is required to understand fully the nature and formation of *Grubenhaus* deposits' (ibid.).

These uncertainties aside, Tipper's analysis of the distribution of finds, and especially pottery, within *Grubenhaus* fills leads him to conclude that 'most of the material in *Grubenhaus* fills was the result of tertiary deposition[55] with no

---

[55] That is, derives from midden deposits that could have been carried some distance across the site to be used as backfill for abandoned buildings.

direct relationship to the function of the buildings' (2004, 160). The implications of this for establishing the chronological development of settlements are considered in Chapter 3. Here, it is the implications for the function of these buildings that need to be considered.

Tipper's analysis notwithstanding, there is good evidence from a number of sites that abandoned *Grubenhäuser* were at least partly backfilled with material from their immediate vicinity. One of the most striking examples comes from the settlement at Radley, Barrow Hills (Oxfordshire) where a *Grubenhaus* had been dug through a Neolithic burial (Bradley 1992, 132 and fig. 5). The fill of the *Grubenhaus* contained bone fragments from the same burial, demonstrating that it had been at least partly backfilled with material originally excavated from the pit— material that had clearly not travelled far. The presence of significant numbers of large, unabraded sherds in *Grubenhaus* fills is, furthermore, not uncommon and also points to secondary deposition rather than tertiary material from middens. SFB 2217 at Brandon Road, Thetford, for example, contained pottery which 'suffered little re-working, suggesting that it reached its final location in a relatively fresh state' (Atkins and Connor, forthcoming). Furthermore, pottery from *Grubenhäuser* at Botolphs was 'unabraded and comprised large sized sherds, a substantial number of which were conjoining. The bone showed little sign of gnawing or erosion' (Gardiner 1990, 239). Finally, a *Grubenhaus* at Wharram Percy contained several mould fragments for casting non-ferrous metalwork. These were extremely friable and 'it is unlikely that they would have survived at all if they had moved far from where they were discarded' (Milne and Richards 1992, 82).[56] The pottery and bone from the same feature, in contrast, did appear to have derived from midden deposits (ibid. 36).

Thus, while it is not possible to correlate finds from *Grubenhaus* fills straightforwardly with function, a significant body of archaeological evidence suggests that it would be unwise to dismiss the material found in *Grubenhäuser* comprehensively as a guide to the activities that went on around, and maybe even in, these buildings. A wide range of specific functions has been attributed to *Grubenhäuser*, and there is now a general consensus that they served a variety of uses (Rahtz 1976, 76; Hamerow 2002a, 31–5; Tipper 2004, 160–85). The most abundant archaeological evidence, however, relates to grain storage and textile production.

Grain storage
The scarcity of special-purpose grain storage facilities on early Anglo-Saxon settlements has already been remarked upon and is in marked contrast to

---

[56] Two fragments of another such mould were found in the fill of *Grubenhaus* 109 at Mucking (Hamerow 1993, fig. 141). The settlement at Lyminge has also produced evidence that *Grubenhäuser* there were being backfilled with relatively 'fresh' refuse (G. Thomas, pers. comm. 2011).

contemporary settlements on the other side of the North Sea, where post-built granaries were common (Hamerow 2002a, 36–8). While there is evidence to suggest that at least some grain was stored in the rafters of earth-fast timber buildings (see above), evidence from a few Continental settlements, notably in the Netherlands, indicates that *Grubenhäuser* could also serve as grain stores (Hamerow 2002a, 34). Comparable evidence has been found at West Heslerton, where several *Grubenhäuser* were found to have contained 'large quantities of carbonized grain on the bases of their pits' (Tipper 2004; Powlesland 1997, 106). Tipper suggests, following Powlesland and others, that 'the air space below the suspended floor could have allowed the free circulation of air beneath the store, creating a favourable cool, dry environment for the storage of grain. The suspended floor would also have helped to resist attack from vermin and other pests' (Tipper 2004, 164; cf. Powlesland 2003, 38). The admittedly slight increase in evidence for barns and granaries in later Saxon settlements coincides with a time when *Grubenhäuser* were becoming less common in rural contexts, which may support the idea that some of these buildings—whether or not they had suspended floors—were used for grain storage. It should be recalled, however, that *Grubenhäuser* and other grain storage facilities are found together on contemporary Continental settlements (Hamerow 2002a, 31–8; Tipper 2004, 164). It may be significant in this connection that, at the Mid Saxon settlement at Yarnton, a probable granary lay in the same part of the site as a group of *Grubenhäuser* (Figs. 2.11, 3.18; Hey 2004).

Textile production
The most common class of artefact found in *Grubenhäuser* after pottery relates to textile production. By far the most numerous of these artefacts are clay loomweights, both fired and unfired, which would originally have been suspended from vertical looms to keep the warp threads taut. Spindle whorls, pin beaters, and other implements made out of a range of materials, but mostly clay, bone, or antler, are also found (Rahtz 1976, 76–9).[57] As already noted, loomweights are sometimes found resting on the base of the pits. Where these are numerous and/or arranged in neat, sometimes overlapping, rows—often in *Grubenhäuser* that had been destroyed by fire—it appears that they dropped directly from a loom onto the floor, or alternatively, had been threaded on sticks for storage (see Tipper 2004, table 55 for examples of this kind of deposit).[58] Nevertheless, Tipper cautions that even 'the

[57] Annular weights made out of lead—a valuable substance unlikely to have been casually discarded—are also on occasion found, as at Barton Court Farm (GH 1190, which contained 16 lead annular weights in an overlapping row), and Mucking (GH 17 and 66) (Miles 1986; Hamerow 1993).
[58] Some artefact assemblages found on or just above the base of *Grubenhäuser* represent so-called 'placed deposits', i.e. the remnants of a ritual act, usually associated with the closure of the structure. Some of these deposits, which are discussed in Chapter 4, contain loomweights. It may not always be

discovery of groups or rows of loomweights in the base of a *Grubenhaus* does not necessarily mean that the structure was a specialized weaving shed nor that weaving had been undertaken in it. The structure could have been used for their storage rather than use' (ibid. 166).[59] He accepts, however, that at least some groups of complete loomweights on the base of *Grubenhäuser* represent 'primary deposits which were destroyed *in situ*' and that 'it seems reasonable to assume that large groups of intact loomweights were deposited close to where they had been used' (ibid. 168). Clearly, some of these buildings were used for cloth production. It is true, however, that even in cases where it appears almost certain that weaving took place inside a *Grubenhaus*, there is no reason to assume that weaving was the only activity which took place inside the building, nor that weaving was not also carried out in earth-fast timber buildings (see Hamerow 2002a, 33 for Continental examples of ground-level buildings used for weaving). Evidence from the other side of the North Sea should, however, make us think carefully before dismissing the idea of *Grubenhäuser* as weaving sheds, although it must be recognized that nothing directly comparable has been found in England. At least one of the *Grubenhäuser* excavated at the seventh- to twelfth-century settlement of Dalem (Lower Saxony) produced convincing evidence that it had indeed been used primarily for cloth production. *Grubenhaus* 9, with a sunken area measuring 4.9m x 3.5m and (like all of the Dalem *Grubenhäuser*) a stone oven in one corner, contained 104 loomweights lying on the floor of the sunken hollow in two double rows. Many still rested on their edge, where they had apparently dropped from the loom when the building burned down, leaving a detailed record of the position of the loom itself. The latter was some 4m wide and would have taken up much of the space inside the building. No evidence of a planked floor appears to have survived (Zimmermann 1982, Abb. 3, 7, 8).

Archaeologists often cite ancient and medieval writers who appear to indicate that cloth production was carried out in special buildings, perhaps even buildings with dug-out floors (Hamerow 2002a, 44–6). These sources—notably Pliny's *Naturalis Historia* (XIX.II.9), certain Carolingian capitularies, and other early medieval legal texts, have arguably led some to interpret structures as weaving sheds on the basis of rather tenuous archaeological evidence. Tipper rightly observes that these sources, while a useful adjunct to the archaeological

---

possible to distinguish them from objects that had been used or stored in the building; whether such deposits reflected the original function of the building is a moot point, but at least some deposits of loomweights may be seen in this light (Hamerow 2006, 17–18; Gibson and Murray 2003, 210–11; Sofield, forthcoming).

[59] The interpretation of certain internal features in a few *Grubenhäuser* as the emplacements for warp-weighted looms or even seats for the weaver (e.g. at Upton; Jackson et al. 1969) are regarded by Tipper as inconclusive, not least because such emplacements are unnecessary for this type of loom (Tipper 2004, 169–70).

record, are by no means conclusive and that an element of circularity has crept into arguments regarding whether *Grubenhäuser* were used as weaving sheds (2004, 173–6).

It is of course likely that weaving also took place in other kinds of buildings. Flixborough provides a good example of a settlement where weaving clearly took place, but apparently not in *Grubenhäuser*, as none was identified within the excavated area and, in any event, such buildings had largely gone out of use on rural sites by the eighth and ninth centuries (Loveluck 2001). The site has additional significance, however, for it provides convincing evidence that 'rubbish was apparently discarded immediately outside buildings in discrete dumps that appeared to relate to the activities that took place inside individual structures', in particular textile production (Loveluck 2001, 91; Tipper 2004, 177). This raises the possibility that a similar pattern of discard existed at settlements where conditions of preservation were less favourable and that, in some cases, the finds in *Grubenhäuser* do derive from activities that took place in and around these buildings.[60]

The relationship between *Grubenhäuser* and earth-fast timber buildings

Recent scholarship has tended to downplay the functional differences between *Grubenhäuser* and earth-fast timber buildings and both are now generally regarded as having served a range of functions. As already noted, if the suspended-floor model is accepted, then *Grubenhäuser* could have had the same floor area as earth-fast timber buildings and their superstructures could have been virtually indistinguishable.[61] Yet despite this, even proponents of the 'suspended-floor model' accept the traditional view that *Grubenhäuser* were ancillary buildings which were generally more numerous and shorter-lived than their earth-fast counterparts, despite the improved air circulation which would be afforded by a suspended floor (e.g. West 1986, 151). Thus the zoning apparent at West Heslerton, where *Grubenhäuser* were found mostly in the northwestern part of the site and earth-fast buildings in the east, is explained as reflecting functional differentiation, with a 'craft and industry' zone and a 'housing' zone (Powlesland 1997, 110–13; Tipper 2004, 184).[62]

---

[60] One potential example of this is the *Grubenhaus* at Wharram Percy which not only contained a 'hearth of vitrified chalk' in the centre of the floor, but also fragments of a mould for making decorative mounts (Milne and Richards 1992, 20). The excavators argue that this evidence, together with fragments of crucibles and tuyères, indicate that the building was used for non-ferrous metalworking, although they acknowledge that this could equally represent 're-use of the structure as a working hollow following its abandonment' (Milne and Richards 1992, 82–3, 85).

[61] Indeed, on a number of sites, the floor areas of the smallest earth-fast buildings are no greater than the sunken areas of the largest *Grubenhäuser*, as at Chalton and Eye Kettleby (Champion 1977; N. Finn, pers. comm.).

[62] It should be noted that the evidence for craft and industry appears to come primarily not from the *Grubenhäuser* themselves, but rather from features such as metalworking furnaces, a malt-kiln, and butchery deposits (Tipper 2004, 184).

Discussion of the functional relationship between these two types of buildings often reflects a tension between, on the one hand, rejection of the idea that the finds from *Grubenhäuser* indicate that these served distinct functions which set them apart from earth-fast buildings and, on the other, that such functional distinctions must have existed: 'We should not assume that there were necessarily clear differences between buildings on early Anglo-Saxon settlements, although the spatial differentiation at West Heslerton indicates that there was also functional differentiation' (Tipper 2004, 184).

This raises a number of conundrums. Why, for example, was it necessary to incur the considerable costs in labour and timber involved in digging a pit and constructing a suspended planked floor, if, in terms of size and external appearance, the two types of building were broadly comparable? If a sub-floor space conferred significant benefits such as extending the life of the main structural timbers, why were not all buildings constructed in this way? Finally, why would greater effort and materials be expended on buildings that were used for storage and/or craftworking, than on dwellings?[63]

We do not as yet have the evidence at our disposal to resolve these apparent contradictions. It is of interest, however, to note that a small number of 'hybrid' buildings have been excavated that appear to display attributes of both earth-fast buildings and *Grubenhäuser*. Buildings D3 and C1 at Yeavering, both of which burned down, preserving detailed evidence of their superstructures, have already been mentioned. Building D3 possessed a sunken floor around 1m deep, but in almost every other respect it resembled a typical earth-fast timber building measuring around 12m x 6m and containing two central, opposed doorways in the long walls. It was ringed by external postholes interpreted by the excavator as representing 'buttresses' (Hope-Taylor 1977, 103–4). Building C1, in contrast, resembled in dimensions and structural detail a fairly typical six-post *Grubenhaus*, apart from the fact that a series of widely spaced postholes lined the ground surface along the northern and southern edges of the sunken area. These are interpreted by the excavator as having accommodated 'the lower ends of rafters set directly into the ground', although the published sections do not indicate whether these posts were inwardly raking (Hope-Taylor 1977, 90).

One *Grubenhaus* at Ryall Quarry was also partly encircled by a series of postholes—considered by the excavators not to be load-bearing—outside the shallow sunken area, and at least two of the *Grubenhäuser* at Eye Kettleby were similarly encircled by postholes (Barber and Watts 2006; N. Finn, pers. comm.). Building 1120 at Flixton Quarry (Suffolk) possessed a shallow, sunken

---

[63] Ever since the discovery of earth-fast timber buildings, it has been widely accepted that *Grubenhäuser* are unlikely to have functioned as dwellings. Of West Heslerton, the excavator says: 'one thing we can be reasonably certain of is that [*Grubenhäuser*] did not provide housing' (Powlesland 1997, 107). Even on settlements where only *Grubenhäuser* have been recognized, it is rarely if ever possible to exclude the possibility that earth-fast timber buildings lay beyond the edges of the excavation.

area with two large gable posts at either end. Outside of this sunken area (which measured 4.0m x 3.2m), along the long sides of the structure, was a shallow foundation trench into which were set a series of postholes, four on the eastern side and three on the west (Boulter 2003; Boulter 2006, 61). At Bonners Lane, Leicester, an incompletely excavated *Grubenhaus*, estimated to have been over 5.5m in width, contained a series of eight substantial postholes more or less evenly positioned around the perimeter of the shallow sunken area. The excavators have argued that these closely resemble the load-bearing posts of an earth-fast building (N. Finn 2004, 15–19). While each of these 'hybrids' is unique, viewed together they suggest that the distinction between *Grubenhäuser* and earth-fast timber buildings may have been less rigid than is usually assumed.

3

Settlement forms and community structures

Establishing settlement form

In 1976, so few Anglo-Saxon settlements had been excavated on an adequate scale that, in his survey published in that year, Philip Rahtz was able to deal in detail only with buildings; the layout and development of settlements were scarcely considered. Since then, publication of a number of extensively excavated settlements has enabled archaeologists to begin to observe certain trends and patterns in the development of settlement forms. The prevailing model for the fifth to seventh centuries is one of shifting settlement, although what exactly is meant by this term can vary. At West Stow, shifting was identified at the level of individual earth-fast timber buildings which, after they were abandoned, were replaced by new buildings sited a relatively short distance away (West 1986, 151). This replacement of what were essentially single generational dwellings was also a widespread phenomenon in later prehistory and relates to the issue of the 'life-cycle' of dwellings considered in Chapter 2. The location of a settlement could thus remain relatively stable even while that of individual dwellings changed as timber buildings were abandoned and replaced. At Mucking, where a much more extensive area was investigated, shifting on a larger scale was identified (Fig. 3.1): the main focus of occupation in the fifth and sixth centuries lay in the southern part of the site, while by the seventh century it had shifted several hundred metres to the north as well as westwards, away from the edge of the gravel terrace overlooking the Thames on which the settlement and its associated cemeteries had been established (Hamerow 1993, 86–91). Whether this involved a gradual 'wandering' as originally postulated by the present writer, or a single discontinuous shift cannot be established with certainty. While the phenomenon of shifting settlements has long been recognized (Taylor 1983, 120–3), the recognition that excavating a relatively small part of an Anglo-Saxon settlement is likely to reveal only one phase of occupation suggests that it is more difficult to determine when a particular settlement was established and abandoned than has often been assumed (Hamerow 1991, 17).

Several objections to this model of 'shifting settlement' have, however, been raised. Because little survives in the way of occupation layers on most rural

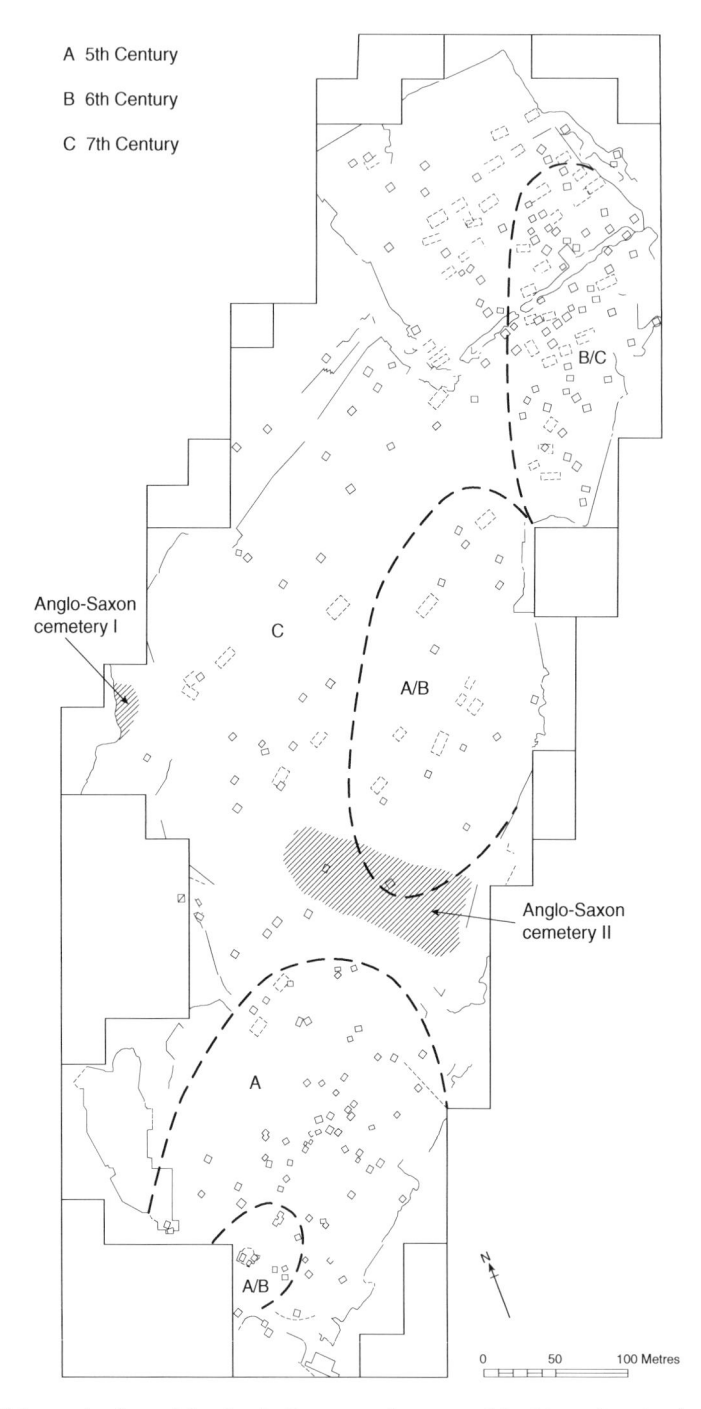

Fig. 3.1. Schematic plan of the Anglo-Saxon settlement at Mucking, showing broad spatial development (after Hamerow 1992).

settlements of this period, archaeologists have relied heavily on datable finds found in pits and buildings—above all in *Grubenhäuser*—to establish the chronological development of these sites. As noted in Chapter 2, recent research suggests that material found in *Grubenhäuser* is largely tertiary—i.e. derived from middens—and therefore cannot be used to date the use of these structures. Nevertheless, the relatively clear spatial patterning in the distribution of finds and pottery of different date at Mucking militates against the idea that middening has completely obscured chronological patterning, as Tipper acknowledges (Tipper 2004, 52). He has, nevertheless, put forward an alternative model for Mucking's development, while cautioning that 'this is not necessarily any more correct than the shifting settlement model' (ibid. 52). He argues that, while *Grubenhäuser* containing fifth-century finds were indeed restricted to the southern end of the site, the fact that sixth-century and, to a limited extent, seventh-century material occurs in both northern and southern areas suggests the existence of two contemporary 'settlements or clusters of structures at opposite ends of the site'. This is not dissimilar to the model put forward in 1993, which recognized that the settlement phases overlapped chronologically and that the settlement would therefore at times have had more than one focus of occupation, i.e. that 'Mucking... is best described... as a shifting hamlet, at times perhaps *more than one*' (Hamerow 1993, 86, 90). Nevertheless, the near-complete lack of seventh-century material in *Grubenhäuser* in those parts of the site dated in the original report to the fifth and sixth centuries, i.e. Phases A and A/B, suggests that by this time the focus of occupation had indeed shifted elsewhere (ibid., fig. 50). This is not inconsistent with the suggestion that the settlement had 'some sort of permanency' as indicated by the rebuilding of some structures very close to, or even cutting, earlier buildings in certain parts of the site (Tipper 2004, 52). Indeed, the clustering apparent in Phase A is suggestive of this, with *Grubenhäuser* 'lying close together, with up to three phases of rebuilding' (Hamerow 1993, 86).[1]

The evidence unearthed at West Heslerton, which has been excavated on a comparable scale to Mucking, has given rise to a model very different to the one just outlined of small settlements shifting on a large scale. The excavator has argued that West Heslerton was established around AD 400 as a single, large, planned settlement, describing it as a 'proto-type town'; this was 'laid out on a grand scale', covering an area nearly 500 metres square, and continued to occupy the same site until the mid ninth century (Powlesland 1997, 110; 2003, 35). While the evidence on which this interpretation is based remains at the time of

---

[1] At Mucking, as at most other early Anglo-Saxon settlements, inter-cutting buildings are relatively scarce, which is itself suggestive of settlement shift (cf. Dodwell et al. 2004, 121).

writing largely unpublished, it is enough to suggest that it would be unwise to assume that the 'Mucking model' of shifting settlement can be universally applied. What can be said is that it remains extremely unusual to find unambiguous evidence of continuous occupation from the fifth to ninth centuries on settlements where only a relatively small area has been excavated, and this itself implies that some degree of settlement shift was common.

As the preceding discussion makes clear, the means by which individual buildings are dated is crucial to understanding the spatial development of settlements as a whole. Earth-fast timber buildings rarely contain datable artefacts, however, and while the use of foundation trenches indicates a seventh-century or later date, it is not usually possible to be more precise than this; the caveats regarding the dating of *Grubenhäuser* based purely on the finds they contain have already been rehearsed.

The difficulties involved in phasing Anglo-Saxon settlements are thus considerable, quite apart from the problem of excavating in their entirety settlements which were dispersed and lacked clear 'edges'. Indeed, air-photographic evidence and remote-sensing surveys in several regions, notably the Vale of Pickering, the Upper Thames Valley, and the area to the west of Thetford have revealed dispersed spreads of what appear to be *Grubenhäuser* covering many hectares (Powlesland, pers. comm.; Hamerow, Hayden, and Hey, 2008; Atkins, forthcoming).[2] Add to this the scarcity of datable artefacts and paucity of stratigraphic relationships between buildings on most settlements, and it is easy to see why it is extremely difficult to provide a 'snapshot' of an Anglo-Saxon settlement at any particular moment in time.

Settlement forms of the fifth to late sixth centuries

Despite these difficulties and the great variability apparent between the layouts of individual settlements, the evidence available thus far suggests that, until the late sixth century, settlements tended to be fairly dispersed and to lack obvious edges, boundaries, or signs of planning. They may nevertheless display certain regularities and even show signs of functional zones. There is little to indicate, however, that they adhered to a generally agreed or imposed plan which involved the setting out of defined plots or surveying, such as the precise alignment or perpendicular layout of buildings (Hamerow 2004). These settlements, furthermore, did not contain obviously focal or exceptionally large buildings, although one can rarely say with certainty that a particular

---

[2] Even at West Stow, recent excavation in advance of development some 100m north-east of the main excavation of 1965–72 has revealed three further *Grubenhäuser*. This, combined with evidence of early Anglo-Saxon settlement found in a small quarry site *c.*600m west of the main excavation is also suggestive of settlement extending along the valley side, rather than a single 'village' as originally supposed (J. Newman, pers. comm. 2007). Piecemeal excavation on the East London gravels between Heathrow and the M4 motorway, comparable in area to Mucking and West Heslerton, is suggestive of even more diffuse settlement (Cowie and Blackmore 2008, 137).

type of feature was absent, particularly in the case of shallow fence-lines or trackways which could so easily have been ploughed away. These earliest settlements are also characterized by a lack of enclosures around, or in direct association with, buildings, although traces of structures that might have been animal pens or paddocks are occasionally identified (as, for example, at West Stow: West 1986, 53). Long-lived enclosures surrounding planned arrangements of buildings, and complexes of paddocks or corrals are not in evidence much before *c*.600.[3] In this respect, early Anglo-Saxon England was unusual compared to other parts of the North Sea Zone, where each household typically occupied a separate enclosure which often contained storage facilities (Hamerow 2002a).

West Stow and Mucking are the best-known examples of this kind of early settlement, but more recently excavated settlements at Eye Kettleby (Leicestershire), Riverdene (Hampshire), and Kilverstone (Norfolk) all appear to conform broadly to this model (Fig. 3.2; Finn, forthcoming; Hall-Torrance and Weaver 2003; Garrow et al. 2006). With so few extensively excavated settlements, it is difficult to assess the size of these fifth- and sixth-century communities, which would, in any case, have fluctuated, but they appear to range from single farmsteads to much more extensive settlements like those at West Heslerton and Mucking, where at times perhaps as many as 100 individuals lived. Most of these sites, however, would have been home to between 30 and 50 people, a figure that accords well with the estimates of the size of early Anglo-Saxon communities based on the more substantial data-set provided by excavated cemeteries (Härke 1997, 140).

How these dispersed, un-bounded settlements consisting of relatively small, undifferentiated dwellings relate to socio-economic structures is difficult to say.[4] Where cemeteries are associated with early Anglo-Saxon settlements, as at Mucking, they clearly indicate that these communities were internally ranked; some individuals were buried with a great deal more wealth than others. This suggests that social ranking, whether defined by gender, age,

---

[3] At Gamlingay (Cambridgeshire) a ditched enclosure around an Anglo-Saxon farmstead consisting of a post-in-trench building and a number of *Grubenhäuser* has been described as 'early Anglo-Saxon' (Murray and McDonald 2005). However, while some sherds of fifth- or sixth-century pottery were retrieved from the settlement, the majority of the evidence points towards a Mid Saxon date and there is no reason to assume that the ditched enclosures pre-date the seventh century (B. Sudds, pers. comm. 2007). Similarly, there is no evidence to suggest that the ditched enclosures and droveway excavated at Cardinal Park, Godmanchester pre-date the seventh century, although the site is dated in the published report to the fifth to seventh centuries, based primarily on the small quantity of Ipswich Ware recovered and the absence of Maxey Ware (Gibson 2003).

[4] It should be noted that even in early Anglo-Saxon settlements, buildings ranged somewhat in size. At Mucking, for example, PHB 1 was somewhat larger than the other buildings found there, although its location and the fact that it contained a compartment suggest that it should be dated to the seventh century, or perhaps even slightly later (see Chapter 2 and below; Hamerow 1993, fig. 54). No exceptionally large buildings, however, have yet been dated to the fifth or first half of the sixth century.

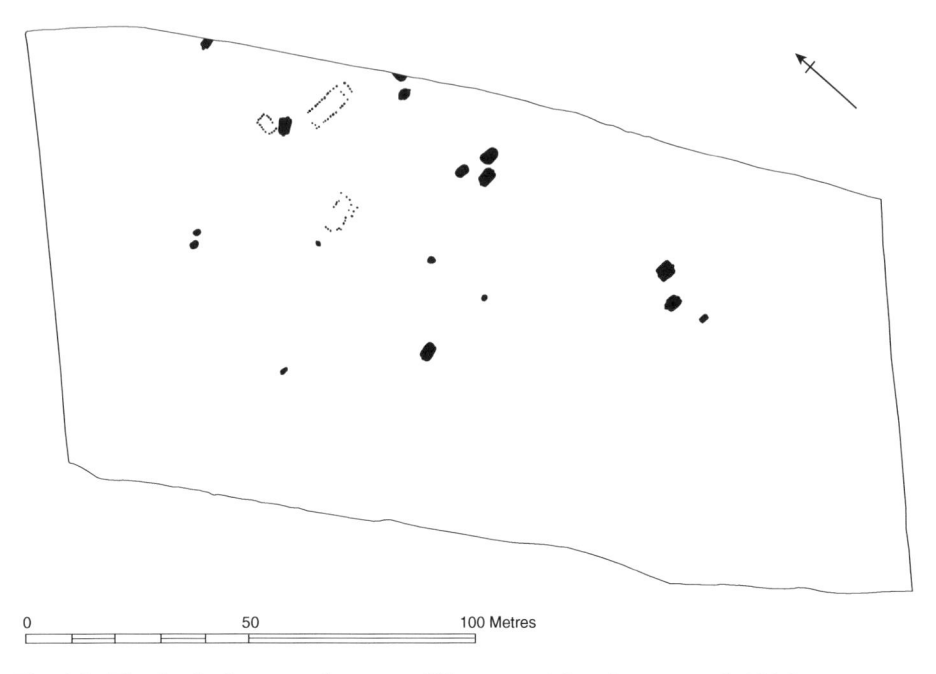

Fig. 3.2. The Anglo-Saxon settlement at Kilverstone (after Garrow et al. 2006).

cult, descent, or—as is likely—a combination of these and other archaeologically invisible factors, was largely expressed within households rather than between them (cf. Welch 1992, 81; Härke 1997). It was apparently not expressed in the size of individual dwellings and thereby in the ability to maintain a particularly large household under one roof. The lack of any clear settlement hierarchy before the seventh and, especially, eighth centuries can in short be regarded as 'an independent indicator of a relative weakness of elites' (Wickham 2005, 545).

Settlement forms of the late sixth to ninth centuries

The diversification of settlement forms that occurred in the course of the late sixth to ninth centuries invites some attempt at classification. Inevitably, however, archaeologists' need to classify is in tension with the complexity and diversity of the archaeological record. In a seminal paper, Andrew Reynolds proposed a classification according to the morphology of the enclosures associated with many settlements of this period (2003). He rightly cautions against adopting the complex classification schemes used for later medieval villages, arguing that a scheme based on the archaeological evidence is needed instead. He identifies two broad categories of settlements with enclosures from the late sixth century onwards: rectilinear and enclosed. Rectilinear settlements include those with rectilinear paddocks, trackways, plots, and field boundaries (Reynolds 2003, 119). Enclosed settlements, on the other hand, have enclosures 'that either surround or are associated with individual buildings' (ibid. 104). While these are useful categories, it is not always possible to make a clear distinction between the two settlement forms, as Reynolds himself recognized. Furthermore, some settlements of this period have yielded no evidence of enclosures of any kind. I have, therefore, elaborated on this scheme slightly by distinguishing between settlements which were established from the outset with rectilinear enclosures; settlements established in the fifth or sixth centuries and which gained enclosures in the Mid Saxon period; and settlements without enclosures. Enclosed settlements (following Reynolds' definition), are considered separately.

Rectilinear settlements

Several Mid Saxon settlements in Cambridgeshire have recently been excavated that appear to have been established from the outset with rectilinear ditched enclosures. At Lordship Lane, Cottenham, an enclosure measuring some 170m in length was constructed during the seventh to eighth centuries (Fig. 3.3; Mortimer 2000). Within the enclosure lay three post-built structures, while a single *Grubenhaus* was identified lying immediately outside. The enclosure appears to have developed piecemeal, but the ditches were re-cut along broadly the same lines. Within the main enclosure, several smaller yards or paddocks were identified. During Phase B, dated to the eighth and ninth centuries, the focus of the settlement shifted to the southeast. A series of ditched enclosures was laid out in a radial pattern around an unseen core lying outside the excavated area to the south-east (Fig. 3.4). This remodelling of the site was accompanied by the digging of deeper, wider, 'more permanent' ditches (ibid. 10). Several poorly preserved sheds or barns were associated with the Phase B enclosures. The compounds 'have the appearance of regularly laid out enclosures'. The excavator sees in this layout 'the beginnings of the toft system of individual tenement plots' with frontages of around 20m each and dwellings lying somewhere to the southeast. This basic structure persisted throughout the Late Saxon period (see below).

At Cardinal Park, Godmanchester (Cambridgeshire), six *Grubenhäuser*, a well, several pits, and possibly three post-built structures were excavated together with two ditched enclosures (Fig. 3.5). Most if not all of these features are likely to date to the seventh century. A droveway some 12m wide and over 110m long ran along the southern edge of one of the enclosures, although the phasing of the ditches is uncertain and at least two

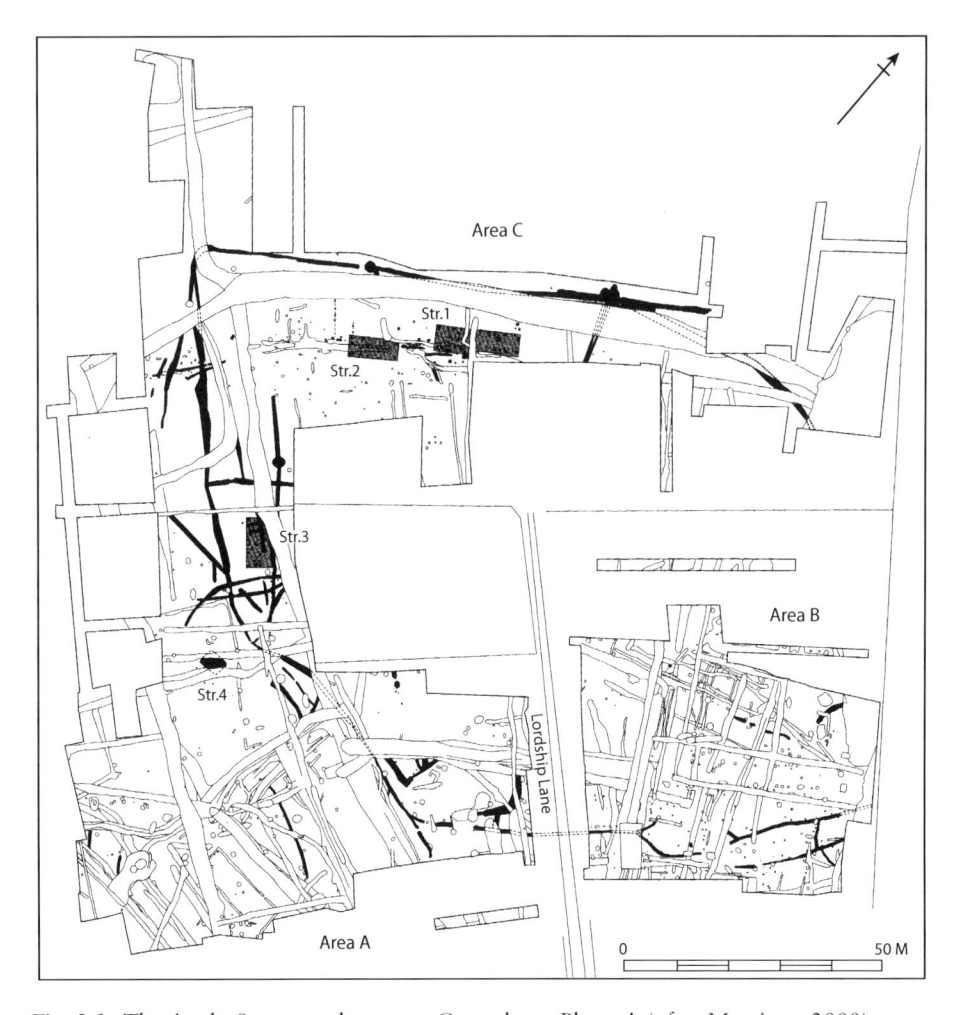

Fig. 3.3. The Anglo-Saxon settlement at Cottenham, Phase A (after Mortimer 2000).

alternative sequences are possible (Gibson 2003, fig. 42). Enclosure 1, which measured at least 100m x 45 m, appears to have been the earliest feature on the site and was defined by a substantial ditch. Enclosure 2 was characterized by shallower, interrupted ditches, defining an area of $c.$125m x 70 m, within which lay all but one of the *Grubenhäuser*. A possible entrance structure was identified, perhaps 'used to funnel and control the movement of animals between Enclosure 1 and the adjacent droveway' (Gibson 2003, 157). The enclosures were in all likelihood broadly contemporary, albeit with somewhat different alignments and possibly serving different functions. The evidence is insufficient, however, to identify Enclosure 2 conclusively as 'domestic' (ibid. 157).

Fig. 3.4. The Anglo-Saxon settlement at Cottenham, Phase B (after Mortimer 2000).

At West Fen Road, Ely (Mortimer et al. 2005), over 3 hectares were excavated to reveal an extensive complex of ditched, rectilinear boundaries—an extraordinary 15–20 km length of ditches and gullies is estimated for all periods (ibid. 7; Fig. 3.6). This profusion of boundaries was the defining characteristic of a settlement that was established in the second quarter of the eighth century and continued into the twelfth, with the major boundaries enduring throughout this period. The ditches defined eight enclosures whose dimensions—mostly around 45m x 60 m—remained remarkably constant over time. Despite the considerable extent of the excavation, only the southern limit of the settlement was defined. Some of the ditched compounds contained small,

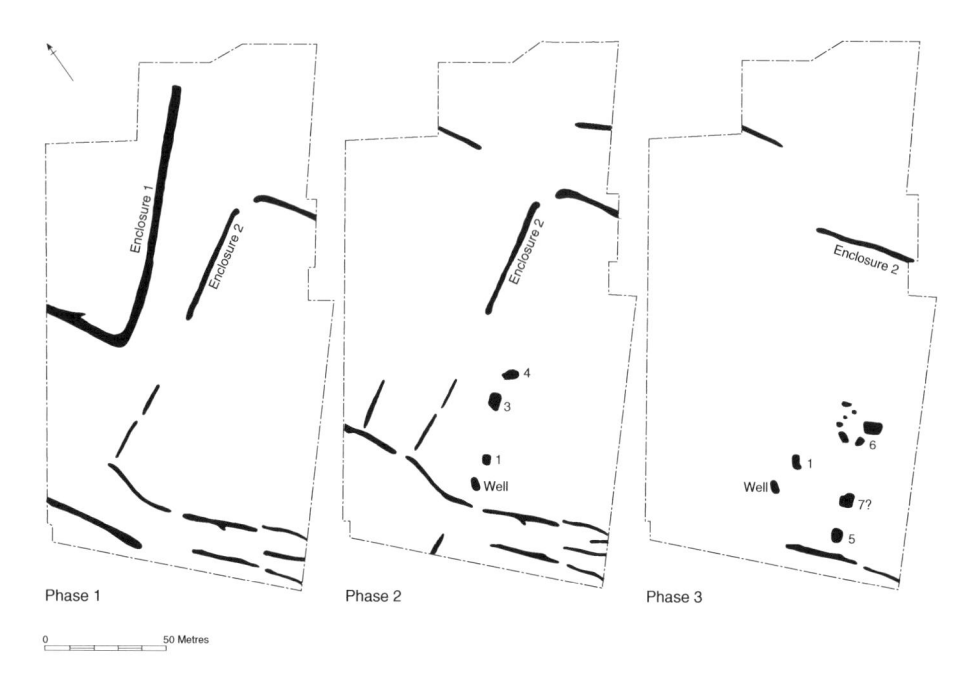

Fig. 3.5. The development of the Anglo-Saxon settlement at Cardinal Park, Godmanchester (one of two alternative sequences) (after Gibson and Murray 2003).

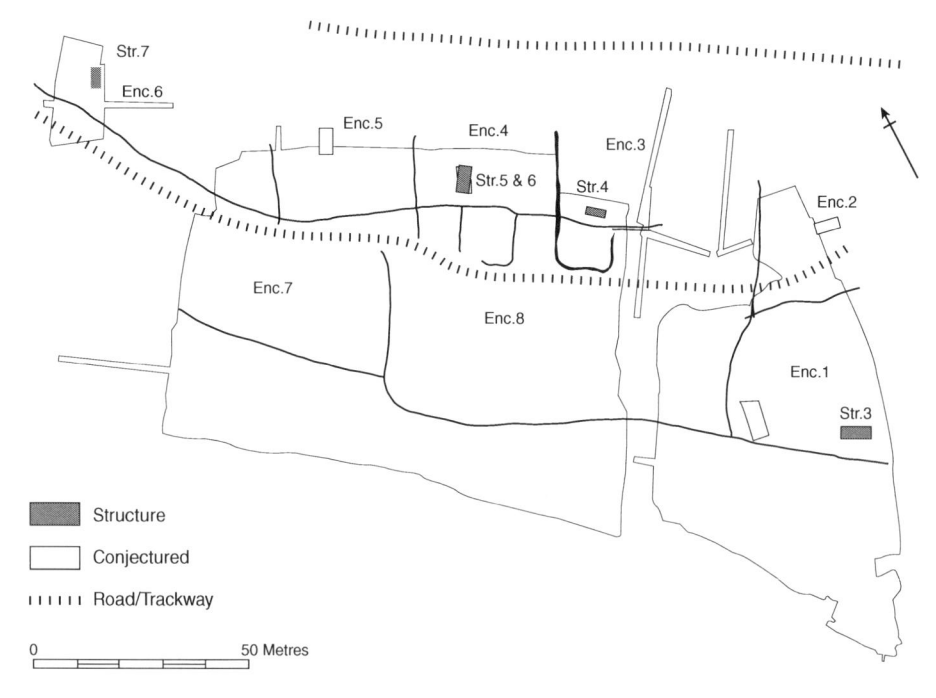

Fig. 3.6. Schematic plan of the main enclosures at West Fen Road, Ely (after Mortimer et al. 2005).

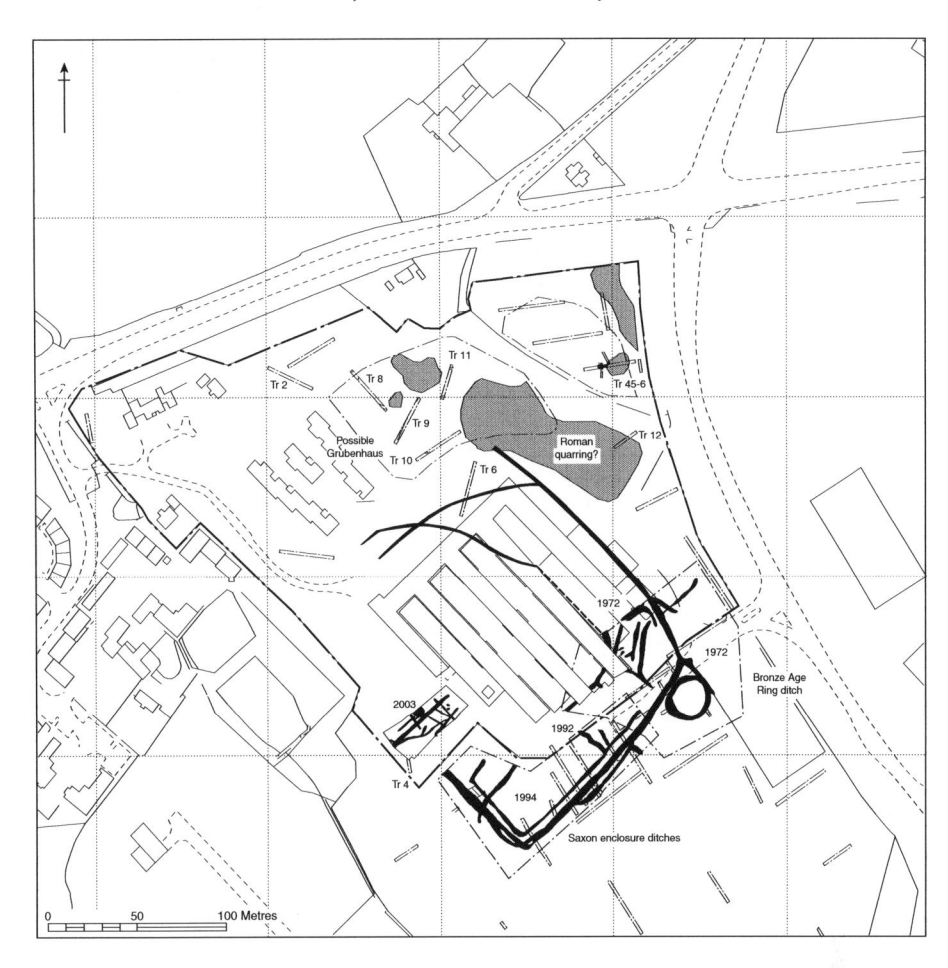

Fig. 3.7. Mid to Late Saxon enclosures at Wolverton Mill (reproduced with kind permission of Northamptonshire Archaeology).

post-built buildings and appear to have been residential, while others may have been pens or paddocks.

Although Cambridgeshire has a particular abundance of rectilinear settlements, comparable sites have been identified elsewhere.[5] At Wolverton Turn, near Milton Keynes in Buckinghamshire, a large ditched complex of Mid to Late Saxon date has been recognized (Fig. 3.7). Analysis of this complex site has been hampered by the fact that, since 1972, excavations have been carried out by no fewer than four separate archaeological units and contractors. It nevertheless appears that a roughly rectangular ditched enclosure, nearly 200m

---

[5] Evidence of yet another rectilinear settlement from Cambridgeshire was recovered from a 'key-hole' excavation near the parish church at Orton Waterville, near Peterborough, where a rectilinear ditched enclosure underwent several modifications between the seventh/eighth and eleventh/twelfth centuries (Wright 2006).

long and over 130m wide, was laid out during the eighth and ninth centuries and underwent several phases of remodelling, to judge from pottery found in the ditches and radiocarbon dates (Preston 2004). Little evidence of contemporary buildings was identified, but a kiln with two chambers connected by a narrow flue is likely to be Late Saxon in date (ibid. 11).

At Warmington, near Peterborough (Northamptonshire), a sequence of ditched enclosures was established on a green-field site, probably in the eighth century (Fig. 3.8). Groupings of postholes suggest the presence of timber structures, although no defined building plans were recorded. By the eleventh century the area appears to have been used exclusively for stock management (Meadows, forthcoming). Phase 1, dating broadly to the eighth to mid ninth century, was represented by a small, roughly square enclosure some 10m across and, to the west and on the same alignment, a straight, shallow ditch, less than a metre wide but 59m long. In the next phase—which continued into the second half of the tenth century—a more clearly rectilinear arrangement of ditches was dug. The dominant feature was a north–south running droveway, leading to a stream just to the north of the excavated area; a second, east–west running droveway may have run perpendicular to it, to the south. Ditches lying to the west of the main droveway may represent internal subdivisions. The enclosures were eventually replaced in the twelfth or thirteenth century by open fields. The medieval village lies some 300m south of the Anglo-Saxon settlement.

Early settlements that acquired enclosures in the Mid Saxon period

A few settlements that were established in the fifth or sixth century gained ditched enclosures in the Mid Saxon period. West Stow and possibly Mucking are both examples of this kind of settlement. In the last settlement phase at West Stow, a sequence of shallow ditched enclosures was constructed, some of which were repeatedly re-cut along roughly the same lines, in some cases six times or more (Fig. 3.9). The fact that the ditches contained Ipswich Ware indicates that they were added to the site in the eighth century. The latest buildings appear to lie outside of these enclosures (West 1986, fig. 300). No Mid Saxon enclosures can be identified with complete certainty at Mucking, although Ditch 15010 contained several sherds of Ipswich Ware and probably dates to this period, along with two other nearby ditches which appear to form an enclosure around the largest timber building on the site, PHB 1. They are, on these grounds, likely to be Mid Saxon in origin (Going 1993b, 22; Hamerow 1993, 22, 294, fig. 186.16; Tipper 2004, fig. C6).[6]

The settlement at Pennyland (Buckinghamshire) also appears to have originated as a scatter of unenclosed *Grubenhäuser*, although it seems likely that only

---

[6] The caption for Tipper's figure C6 indicates that it shows a series of 'Anglo-Saxon enclosures' at Mucking. However, as the text notes, it is in fact 'possible that the ditches post-dated the Anglo-Saxon settlement…and may have formed field boundaries…', with the exception noted here (Tipper 2004, 38).

Fig. 3.8. The development of the Anglo-Saxon settlement at Warmington. Provisional plans (reproduced with kind permission of Northamptonshire Archaeology).

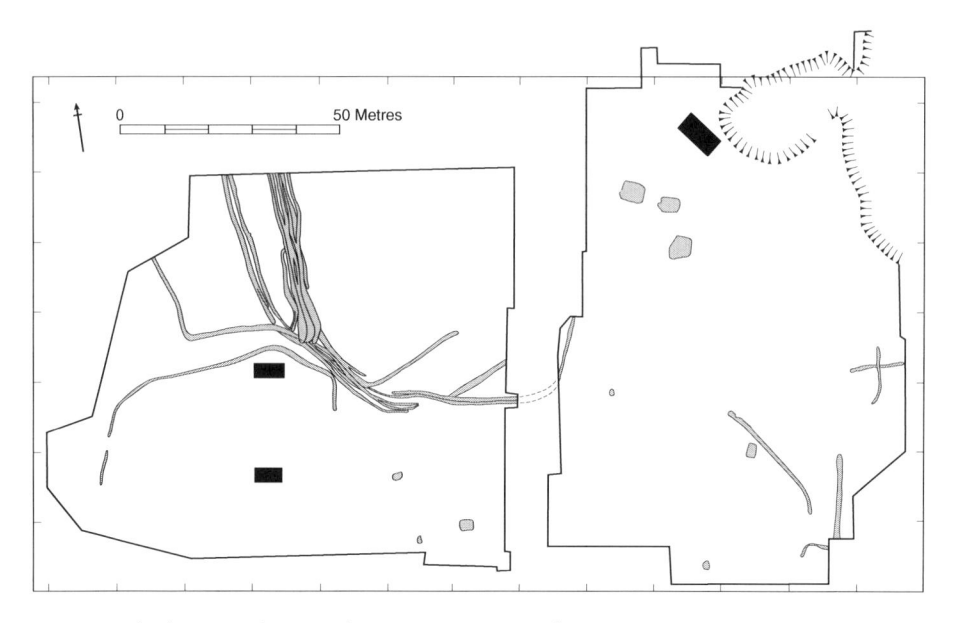

Fig. 3.9. The latest settlement phase at West Stow (after West 1986).

part of this early phase has been uncovered (Williams 1993). Probably in the seventh century, paddocks, a well, at least one trackway, and enclosures seemingly defining house-plots were added (Fig. 3.10). By the mid eighth century, to judge from the presence of Ipswich Ware, the enclosures had been abandoned, or at least had ceased to be actively maintained. Only four *Grubenhäuser*, a well, and several four-post structures which presumably represent granaries—all lying outside the earlier enclosures—were dated to this final phase of the settlement.

A comparable example of radical remodelling may be seen at Gamlingay (Cambridgeshire), where a sequence of ditched enclosures, timber buildings, and a cemetery were uncovered (Murray 2006). Phase A consisted of an enclosure measuring over 130m north to south, with one wide entrance and three narrower entrances, one of which possessed a gate (Fig. 3.11). The ditch was quite shallow and no more than 0.5m wide. A ditch leading off from Enclosure 1 to the east is likely to represent one edge of a trackway leading into the enclosure. Twelve *Grubenhäuser* have also been dated to Phase A and a small quantity of pottery contained in some of their fills dates to the fifth or sixth century. As already noted, however (see above, n. 3), there is no reason to assume that Enclosure 1 pre-dates the seventh century, although some of the *Grubenhäuser* could pre-date it. In the next phase, the settlement took on a new, rectilinear form. A droveway some 4–5m wide led into an enclosure within which lay a small earth-fast timber building[7] aligned with,

---

[7] It seems most unlikely that this structure was a church as suggested in the published report; in any event, the main burial ground clearly post-dates it (Murray 2006, 266–8).

Late 6th century - late 7th century

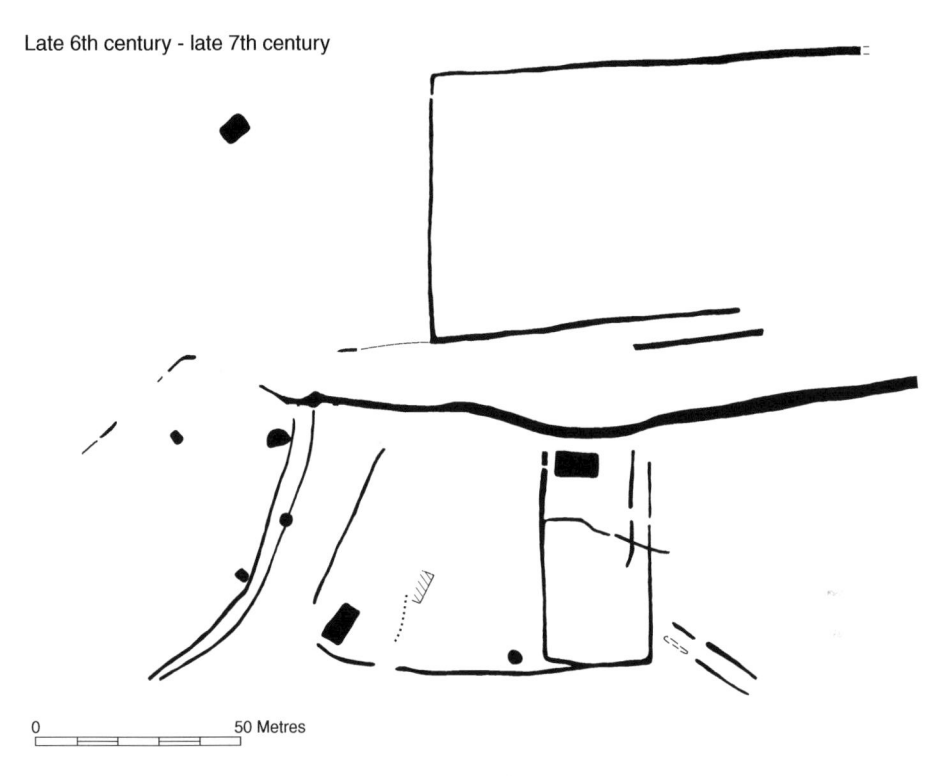

Fig. 3.10. The late sixth- to late seventh-century phase at Pennyland (after Williams 1993).

and immediately adjacent to, another rectangular structure (*c*.9.6m x 4.8m). The latter was tentatively identified by the excavators as an animal pen, although its dimensions suggest that this may in fact have been the poorly preserved remains of another building. A six-post structure, probably a granary, lay some 15m from the building and may be contemporary with it. Phase C saw the construction of a new rectilinear enclosure in the southern part of the excavated area, consisting of two parallel ditches, lying some 52–57m apart. The orientation of the ditches differs markedly from those of the preceding phase, and the excavator suggests that these were laid out 'after at least some elements of the early farmstead had been abandoned' (Murray 2006, 197). Phase D, which is likely to date to the eighth or even ninth century, saw the construction of a new, seemingly curvilinear enclosure, only a small section of which was excavated, and two *Grubenhäuser*. A cemetery of over 100 west–east aligned, unfurnished inhumations, mostly laid out in seven rows, is probably contemporary with this last phase of occupation, although it respects the alignment of an enclosure ditch of Phase C. While several of the graves contained sherds of Mid Saxon pottery in their fill, in the absence of radiocarbon dates, the exact date of the cemetery remains unclear. The near-complete

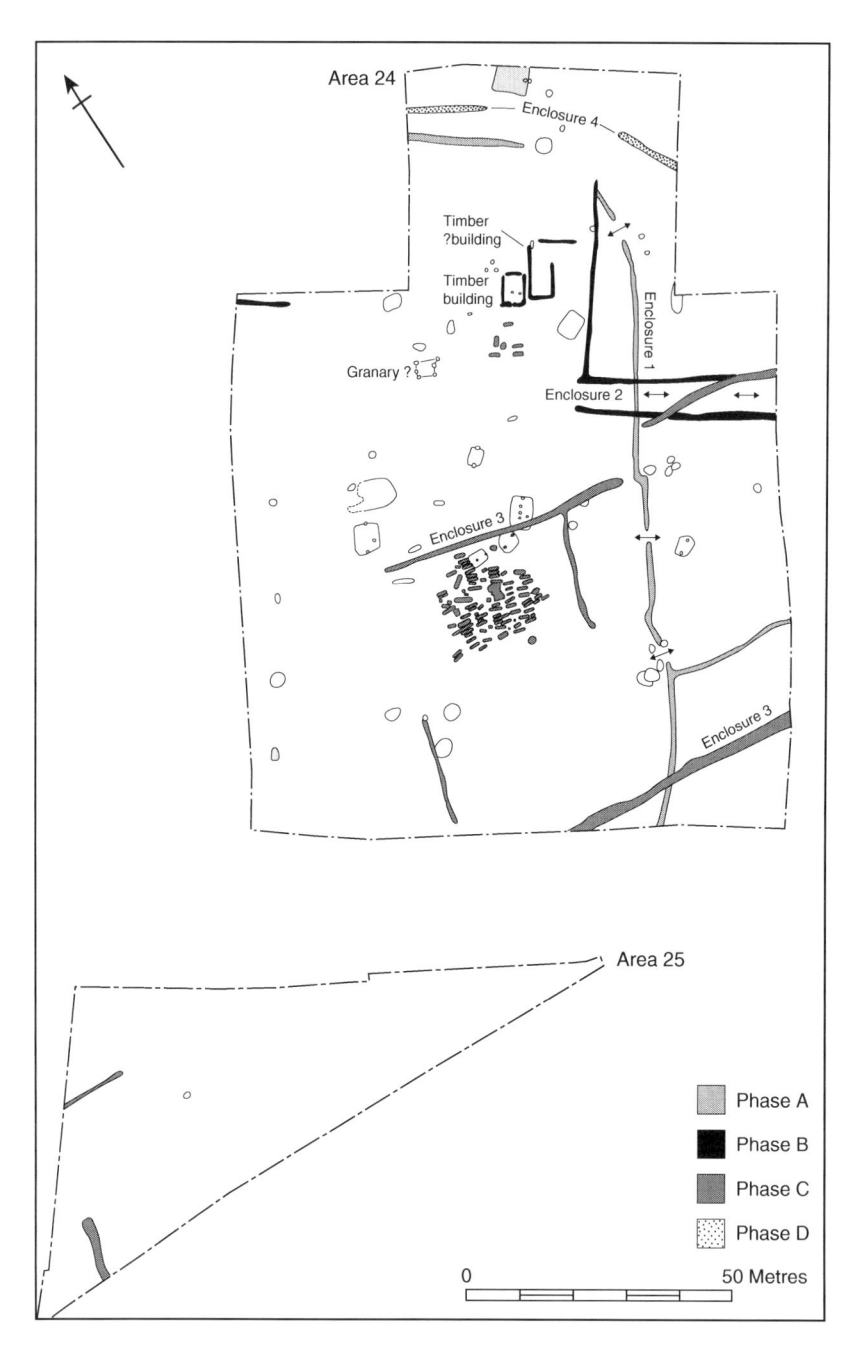

Fig. 3.11. Phased plan of settlement and burials at Gamlingay (after Murray 2006).

absence of dress items or grave goods, however, suggests a Late Saxon date (see Chapter 4 for further discussion of the cemetery).

Settlements without enclosures

While the Mid Saxon period saw the emergence of a range of new settlement forms, it should be recalled that some communities in this period lived in settlements that, at least in terms of their layout, looked much like those of the fifth and sixth centuries. Although never fully published, the settlement at New Wintles, Eynsham (Oxfordshire) spanned the sixth to (at least) early eighth centuries, yet appears to have consisted throughout of widely scattered *Grubenhäuser* with no more than four post-built structures, a possible trackway, and 'many isolated pits and hearths' (Hawkes and Gray 1969; Gray 1974). Although only a small part of the Mid Saxon settlement at Cadley Road, Collingbourne Ducis (Wiltshire) was excavated, it too produced no evidence of enclosures (Pine 2001). Had there been no datable finds or radiocarbon dates to indicate otherwise, it is likely that these settlements would have been assumed to date to the early Anglo-Saxon period.

Settlement forms of the tenth and eleventh centuries

The settlement forms established in the Mid Saxon period largely persisted into the Late Saxon period and sometimes beyond. This can be seen, for example, at Cottenham, where the radial layout established in the Mid Saxon period continued into the tenth and eleventh centuries, expanding somewhat, but essentially retaining its earlier form.[8] One of the ditches established in Phase 2 was extended beyond the excavated area towards the fen, perhaps to 'establish crofts which lie behind the tenement plots' (Mortimer 2000, 12). Three timber buildings and a probable granary were associated with this phase. Not until the twelfth or thirteenth century was the site abandoned and replaced by a village to the east.

The Mid Saxon settlement at Yarnton is described in some detail later in this chapter. In the tenth century, a new system of ditches was laid out over the earlier settlement, forming seven enclosures to the north and south of an east–west running trackway (Fig. 3.12; Hey 2004, fig. 8.1). This system of enclosures extended to the north and east of the excavated area, where geophysical survey has revealed the existence of a rectilinear field system. A number of pits, waterholes, and a possible timber structure were associated with the excavated enclosures but, although they have been described as 'toft

---

[8] The place-name suggests that Cottenham was a settlement of *kotsetla*, or 'cottars'—described by Stenton as forming 'the base' of Anglo-Saxon peasant society' (Stenton 1971, 473).

84   *Settlement forms and community structures*

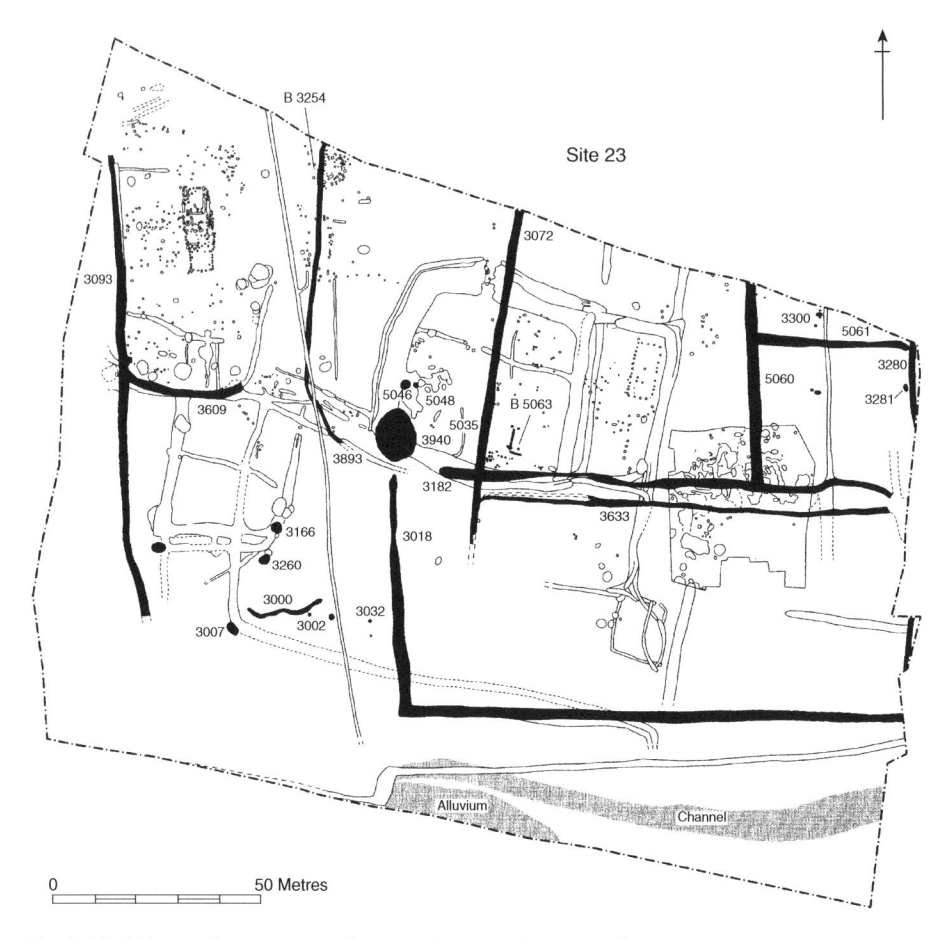

Fig. 3.12. The tenth-century settlement phase at Yarnton (after Hey 2004).

like', evidence of domestic occupation was limited, suggesting that 'the focus of settlement had by this time moved beyond the area excavated' (Hey 2004, 51, 167).

The first phase of occupation at Hall Farm, Baston (Lincolnshire), spanned the ninth to mid twelfth centuries. A rectilinear system of ditches and gullies, many of which had been re-cut, was identified along with cess and refuse pits, suggesting that dwellings lay nearby, though none was recognized within the excavated area. A row of pits 'probably delineated, or were located alongside, the back boundary of a croft or crofts' (Taylor 2003a, 15). A small, square timber building has been tentatively identified as a barn or stable. A Saxo-Norman metalworking zone that included a feature interpreted as a smithy, with slag, hammerscale (implying the presence of an anvil), hearth lining, and some iron objects, lay a short distance from the occupation area.[9] The excavator has suggested that in the late ninth century, the area was 'divided up into fields and crofts bounded by ditches', an arrangement not dissimilar to that seen at West Fen Road, Ely. There, the mid ninth to eleventh centuries saw a broad continuation of the ditched enclosures, most containing timber structures, established in the Mid Saxon period (see above). Such stability is, as at Cottenham, suggestive of legally constituted ancestral properties that passed from generation to generation. This phase also saw new developments: a series of small sub-enclosures established within Enclosures 13 and 14 'were patently stock control areas with...access to the trackways, and appear to have been shared between the surrounding domestic enclosures' (Mortimer et al. 2005, 129 and fig. 3.3). The site appears by this stage to have represented part of an extensive zone of suburban occupation outside the precinct of the abbey at Ely.

Rural or urban?

West Fen Road, Ely illustrates a certain ambiguity in the archaeological record with regard to the distinction between rural and urban settlements in the Late Saxon period. Its extent, density, and longevity have led its excavator to describe the settlement as '[occupying] an ambivalent place between our notions of urban and rural conditions', with an economy geared towards producing food and other products for consumption in the 'monastic town' founded at Ely c.673 by St Etheldreda (Mortimer et al. 2005, 148; Blair 2005, 255–6). Similar questions arise concerning the settlement at Market Field, Steyning, in Sussex. Written sources indicate that Steyning was a small town by the time of Domesday Book, and it has been described as an 'incipient minster-town' in the Late Saxon period (Blair 2005, 337).

---

[9] While many Anglo-Saxon settlements produce traces of iron smithing, such evidence is rarely substantial, the exception being a small number of sites with ecclesiastical and/or royal connections (Hinton 1998, 17–18; Hamerow 2002, 189). Evidence recovered at the settlement of Bloodmoor Hill (Suffolk) is, therefore, all the more remarkable (see Chapter 4 for a description of the site). One surface deposit yielded 26.5 kg of iron slag, a large amount of hammerscale, crucibles, and tuyère fragments, and 'was clearly being used as a dump by at least one smithy' (Cowgill in Lucy et al. 2009, 373). A *Grubenhaus* containing primary smithing debris derived from a slag heap may have been associated with a smithy (ibid. 374). The fact that the by-products of ferrous and non-ferrous metalworking were discarded together suggests that 'iron and non-ferrous metalworking were undertaken to some extent in the same workshop/smithy' (ibid.). Smithing and smelting had also been carried out near, though not within, the excavated area at Flixborough (Evans and Loveluck 2009, 324). One of the metalworking zones at Bloodmoor Hill appears to have lain at the core of the occupation area. While this may seem surprising, Cowgill notes that a smithy need not have posed a major fire hazard: 'fire control is fundamental for a smith's work, [smithies] emit no noxious fumes and are not particularly dusty' (ibid. 380). The recently identified area of iron working lying adjacent to the Mid Saxon settlement at Lyminge, Kent, will undoubtedly extend our understanding of the settlement context of such activity still further (G. Thomas, pers. comm.).

86   *Settlement forms and community structures*

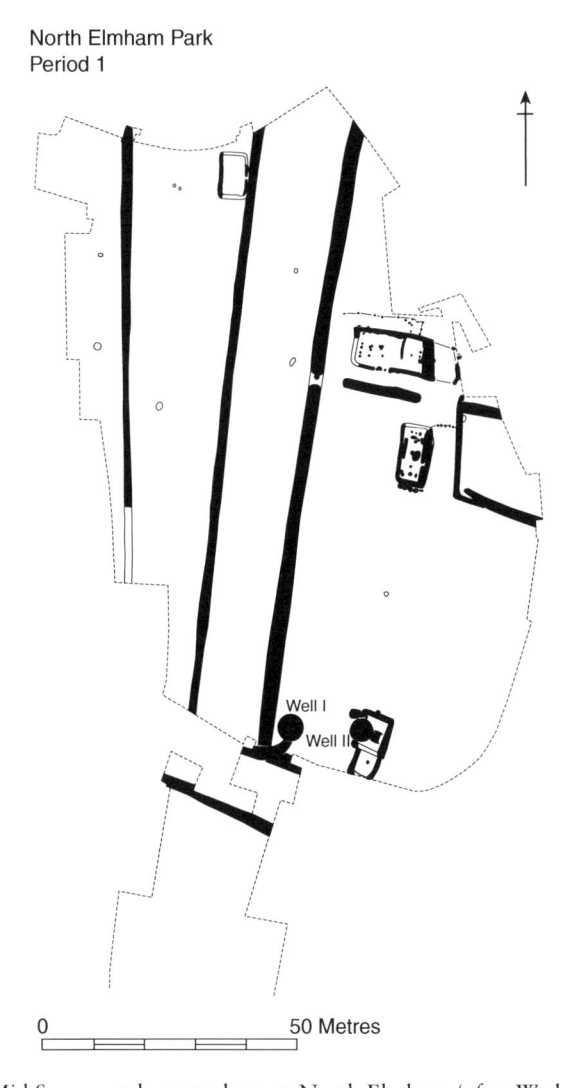

Fig. 3.13. The Mid Saxon settlement phase at North Elmham (after Wade-Martins 1980).

Yet excavations to the north-east of St Andrew's church uncovered a large part of a tenth- to eleventh-century enclosed settlement whose layout is similar to a number of other rural settlements of that period (albeit ones of comparatively high status; see the discussion of enclosed settlements below; Gardiner 1993; Gardiner and Greatorex 1997). Market Field may indeed represent a 'farmstead…on the periphery of the town', but, as John Blair has observed, excavation has demonstrated that even within Late Saxon towns, land appears to have been 'mainly divided into large, open-ground tenements (*hagae*), resembling farmyards and still supporting relatively low populations' (Gardiner and Greatorex 1997, 168; Blair 2005, 337). Certain

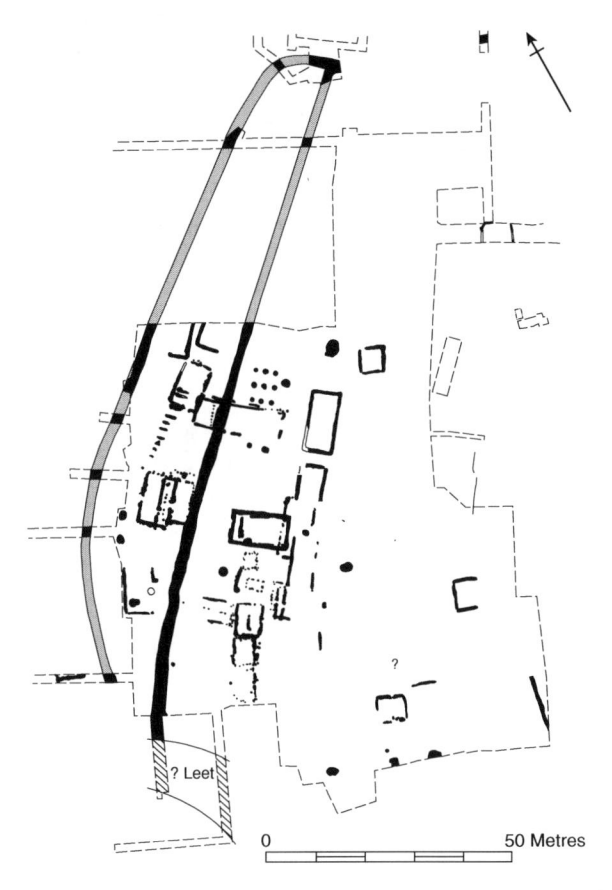

Fig. 3.14. The Mid Saxon settlement phase at Wicken Bonhunt (after Wade 1980).

aspects of the settlement at Bishopstone—notably its density and methods of waste management—have led the excavator to suggest that it too may have had a 'proto-urban' character (Thomas 2010, 209). For the Mid Saxon period, similarities in the layouts of the *emporium* of *Hamwic* and the broadly contemporary phases of the high-status rural settlements at North Elmham and Wicken Bonhunt—all of which made use of long, straight ditches to mark out lanes, with wells and buildings scattered amongst them—raise further questions about whether it is possible to draw clear distinctions between rural and urban layouts at such an early date (Figs. 3.13, 3.14; Reynolds 2003, 121–2).

From Anglo-Saxon settlement to medieval village

The examples cited above tend to support Reynolds' contention that 'the use of 1066 as a defining horizon is not particularly helpful' in understanding the development of early medieval settlement forms and that, furthermore, 'it was not until the twelfth and thirteenth centuries that new forms of settlements additional to pre-Conquest types (such as "green" villages) came into existence' (Reynolds 2003, 100).[10] To what extent, then, can settlement forms which originated in pre-Conquest England be seen as the precursors of medieval villages? 'Rectilinear' settlements such as Cottenham, Hall Farm, Baston, West Fen Road, Ely, and Raunds Furnells appear to foreshadow in some respects the 'classic' medieval village with a regular plan of tofts and crofts. Reynolds has suggested, furthermore, that settlements associated with some manorial sites also displayed 'regular "village-type" plots' (2003, 130) and cites Wicken Bonhunt as a prime example: its Saxo-Norman phase consisted of 'regular plots of classic "medieval" type', three of which measured roughly 100 metres by 5 to 10 metres (Wade 1980, fig. 40; Reynolds 2003, 125). Nevertheless, we have yet to excavate an Anglo-Saxon settlement 'which resembles the type of settlement familiar from the fourteenth century onwards with a series of closely set buildings facing on to a central road or green' (Gardiner 2011, 207). While some Carolingian villages adopted such layouts as early as the eighth century (Hamerow 2002a, 62–75), Anglo-Saxon settlements tended to be more dispersed and lacked the densely occupied street frontages seen in so many English villages during the central Middle Ages.

Settlement morphology: social and economic implications

Rectilinear enclosures

From the preceding examples[11], it is clear that the Mid Saxon period saw the emergence—at least in eastern England—of settlements characterized by systems of ditched enclosures. Although they varied considerably in size, shape, and presumably function, these enclosures shared certain characteristics, namely relatively insubstantial ditches (albeit probably augmented with banks and hedges), evidence of repeated re-cutting, indicating maintenance over relatively long periods of time, and in many cases, extensive reconfiguration or remodelling of enclosures to meet changing needs. What those needs were remains a matter for conjecture, although there can be little doubt that the introduction of such semi-permanent boundaries in settlements of the seventh and, especially, eighth centuries, marked a real social and

---

[10] At Wharram Percy, for example, a lynchet—a bank of ploughed earth—defining the back of tofts along a row of houses in part of the planned village has been dated to the twelfth century, suggesting that this may be when the planned layout originated (Stamper and Croft 2000).

[11] There are, of course, other sites that could be added to the preceding discussion of rectilinear settlements, such as Cottam, in Yorkshire (Richards 2000).

economic watershed. The widespread appearance of ditched enclosures has sometimes been attributed to a shift by some farmers towards more intensive stock-rearing practices and away from a broadly based regime geared towards self-sufficiency (e.g. Blinkhorn 1999, 16; see also Chapter 5). It is worth examining this proposition more closely, as in order to understand the changing form of individual settlements it is necessary to consider their relationship with the wider farmed landscape.

What, then, could explain the sudden appearance in the Mid Saxon period of enclosures and droveways directly associated with settlements? It would, after all, always have been necessary to prevent farm animals from getting too close to buildings and damaging them—by nibbling at thatched roofs, for example. This was presumably achieved in the early Anglo-Saxon period by 'hefting', that is, keeping animals outside year-round, on large tracts of unfenced grazing land well away from the settlement (Hart 2004).[12] The appearance of enclosures and droveways indicates at the very least that animals were, for some reason, being kept closer to settlements than they had been previously, and that droveways and paddocks were therefore necessary to keep them safely away from buildings.[13] At Catholme, for example, the convergence of trackways T1, T2, and T3 and the position of trackways T5–T8 at the edge of the terrace where cattle would have been led down to the river for watering suggest that these functioned at least in part to control the movement of livestock as they were driven past the settlement (Losco-Bradley and Kinsley 2002, 31–2 and fig. 3.97).

If the general principle is accepted that farmers enclose crops rather than animals unless absolutely necessary—as implied by an oft-cited late seventh-century law referring to the obligation to fence one's arable to keep out cattle (*EHD* 32.42)—then one possible explanation for the need to keep animals closer to settlements is a shortage of readily accessible pasture, perhaps as arable expanded over terraces and onto heavier soils. The apparent concentration of settlements with rectilinear enclosures near the fen edge in Cambridgeshire could, for example, reflect the need to keep stock near settlements in a landscape that was too wet for winter grazing.[14] An increase in the

---

[12] Gardiner has recently drawn attention to archaeological evidence for Late Saxon transhumance in the form of possible herders' huts and isolated rectilinear enclosures in valley bottoms and in some cases valley sides, which were presumably used for sheep. Few, however, have been excavated and they are poorly dated (Gardiner 2011).

[13] This situation is reflected in Ine's late seventh-century laws which state that a *ceorl* is obliged to fence his homestead and that if his neighbour's cattle get in through a gap in the fence, the *ceorl* has no right to compensation for the damage done (*EHD* 32, 40).

[14] Anxiety about environmental determinism has led to a reluctance to attribute variability in the settlement record to anything other than human agency. Nevertheless, a number of researchers have recently and persuasively reiterated the importance of the local environment in shaping early medieval settlements and landscapes (e.g. Williamson 2003; Rippon 2008).

size of flocks as well as the number of plough oxen being kept could also help to account for such a shortage (see Chapter 5). It is interesting to note in this connection a striking prehistoric parallel, namely the appearance of stock enclosures and droveways in the same region of eastern England in the Bronze and early Iron Ages (Pryor 1996).

The establishment of hay meadows (which would have provided better winter feed for oxen) in the Mid and Late Saxon periods may also have been a factor in the appearance of enclosures, as animals would have to be kept off these meadows until the hay had been cut; the movement of stock would therefore have to be closely controlled (see Chapter 5 for a discussion of the evidence for hay meadows). It is likely, of course, that the appearance of enclosures was the result of the interplay between these and other environmental and social factors, as farming methods underwent a general process of elaboration and, probably, intensification.

The establishment and maintenance of extensive systems of enclosures and droveways also points to an increased investment of labour and material capital. It is likely that the mouldboard plough drawn by a team of oxen—shared between several farmers—came into more widespread use in the Mid Saxon period in order to grow crops, especially bread wheat, on heavier soils.[15] The palaeobotanical and other evidence for such a suggestion is discussed in Chapter 5; its relevance here is that a need to create larger fields and invest in traction animals may have encouraged the development of a co-operative system of shared enclosures.

The geographical distribution of rectilinear settlements, with its emphasis on eastern England, is suggestive. While to some extent it reflects the distribution of large-scale excavations, it may also indicate the different farming strategies required on the heavy clays of the fen-edge, near which settlements such as Ely, Godmanchester, and Cottenham were sited. Williamson (2003) has argued that farmers on heavy clays needed to be able to bring together plough-teams quickly because of the short time available for spring ploughing before 'puddling' occurred; they would therefore have needed to keep their oxen close to their farmsteads rather than scattered across the landscape. The occurrence of some rectilinear settlements on lighter soils at sites like Yarnton, Riby Crossroads, and Wolverton suggests, however, that we should avoid being overly deterministic in explaining their appearance and should recall that the process of nucleation and innovations in farming also had an important social dimension (see Dyer 2004). Regardless of the relative importance of environmental factors versus 'agency', it is probably not a coincidence that such layouts emerged most clearly in a region which was prosperous and commercially developed, as indicated by the distribution of Mid Saxon coinage, metalwork, and imports.

---

[15] To gain maximum yields from bread wheat, the crop must be kept dry; for this, the ridge and furrow achieved by the use of a mouldboard plough was needed (see Banham 2010).

Rectilinear settlements with regular domestic enclosures

There is growing evidence for the existence of what Roberts has called 'informally regular' (in contrast to 'geometrically rigid') plots, in some cases domestic, associated with settlements of the Mid Saxon period (Roberts 2008, 125). At Quarrington, a series of rectilinear enclosures was established in the second phase of occupation and the roundhouses described in Chapter 2 were replaced by three rectangular, post-built timber buildings lying close together, with two apparently abutting a fence-line, suggesting that this area may have constituted a habitation zone or compound (Fig. 3.15; Taylor 2003b, 273, fig. 7). The layout established in this phase displays considerable regularity, and includes three evenly spaced, east–west aligned ditches defining parcels of land—possibly fields or paddocks—*c.*23m wide (Figs. 3.15, 3.16).[16] The settlement appears to have gone out of use by the ninth century, although remains of later ridge-and-furrow indicate that ploughing in the later medieval and post-medieval periods followed the same orientation as the Mid Saxon enclosures. While the excavation produced no evidence to indicate that these early boundaries were actively maintained, it nevertheless appears that the 'general structure of the landscape' originated in this period (ibid. 274).

The establishment and maintenance of rectilinear settlements such as Cottenham and West Fen Road, Ely was also clearly a co-ordinated exercise. The size of enclosures, furthermore, remained remarkably consistent over time, suggesting a measure of legal control over the passing down of properties. Indeed, in the view of the excavator of West Fen Road, 'the longevity of most of the enclosures suggests that individual farmsteads lay within them, possibly with the property passing from one generation to the next' (Mortimer et al. 2005, 129). Further evidence for the existence of enclosed, ancestral properties comes from the settlement of Catholme, which was established, probably in the seventh century, as a series of enclosed farmsteads and trackways (Fig. 4.3). The repeated re-cutting of the enclosure ditches as well as the placement of a single human burial at the entrances to two of the enclosures strongly suggest that these enclosures served to demarcate ancestral properties (Hamerow 2002b).

How should such regular plots and enclosures be interpreted? By the tenth century, regular house-plots presumably reflected some form of assessment. There has been a tendency to assume that the earlier planned layouts and systems of enclosure associated with Mid Saxon settlements were also reflections of lordship. Reynolds, for example, has argued that the planning implicit

---

[16] The excavator notes that these widths may be based on a perch of 4.65m even though, as he admits, this unit of measurement 'has no documented history in England' (Taylor 2003b, 274). John Blair is, at the time of writing, however, undertaking research which suggests that a range of Mid and Late Saxon communities used a fifteen-foot 'perch' to lay out their settlements. I am grateful to him for discussing this evidence with me in advance of publication.

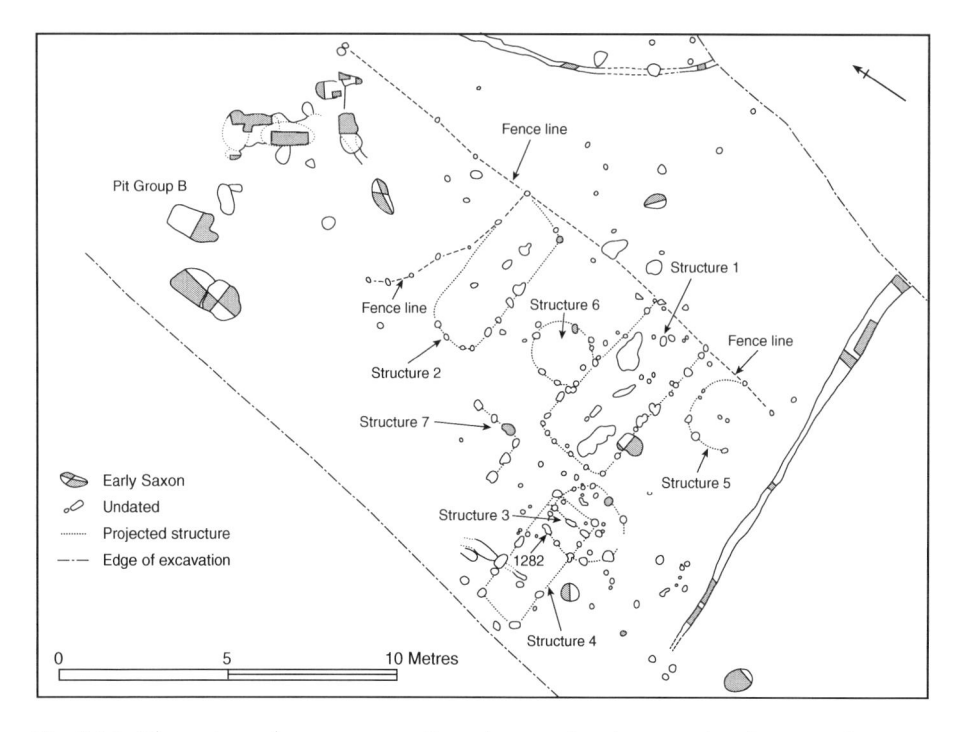

Fig. 3.15. The main settlement zone at Quarrington, showing round and rectangular structures (after Taylor et al. 2003b).

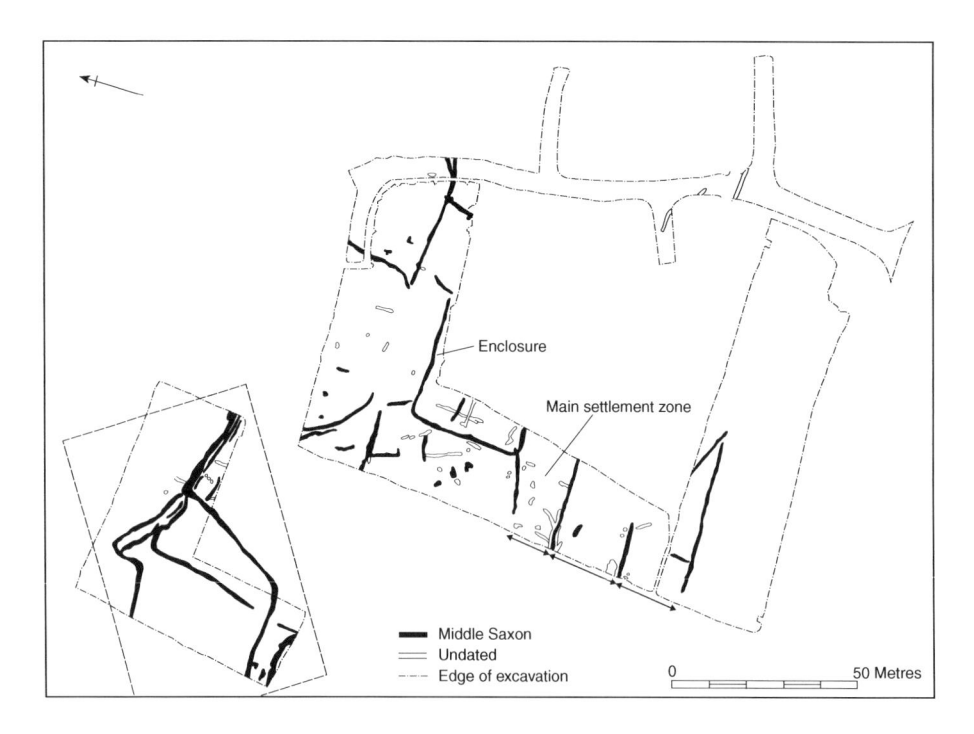

Fig. 3.16. Overall plan of Mid Saxon enclosures at Quarrington (after Taylor et al. 2003b).

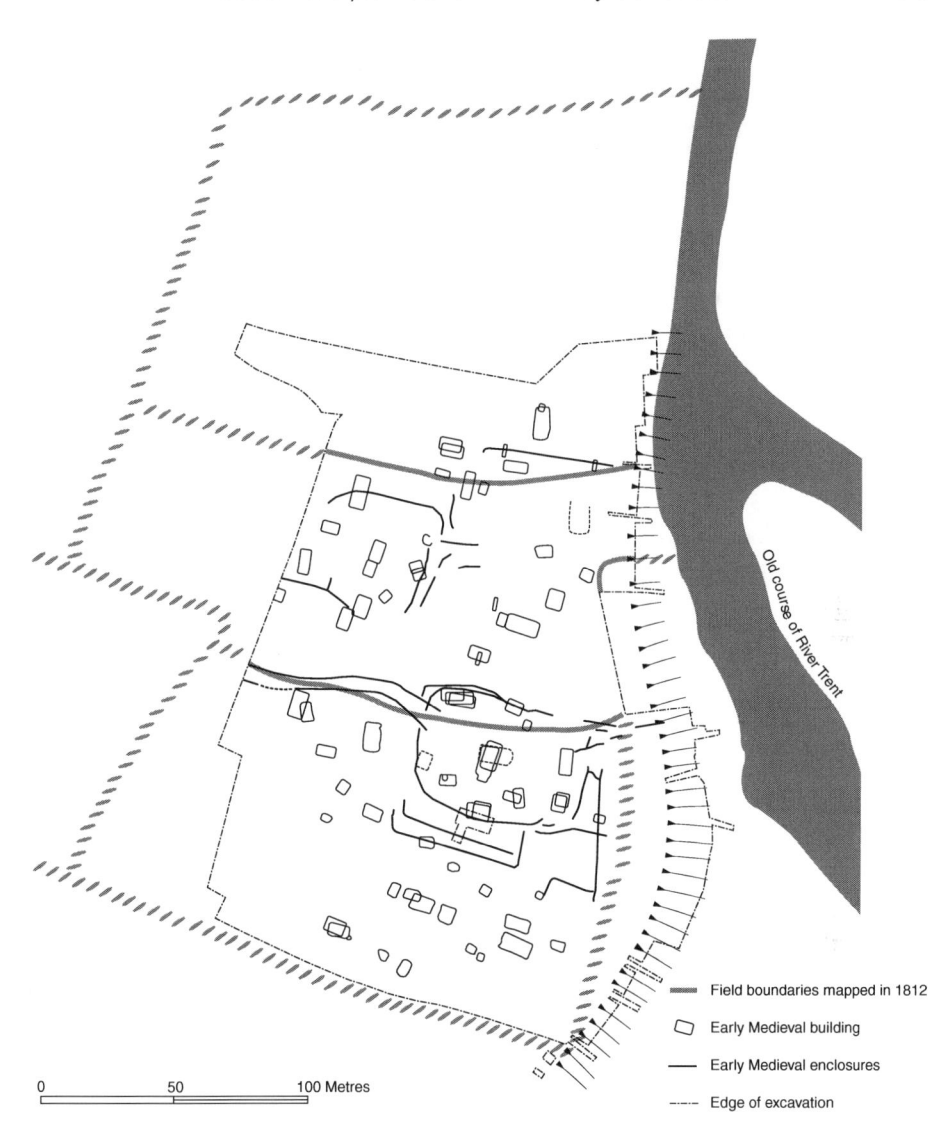

Fig. 3.17. A schematic plan of the settlement at Catholme in relation to field boundaries mapped in 1812 (after Losco-Bradley and Kinsley 2002).

in rectilinear enclosures '[required] either widespread consent or enforcement', and such settlements were 'surely founded under lordly control and look towards a new social rigidity including increasingly quantified territory' (2003, 131). Similarly, Blair has hypothesized that the radical reorganization that occurred at Yarnton around AD 700 marked its transfer to monastic control (Blair 2005, 255).

The question of the role of lordship in the organization of individual settlements is linked to a much wider debate concerning whether the creation of common fields was a gradual, drawn-out process (cf. Lewis et al. 2001) or involved a dramatic restructuring of the landscape overseen by lords who replaced small, scattered farms with nucleated villages (cf. Audouy and Chapman 2009).[17] This debate is far from resolved and, as Steve Rippon has succinctly observed, we still 'do not understand the actual process whereby a landscape of dispersed settlement was transformed into one of villages and common fields' (2008, 20). We should be cautious, therefore, about assuming that lords were able to exercise such a high degree of control over peasant communities in the eighth and ninth centuries, or indeed that these same communities were incapable of establishing and maintaining such layouts themselves.[18] At the very least, the emergence of such settlements in the Mid Saxon period militates against the argument that, in the 'central zone' of England at least, the process which led to the formation of nucleated settlements only commenced post-850 (Lewis et al. 2001, 191–2; Lewis 2010, 104–5; cf. Williamson 2003, who argues for the formation of nucleated villages in the ninth century or even earlier).

'Service features' and functional zones

The Mid and Late Saxon periods saw an increase in the frequency of 'service features' in settlements, namely wells, pits, ovens, cesspits, and latrines (Reynolds 2003, 130). Pits occur on many early Anglo-Saxon settlements, but are found in increasing numbers in the Mid and Late Saxon periods. Those containing animal bone and pottery are sometimes referred to as 'rubbish pits' by their excavators, yet true refuse pits are actually quite rare in Anglo-Saxon settlements (e.g. Tyler and Major 2005, 148). In the early Anglo-Saxon period in particular, most refuse appears to have ended up in the abandoned hollows of *Grubenhäuser*. In truth, it is usually impossible to assign a specific function to pits, although certain regular types are apparent. At Eye Kettleby, where more than sixty Anglo-Saxon pits were excavated, twelve were 'fire-pits' filled with scorched stones and charred wood believed to have been used for cooking (N. Finn, forthcoming). Two nearly identical fire-pits at Nettleton Top (Lincolnshire) were shallow, oblong, and 'lined with small pieces of ironstone, many of which were very reddened by heat', and similar features were found at Catholme; their function, however, remains a mystery (Field and Leahy 1993, 11), as does that of seven 'flint burning pits' containing up to 450 kg of burnt flint and scorched subsoil excavated at Kilverstone, although it has been suggested that such pits may have been used for cooking large quantities of meat,

---

[17] This debate has most recently been set out by Rippon (2008).
[18] Even for the thirteenth century, the relative roles of 'communal agreement' versus 'seignorial power' in explaining the sometimes radical changes seen in settlement are difficult to assess (Harvey 1989).

(Crowson et al. 2005; Garrow et al. 2006). Seven rectangular early Anglo-Saxon fire-pits excavated at Gravesend (Kent), two of which were archaeomagnetically dated to between 485–510 and 500–30, appear to have been used for smoking meat, including cod and pork (Gaimster and O'Connor 2005, 379). In the Late Saxon period, sub-rectangular pits became particularly common as, for example, at Bishopstone, where the largest such pit—measuring 1.4m x 0.9m—contained a nearly complete pot and a substantial quantity of animal bone, while others contained nearly a metric ton of burnt building material (Thomas 2010, 194 and pers. comm.). Detailed analysis of the fills of these pits indicates that their function could change over time; thus 'latrines were often capped off with chalk and then filled up with hearth sweepings, kitchen waste and redeposited surface middens' (Thomas 2011b, 45).

Pits were sometimes used to form or give emphasis to a boundary, as at Hall Farm, Baston, Bishopstone, and Springfield Lyons, in a manner similar to that seen at *emporia* such as *Hamwic* (Andrews 1997, 179; Taylor 2003a, 15; Tyler and Major 2005; Thomas 2010, 209). In a small number of cases, sites have been identified that appear to have consisted almost exclusively of pits. Thus, at three adjacent sites near Dorney (Buckinghamshire) in the middle Thames valley, no fewer than 123 pits of Mid Saxon date were excavated, yet almost no other contemporary features were identified (Foreman et al. 2002). The conclusion reached by the excavators—as much through the elimination of a range of alternative possibilities as through the discovery of conclusive evidence—was that the site represents a periodic meeting place where trade and perhaps some craft production occurred, rather than a settlement per se.[19]

Thanks in part to the proliferation of 'service features' it is possible to see the emergence of functional zones more clearly in Mid and Late Saxon settlements. At Steyning, for example, wells were primarily sited to the south of the buildings while rubbish pits lay to the north (Gardiner 1993). At Bishopstone and Lyminge too, 'disposal of human and domestic waste appears to have taken place within prescribed zones' (Thomas 2011b, 45). Large-scale excavation in advance of gravel extraction around the villages of Yarnton and Cassington (Oxfordshire) revealed the remains of three Anglo-Saxon settlements, the most extensive being at Yarnton itself. Here too, functional zones are discernible. Traces of early Anglo-Saxon settlement were uncovered in the form of five *Grubenhäuser*, but the more substantial Mid Saxon phase, which was established *c.*700 and covered over 3 ha, lay to the east of these (Fig. 3.18; Hey 2004, 21). It is likely that the excavated features represent most of the Mid Saxon settlement (ibid. 45).[20] In the course of the eighth century, two earth-fast

---

[19] For a wider discussion of the evidence for open-air meeting places in the Mid and Late Saxon periods see Pestell and Ulmschneider 2003 as well as Pantos and Semple 2004.
[20] Yarnton also provides a particularly clear example of a gradual shift of occupation from west to east over time, from the Roman settlement to the medieval village (Hey 2004).

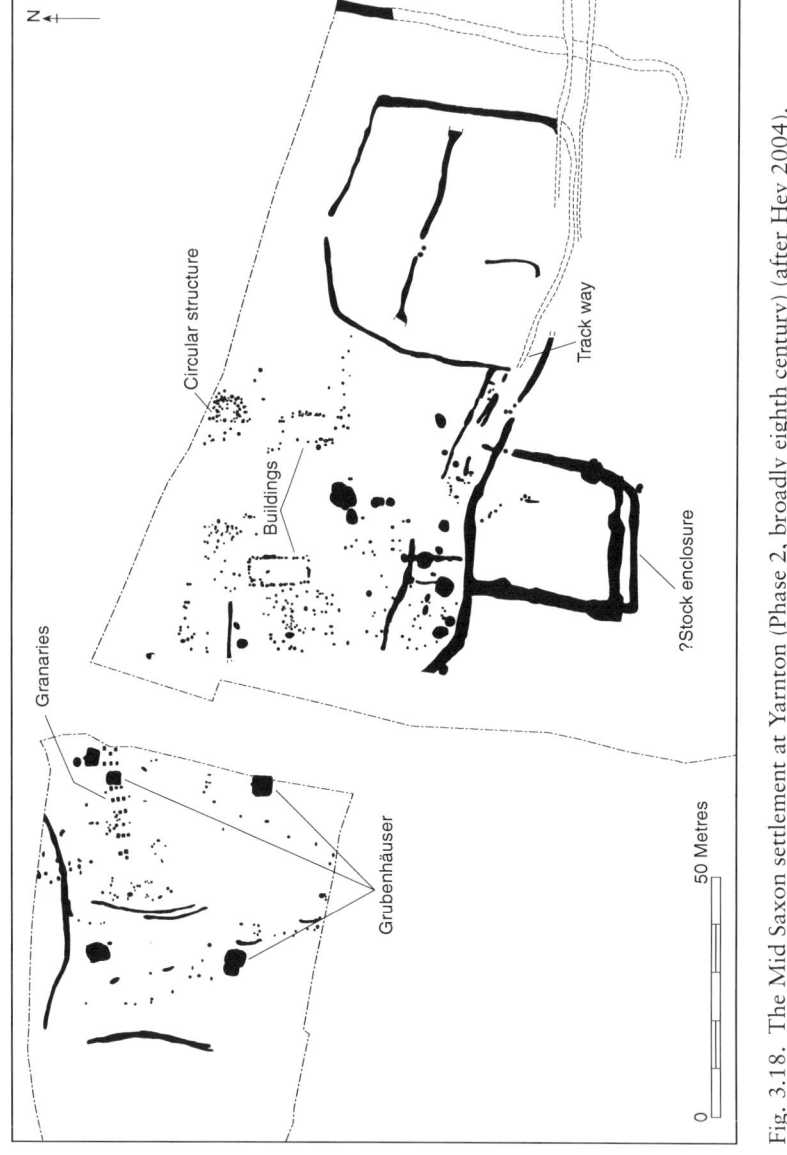

Fig. 3.18. The Mid Saxon settlement at Yarnton (Phase 2, broadly eighth century) (after Hey 2004).

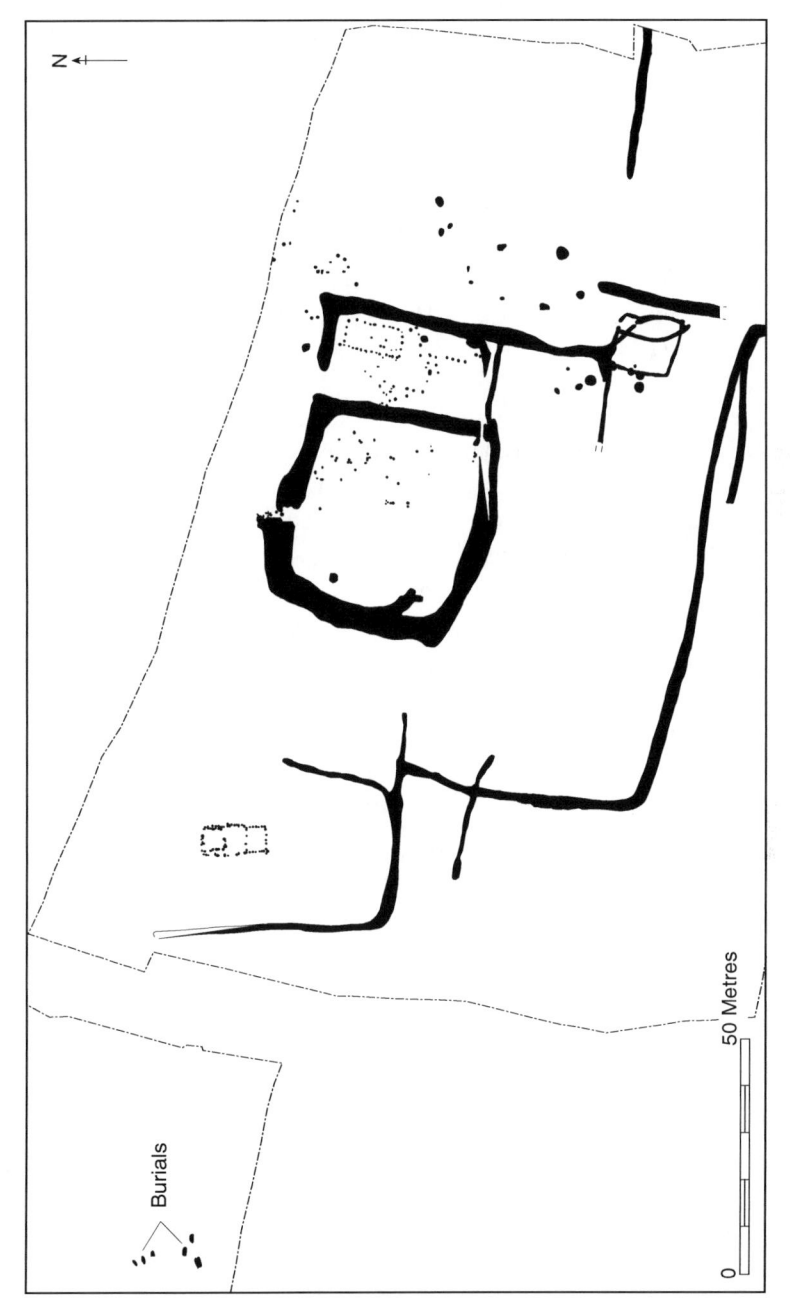

Fig. 3.19. The Mid Saxon settlement at Yarnton (Phase 3, broadly ninth century) (after Hey 2004).

timber buildings were constructed in the central part of the site; six *Grubenhäuser* as well as one or more granaries lay to the west in an area interpreted as an agricultural processing and craft zone. Pits, wells, and a probable stock enclosure lay to the south, and one or more larger enclosures—again presumably for stock—lay to the east. Two parallel ditches demarcating a probable track or droveway entered the settlement from the west, leading towards the central enclosure. The slightly larger building to the west was associated with a range of rectangular buildings and a circular timber structure tentatively identified as a fowl house. During Phase 3, dated broadly to the ninth century, the ditches demarcating the enclosures became wider and deeper. What began as a relatively minor enclosure in Phase 2 became 'the main focus of occupation' (Fig. 3.19; Hey 2004, 46). An earth-fast timber building was set within an 'annexe' to the east of the main enclosure which appears to have been part of the original layout, and not a later addition (ibid. 155). The main enclosure contained several subdivisions whose functions are uncertain. Some *Grubenhäuser* may have remained in use into the ninth century, but the focus of activity moved to the south of the large enclosures, where two wells were dug and small ditched enclosures were formed.[21] Twenty-two pits, mostly in the southeastern part of the site, were dated to this phase.

The increased frequency of service features may well mark some form of 'social transformation', as Andrew Reynolds has suggested (2003, 130). Indeed, their presence has in itself sometimes been seen as an indicator of status. This brings us to an issue already alluded to, namely the degree to which apparently 'high-status' settlements dominate the archaeological record of the Mid and Late Saxon periods and the question of how the status of rural settlements in this period should be defined in the first place.

Defining the status of Anglo-Saxon communities

As already observed, the emergence of settlements with boundaries and enclosures has often been regarded as 'the first stage of the journey towards the highly regulated patterns of social space observed into the middle ages and beyond' and, furthermore, as marking 'the development of an increasingly ranked and polarized society' in which social roles were more closely regulated (Reynolds 2003, 131). Indeed, as documents such as the *Rectitudines Singularum Personarum* (Liebermann 1903, i; Swanton 1975) clearly indicate, Late Saxon society was 'strongly hierarchical and marked by considerable inequalities of wealth' (Gardiner 2011, 198). It is not unreasonable, therefore, to expect that excavated settlements will, to some degree, reflect these inequalities.

---

[21] Wells appear to be found with greater frequency in Mid and Late Saxon settlements and often lay within enclosures, as at Yarnton, Pennyland, and Godmanchester. This is not inconsistent, however, with such enclosures being used to hold stock (Pryor 1996).

Establishing the status of a settlement is, however, often extremely difficult in practice given the paucity of both artefacts and environmental remains found at most sites, even those identified in written sources as having been of high status (such as the royal vill at Yeavering; see below). Partly for this reason, excavations at the settlement of Flixborough, south of the Humber estuary in Lincolnshire, have assumed particular importance (Loveluck 2007). Between 1989 and 1991, excavations uncovered traces of some forty buildings dating to the Mid and Late Saxon periods. What makes the site truly exceptional, however, is the preservation of very large quantities of artefacts (some 15,000) and hundreds of thousands of animal bone fragments contained in refuse middens which were subsequently sealed by blown sand. This has enabled archaeologists to argue for clear and sometimes radical changes in the character and status of the settlement during the eighth to tenth centuries, thereby prompting a renewed debate about how the status of settlements should be defined.

Despite the considerable extent of the excavation, only a fraction of the settlement was uncovered and its core probably lay outside the excavated area; indeed, field survey has demonstrated that Saxon activity extended north and south of the excavated site. Nevertheless, the detailed stratigraphic sequences allow 'changing trends in the use of space between the Mid and Late Saxon periods' to be observed (Loveluck 2007, 66). These include the increasing use of boundaries (although the evidence for boundaries again declines in the tenth and eleventh centuries), increasingly formal organization, and increased zoning, for example of burial, refuse, and craft production. Some phases, such as the mid ninth century, saw deliberate clearance and remodelling of the settlement. Another transformation occurred in the first half of the tenth century, when the relatively small buildings of the preceding period were demolished and replaced by much larger buildings, one of which was nearly 20m in length.

Marked changes in animal husbandry practices occurred in the ninth century, including the introduction of new breeding stock, while the period from the late eighth to mid ninth centuries is characterized by increasing diversity and output of craft production, with more textile-production equipment deriving from this phase than any other. The finds demonstrate that, by the seventh century, the community at Flixborough was already part of a network of contacts across the North Sea and English Channel. By the eighth century, glass fragments representing some 60 Carolingian drinking vessels and 20 silver coins known as sceattas (most of which were minted on the Continent) attest to the community's integration into an international trade network. Despite the fact that Continental coinage had ceased to arrive by the ninth century, lead (presumably imported from the Peak District), Ipswich Ware from East Anglia, and coinage from south-eastern England were reaching the settlement. Indeed, Chris Loveluck has argued that the community was 'in receipt of greater quantities of imported raw materials and artefacts in the first half of the ninth century than at any other period' (2007, 118). The evidence for the later ninth and tenth centuries suggests that exchange was severely disrupted, presumably as a result of Viking activity. A small number of coins continued to arrive, however, and the presence of pottery from Lincoln and perhaps Torksey reflects growing contact with urban centres.

The question of whether Flixborough represents an undocumented minster has generated considerable debate, particularly as the written sources provide no 'clues as to how the rich range of finds should be interpreted' (Foot, in Loveluck 2007, 136; this debate is summarized in Blair 2005, 206–12). Because historically attested monasteries such as Monkwearmouth, Jarrow, and Hartlepool have tended to be targeted for excavation, Loveluck rightly warns that there is a danger of circularity in arguing that the finds they produce—such as styli and window glass, both of which are present at Flixborough—are *exclusively* markers of such communities.

Loveluck's conclusion is that, in the eighth century, Flixborough was an aristocratic estate centre marked by conspicuous consumption; it became monastic (or part of a monastic estate) in the early to mid ninth, when the evidence for literacy is most marked and craft production reached its peak; it then became 'secularized' in the later ninth and early tenth centuries, when it appears to have been of ordinary status. Sometime later in the tenth century, the presence of large buildings and evidence for hunting and feasting suggest that the community regained its elite status. As remarkable as the evidence from Flixborough is, such 'dynamic change' is not entirely surprising, as written sources for the period clearly indicate that minsters could be 'secularized' (see Blair 2005, 186–7, 279–90, 323–9).[22]

Quite apart from the issue of whether the settlement housed a monastic community is the controversial suggestion that the 'profligate' discarding of material goods—including iron tools, widely assumed to have been of very high value in early medieval society—which is so marked at Flixborough, may not have been restricted to high-status sites, at least not in the comparatively rich, eastern part of the country. Indeed, Loveluck suggests that the scarcity of metal objects in the archaeological record, generally assumed to be the result of recycling, is in fact largely due to post-depositional factors. His argument in essence is that the numbers of imports, coins, and other 'high-status' finds at Flixborough reflect exceptional preservation conditions, not necessarily exceptional status.[23] If

---

[22] A change from secular to monastic (rather than vice versa) in the ninth century would, however, make Flixborough unique in an English context, to judge from written sources (Blair 2005, 279–90, 323–9). Bishopstone provides another example of a Late Saxon settlement whose status is ambiguous. Excavations adjacent to the Anglo-Saxon church of St Andrew, which may have pre-Viking origins, have revealed dense occupation and substantial buildings, although no enclosure as far as can be determined. An inhumation cemetery, a tower (see Chapter 2), a gate structure, and evidence for non-ferrous metalworking were found, all indicating a community of considerable status. It is not possible to establish with certainty, however, whether this was the settlement of a *thegn* or, for example, of unreformed minster clergy (Thomas 2004; 2010, 205–6).

[23] Though see Blair 2011 for a cautionary note.

correct, this has enormous implications for our interpretations of other, less well-preserved settlements. It is certainly reasonable to question whether certain types of imports and other 'luxuries' should necessarily be regarded as indicators of high status and, conversely, whether the lack of such items can necessarily be taken as evidence of impoverishment. Even Flixborough, despite being interpreted as of high status in the later tenth century on the basis of its large buildings, produced very little metalwork dating to this period.[24]

On the basis of the evidence from Flixborough, Loveluck urges archaeologists to abandon labels such as 'high-status' and instead to adopt a model of 'dynamic change'. Unfortunately, the overwhelming majority of excavated settlements simply do not produce the kind of preservation that enables such changes of status to be either demonstrated or disproved. It is true that a suspiciously high proportion of excavated Anglo-Saxon settlements of the Mid to Late Saxon periods display at least some trappings of high status in terms of their layout, buildings, and/or material culture. Loveluck's scepticism regarding whether imported goods, certain kinds of dress items, and other artefacts should *necessarily* be seen as 'badges of wealth and rank' (2007, 147) is therefore entirely reasonable.[25] The explanation for the apparently large proportion of high-status settlements may, as he suggests, lie in our interpretations of the archaeological record. Yet the alternative possibility, that the settlements of later Anglo-Saxon peasants may be all but invisible in archaeological terms, should not be discounted. It is interesting to consider what would have happened to those farmers who were unable to participate in a system which required the investment of considerable capital in terms of plough oxen and the construction of extensive systems of enclosures. It may be that only the settlements of more prosperous farmers are readily identifiable in the archaeological record. In short, until more well-preserved sites are excavated, it is impossible either to establish what was 'normal', or indeed to make meaningful comparisons with documented monasteries.

---

[24] This cannot, however, be due to a general paucity of ornamental metalwork in the region (Loveluck 2007, 156), as dozens of items of tenth-century metalwork, including imports, have been found by metal-detectorists in rural Lincolnshire (Kershaw, forthcoming).

[25] The settlement at Riby Cross Roads which, like Flixborough, lies just south of the Humber estuary, provides further support for such scepticism. Here, aerial photographs revealed at least seven interconnected and potentially contemporary ditched enclosures covering an area of some 2.3 hectares as well as at least two main trackways (Steedman 1995). A long, narrow strip excavated in advance of a gas pipeline revealed these to be Mid Saxon in date (although some pottery could be as early as the later sixth century, none of the other finds pre-dates the seventh). Parts of five probable *Grubenhäuser* were uncovered, and a substantial quantity of pottery and animal bone was recovered, suggestive of domestic occupation. Riby Cross Roads also proved to be remarkably finds-rich, despite the limited scale of the excavation. Some of the finds, such as horse gear, a folded lead vessel, several imports, and dress items, are often regarded as indicators of high status. The evidence from Riby Crossroads suggests, however, that such goods may have been abundant in this region, which is exceptionally well situated to benefit from commercial activity, close to the confluence of the Trent—the main artery to and from Mercia—and the Humber.

The emergence of high-status settlements, c.600–800

While distinguishing between 'ordinary' and high-status settlements in Mid to Late Saxon England is thus far from straightforward, the first half of the seventh century saw the establishment of a small number of settlements characterized by large buildings associated with enclosures and carefully planned layouts whose special status can hardly be doubted. These were radically different from anything that had preceded them. Lying at the heart of each were one or more exceptionally large buildings, surely the 'Great Halls' referred to in Anglo-Saxon poems such as *Beowulf*, places where feasting, drinking, and boasting were de rigueur, and where the public presentation of prestigious gifts to followers cemented the loyalty of the war band (Herschend 1998). These settlements were the homes of newly dominant families—those of the first Anglo-Saxon kings and their followers—and their new and distinctive buildings and layouts resonated with power.[26]

The first and most remarkable of these settlements to be identified and excavated was at Yeavering (Hope-Taylor 1977). It was here, at *Ad Gefrin*, according to Bede, that the Bernician King Edwin had a *villa regia*, and here that he received the Christian missionary Paulinus, who carried out a mass campaign of baptism in the waters of the river Glen in the year 627 (*HE* II.14; Colgrave and Mynors 1969). Since the excavations at Yeavering, several more early Anglo-Saxon royal, or at least 'princely', settlements have been identified, allowing certain shared features regarding their layout and use of enclosures, as well as the role of cultic activity, to be recognized.

Layout: alignment and 'ritual symmetry'

The main buildings at Yeavering were arranged with great precision and in a manner that clearly required surveying. Certain buildings were carefully aligned along their long axes and laid out according to an established unit of measurement, dubbed the 'Yeavering foot' (Hope-Taylor 1977). Similar care over alignment was taken at the settlements of Cowdery's Down and Chalton, far to the south in Hampshire, where, in addition to axial alignment, certain buildings were arranged in a perpendicular fashion within fenced enclosures to form courtyards, an arrangement which became characteristic of manorial complexes of the Late Saxon period and beyond (Addyman and Leigh 1973; Millett and James 1984; Thomas 2010, 204–5, fig. 8.5). Recent fieldwork at Sutton Courtenay has shed light on another directly comparable high-status complex (Hamerow, Hayden, and Hey 2008). While the position of the large timber buildings has had to be

---

[26] Halsall has argued that, on analogy with Gaul, the existence of 'kings' in lowland Britain in the fifth and sixth centuries (albeit unrecorded and leaving no archaeological trace) cannot be ruled out (2007, 313–15). It is, nevertheless, clear that the decades around 600 marked a real watershed in sociopolitical organization.

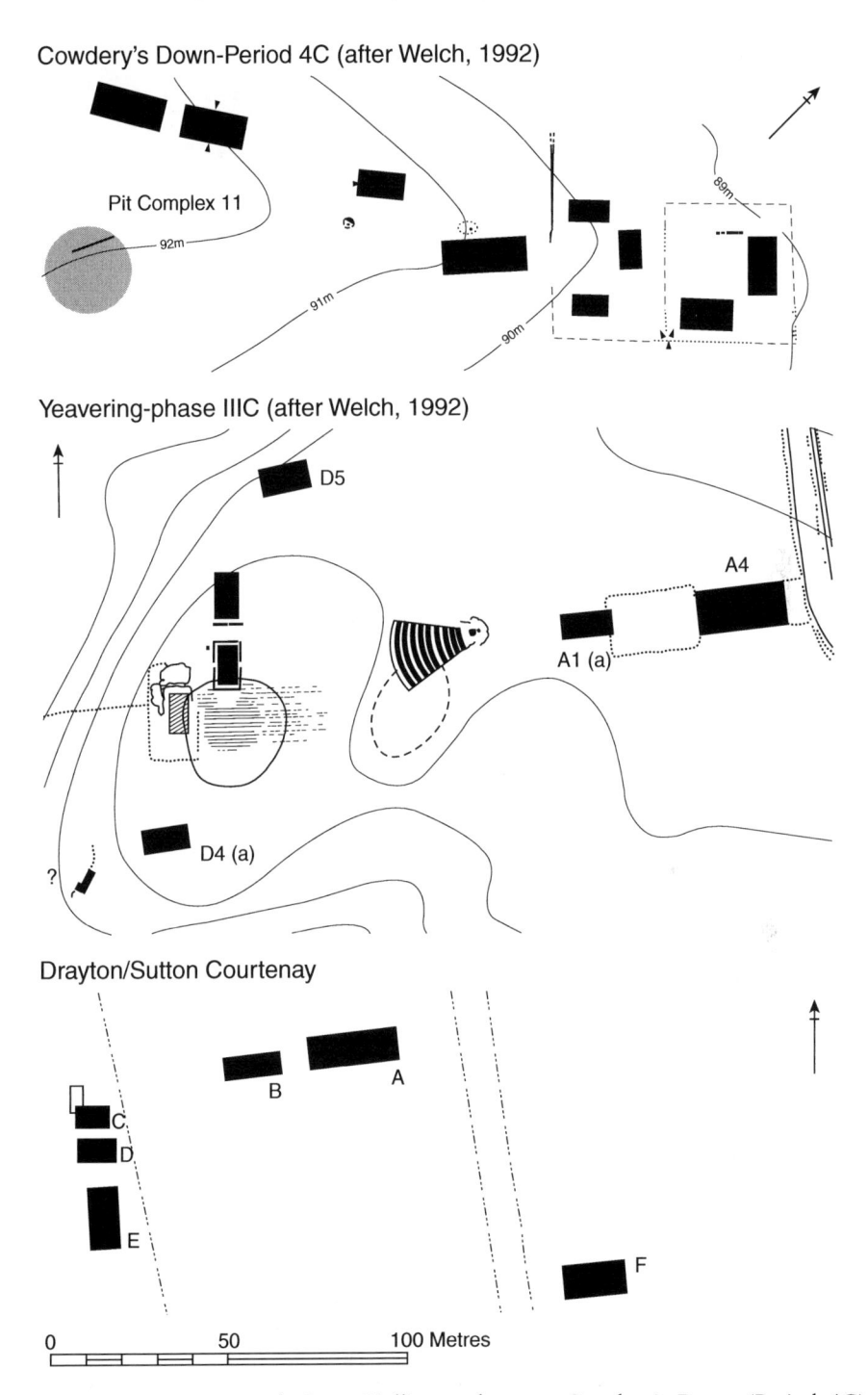

Fig. 3.20. A comparison of 'Great Hall' complexes at Cowdery's Down (Period 4C), Yeavering (Phase IIIC) and Drayton/Sutton Courtenay (after Hamerow, Hayden, and Hey 2008).

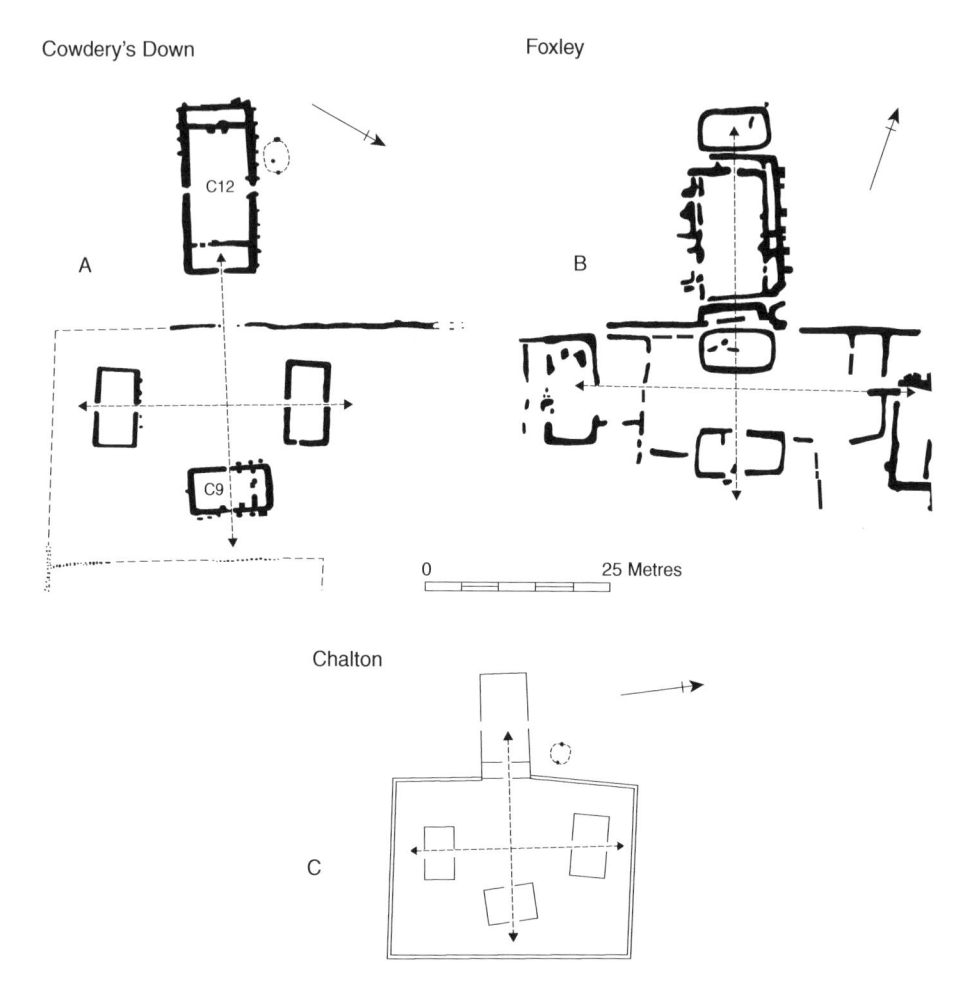

Fig. 3.21. Symmetrical arrangements of buildings, courtyards, and entrances (after Reynolds 2003).

established largely from aerial photographs, a comparison of Sutton Courtenay with Cowdery's Down and Yeavering reveals strikingly similar layouts (Fig. 3.20). In most cases, we simply do not know what determined the alignment of these buildings, although at Yeavering, one of the halls was clearly aligned on a prehistoric ring ditch within which a timber post had been set (Hope Taylor 1977, figs. 31, 33). It is also possible that one hall acted as a 'founder' building on which others were subsequently aligned.[27]

---

[27] 'Phase 2' of the Mid–Late Saxon settlement at Hatton Rock (Warwickshire), known almost entirely from aerial photographs, resembles Sutton Courtenay and Yeavering both in layout and building size (Hirst and Rahtz 1973). In fact, it seems more likely that features originally (and tentatively) assigned to 'Phase 2' actually belong to the earlier, perhaps seventh-century, phase of occupation, while 'Phase 1' resembles more closely a Late Saxon 'long-range' complex of the kind seen at Raunds and elsewhere (see below). In the absence of further excavation, of course, this can be nothing more than speculation.

Andrew Reynolds has noted that at Cowdery's Down, as well as two other broadly contemporary sites at Foxley (Wiltshire) and Chalton, the entrances into buildings were carefully aligned with the entrances into enclosures (Fig. 3.21).[28] Such alignment, as well as the symmetrical layout of the buildings generally—something not seen at ordinary settlements of this period—seems likely to have been done in order to facilitate procession between and through buildings and enclosures.[29] Indeed, Reynolds observes that these symmetrical arrangements are 'strongly suggestive of a ritually organized space' (Reynolds 2003, 106). It is also likely that the layout of buildings and enclosures was used to control access to, and restrict visibility of, certain spaces within the complex. It is striking that some of the earliest Christian sites in Anglo-Saxon England, including the monastery at Jarrow, made similar use of axial alignment. John Blair has suggested that the layout of these monasteries may even have been modelled in part on the slightly earlier princely settlements (Blair 2005, 199–200, fig. 24).

Association with ancient monuments

It has long been recognized that early Anglo-Saxon burial sites were often placed near earlier monuments (especially Bronze Age barrows), a practice that became more common in the seventh century (Williams 1997). Howard Williams and others have argued that monument re-use of this kind reflects the ideological significance in Anglo-Saxon society of 'ancestors' from the remote past (ibid.; see also Bradley 2002). Such association with earlier monuments—and especially complexes of monuments—also appears to have been characteristic of high-status Anglo-Saxon settlements and assembly places, both secular and religious (Blair 1994, 32; Semple 2004).[30] At Yeavering, as already noted, a Bronze Age ring ditch and stone circle appear to have conditioned the layout of the settlement, while the positioning of the 'Great Halls' at Sutton Courtenay immediately adjacent to a group of Bronze Age ring ditches is unlikely to have been coincidental.[31] At Milfield in Northumberland, a large building and palisaded enclosure visible in aerial photographs have been identified as the probable site of *Maelmin*, the successor to the royal vill at Yeavering, according to Bede (*HE* II.14). Excavation has demonstrated that prehistoric henge monuments on the

---

[28] Such alignment may also be seen later, in the ninth- to early tenth-century phase at Raunds Furnells, where opposed northern and southern entrances into a ditched enclosure were aligned on the opposed entrances through a large timber building which lay to the north of the enclosure (Audouy and Chapman 2009, 31).

[29] The function of the enclosures attached to some 'Great Halls' remains unclear, although it is striking that the layout and subdivision of the rectangular enclosure into which Yeavering A2 intrudes mirrors that of the building itself (Hope Taylor 1977, fig. 76).

[30] The location of some ordinary settlements, however, was arguably also influenced by the prehistoric monumental landscape, as will be discussed in Chapter 4.

[31] Two prehistoric ring ditches immediately adjacent to the settlement at Cowdery's Down, however, are likely to have been house gullies, not barrows (Millett and James 1984, 170–2).

western and northern edges of the early medieval complex were still visible when the site was occupied, and indeed attracted burials in the sixth and seventh centuries (Scull and Harding 1990).[32] Such juxtaposition of Anglo-Saxon centres with prehistoric monuments is unlikely to be an expression of ritual continuity spanning many centuries, as Richard Bradley has pointed out in relation to Yeavering and Milfield (Bradley 1987; 1993, 117–19). Rather it suggests the appropriation of ancient monuments and their supernatural associations by an emergent Anglo-Saxon elite seeking to legitimize its control over a region through reference to the past, and through an ideology in which elites were perceived as essentially timeless.

Cultic activity

The analogy drawn between these 'princely' settlements and some of the earliest monasteries is strengthened by evidence for cultic activity at some of these settlements. While evidence of ritualized behaviour is by no means confined to 'special' sites (see Hamerow 2006), it is particularly marked at high-status settlements. The most abundant and striking evidence again comes from Yeavering. This includes a large number of cattle skulls placed in a large pit dug into the foundations of Building D2 immediately north of the eastern entrance to the building; D2 also acted as a focus for human burials and was interpreted by the excavator as a 'temple' (Fig. 3.22; Hope-Taylor 1977). A second deposit of quite different character was found associated with Structure D3, which was broadly contemporary with and only some 5 metres distant from D2. As already noted in Chapter 2, a 'working hollow' and nearby pits contained numerous bone fragments, mostly of ox long bones that had been 'invariably cut and split' (Hope-Taylor 1977, 105). Structure D3 was unusual in having a clay floor and two hearths and was interpreted by the excavator as a kitchen. The lack of teeth or skull fragments from Building D3, the working hollow and pits, suggests a connection with Building D2 and its stack of ox skulls. These deposits must surely be the result of ritual consumption, where the remains of one or more feasts have been carefully sorted and deposited.

Human burials were also associated with several other buildings at Yeavering. Grave AX contained an extended inhumation and an enigmatic object tentatively identified by the excavator as a form of surveying device or staff used in the Roman world; an animal skull, possibly that of a goat, had also been put in the grave. The grave was placed immediately outside the eastern entrance of a 'Great Hall' (Building A4) and was carefully aligned along its main axis (Hope-Taylor 1977, 67–9; Fig. 3.23). An alternative—and

---

[32] The status of the Mid Saxon settlement at Polebrook, where six substantial buildings apparently associated with ditched enclosures have been partly excavated, remains unclear. The buildings lie immediately to the south of two Bronze Age barrows, and near a cursus-like feature, although whether any of these features was visible in the Anglo-Saxon period is not known (Upex 2002).

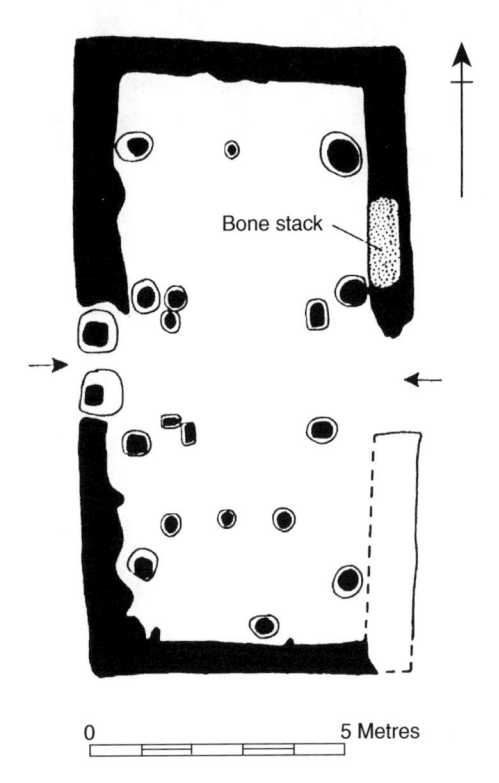

Fig. 3.22. Building D2 at Yeavering, showing position of the deposit of cattle skulls (after Hope-Taylor 1977).

compelling—interpretation is suggested by two Viking Age poems contained in the *Poetic Edda*: *Baldrs draumar* describes the burial place of a sorceress (interestingly, a *volva*, or, 'staff-bearer') as lying by the east doors of *Niflhel* (a region of Hell), while in *Grógaldr* 1, a sorceress is buried 'by the door of the dead' (Price 2002, 113).[33] Religious activity is also indicated in the settlement's final phase, when what appears to have been a small church or chapel was erected over an earlier group of burials (Hope-Taylor 1977). At Cowdery's Down, a pit containing an articulated cow skeleton and a fragment of ?boar skull lay immediately next to the western entrance of the 'Great Hall', Building C13 (Millett and James 1984).

It must be admitted that these early Anglo-Saxon high-status settlements lack the rich material culture associated with their counterparts in southern Scandinavia. Gudme, on the island of Fyn, Tissø on Zealand, and Uppäkra in southern Sweden have all produced impressive deposits of precious metal objects, carefully placed in and around major buildings. It should be noted, however, that at Yeavering a base gold coin—a forged Merovingian *triens*—was found

[33] I am grateful to John Blair for drawing this to my attention.

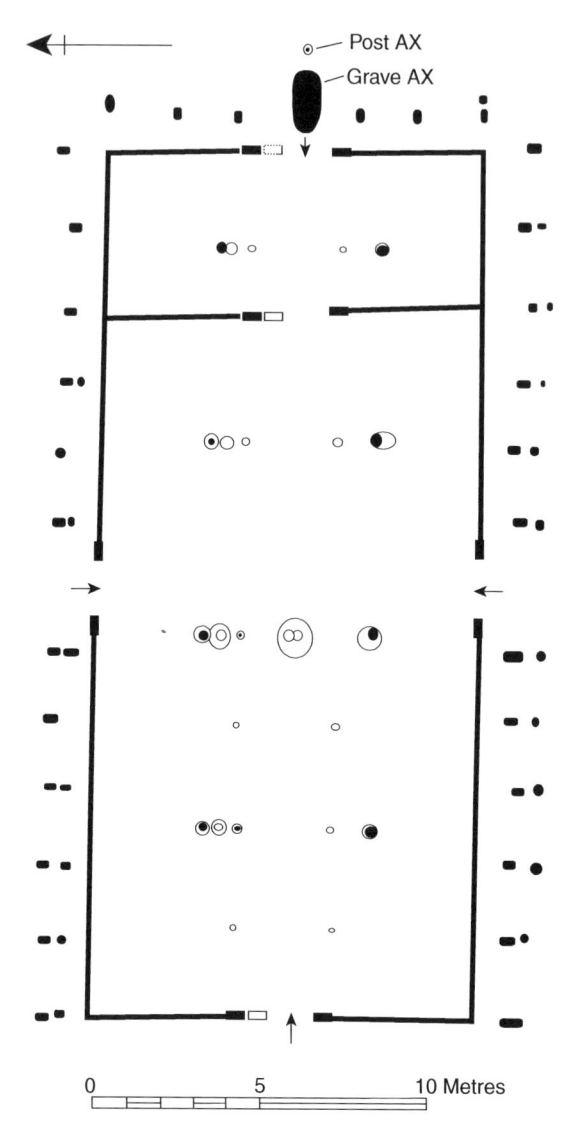

108   *Settlement forms and community structures*

Fig. 3.23. Building A4 at Yeavering, showing the position of Grave AX and Post AX (after Hope-Taylor 1977).

standing vertically against the inner edge of the foundation trench of Building A3(b); it was interpreted by the excavator as a casual loss, but the possibility that it was deliberately placed cannot be ruled out. A tiny ring of beaded gold wire found in the fill of one of the internal roof-supporting posts of the Great Hall, Building A4, may also represent a deliberately placed deposit (Hope-Taylor 1977, 57, 182; Hamerow 2006). At Sutton Courtenay, two small pieces of cut gold sheet and three droplets of gold alloy were recovered by metal-detector users and subjected to trace-element analysis (Hamerow, Hayden, and

Hey 2008). One of the droplets was almost pure gold, while the other two contained significant quantities of copper. As the addition of copper to gold would lower the melting point of the alloy, these two pieces are likely to be solders. Given the multi-period nature of activity at Sutton Courtenay, extending back at least to the Neolithic, it would be unwise to make any assumptions about the date of this material. Nevertheless, given the obviously high-status nature of the early medieval phase of occupation, this material seems most likely to derive from the activities of an Anglo-Saxon goldsmith.

The preceding discussion is by no means a comprehensive survey of all the evidence for cultic activity at high-status Anglo-Saxon settlements; Yeavering alone has provided more than enough evidence of this kind for a lengthy study in its own right. It does, however, serve to demonstrate that—even in the absence of a rich material culture—power and cult are clearly signalled at early Anglo-Saxon high-status settlements and that control over certain rituals appears to have been used to consolidate the positions of the earliest ruling families. It should be remembered, however, that, extraordinary as they were, these 'Great Hall complexes', were—like the princely barrow burials with which they were broadly contemporary—a short-lived expression of power and that remarkably little is known of the royal residences that succeeded them.

Enclosed settlements

The number of archaeologically investigated settlements for which high status can be claimed nevertheless increases markedly from the ninth century. This is probably largely due to the introduction of the practice of leasing land to the laity, who were thereby able to accumulate landed wealth.[34] Royal grants enabled the grantee to obtain more from his tenants than he paid to the king, as more productive farming systems generated ever growing incomes (Wickham 2005, 348–50; see Chapter 5). The proliferation of local lords imposed upon peasant communities appears to be reflected in the emergence of 'enclosed settlements', in which dwellings and associated buildings were surrounded by a substantial earthwork (Reynolds 2003, 104). The association between such enclosures and high status finds considerable support in the written sources. Simon Draper has drawn attention to the definition in the Laws of Ine, King of Wessex (688–726) of a crime referred to as *burh-bryce*, or 'breaching a *burh*'. In the clause in question, fines are specified for breaking into the defended (i.e. enclosed) premises of a king, a bishop, an *ealdorman*, a king's *thegn*, and a nobleman who holds land (*EHD* 32.45; Whitelock 1955). As Draper notes, this law contains 'the tacit implication that only noblemen...owned enclosures around their dwellings' (Draper 2008, 248). In the Laws of Alfred

---

[34] In contrast to the earlier, short-lived 'princely settlements', at least some these later settlements persisted for a century or more.

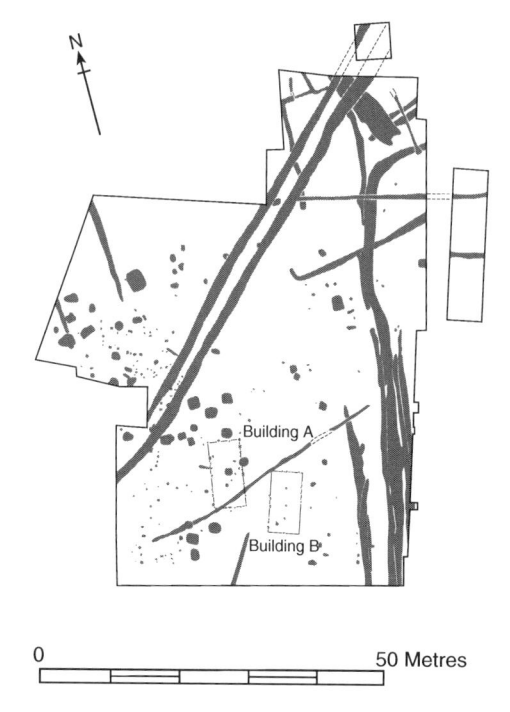

Fig. 3.24. The Late Saxon settlement at Steyning (after Gardiner and Greatorex 1997).

(871–99), the crime of breaking through the enclosure of a free peasant (*ceorl*) was described not as *burh-bryce*, but as *edor-bryce*, breaching a hedge or fence' (ibid.; *EHD* 33.40). Draper goes on to observe that this implies that a *burh* was a more substantial enclosure than merely a hedge or fence. It is not unreasonable, in light of this evidence, to see substantial ditched (and presumably banked) enclosures around settlements of the Mid and Late Saxon periods as in themselves indicators of status.[35]

Archaeologists and historians have often assumed that 'thegnly' residences should, in addition to being enclosed, possess those characteristics enumerated in the early eleventh-century text known as the *Geþyncdo*, namely a *burh*-gate, a 'bell house', a church, and a kitchen, although Mark Gardiner has noted that these were probably chosen as much for their assonance as for their role as 'status symbols' (Gardiner 2011).[36] The role of special-purpose buildings such as

---

[35] It should be noted, however, that the manorial complex at Faccombe Netherton appears not to have been enclosed until the late tenth century (Fairbrother 1990, 62–5).

[36] In another eleventh-century text, *Gerefa*, the reeve is enjoined to 'make walk-ways between the houses' on the lord's farm (Swanton 1975, 26). It is of interest to note in this connection that some of the best evidence for prepared ground surfaces from rural settlements comes from the 'thegnly' settlement at Portchester Castle, where 'a spread of finely crushed chalk had been laid' to the west of Building S11, while to the north, between S11 and an adjacent building, the ground surface 'had been consolidated with metalling' (Cunliffe 1976, 31).

kitchens and towers as indicators of status has already been discussed in Chapter 2. The evidence for gated entrances into enclosed settlements is also worth examining.

Gated entrances into ditched enclosures have been identified on a number of Mid and Late Saxon settlements. These often take the form of two outer posts with a smaller post set between them, which Gardiner interprets as a 'catch-post' for a two-leaf gate (Fig. 3.30; Gardiner and Greatorex 1997, 169). An example of such a 'gated enclosure' was identified at the tenth-century settlement at Steyning, which was enclosed by a bank and ditch (Fig. 3.24). Access was gained via two causeways, one wider (perhaps to accommodate animals), the other narrower and fitted with a double gate (Gardiner 1993, fig. 4d). Virtually identical gates were identified at the Late Saxon enclosed settlement at Little Paxton (Huntingdonshire) and at the royal vill at Cheddar, where the eastern entrance into the ditched enclosure was given further emphasis by the presence of what the excavator suggests was a flagstaff immediately outside the double gate (Fig. 3.30; Rahtz 1979, 166–7, fig. 58; Gardiner 1993, 28 and fig. 6). The excavated area at Steyning contained three wells, two cesspits, and eleven refuse pits, as well as two timber buildings. The excavator suggests that the enclosure was divided into two zones: a domestic side containing the buildings and pits and an apparently empty side which may have been an area of pasture (Gardiner 1993, 28). The initial judgement that this was 'a typical Late Saxon farmstead' has since been revised, and its position within a gated enclosure, as well as the discovery in a pit of a gold inscribed finger ring, strongly suggest that this was in fact a settlement of some status (Gardiner and Greatorex 1997).

The Late Saxon settlement at Springfield Lyons has tentatively been identified with the Domesday manor of Cuton Hall (Tyler and Major 2005, 200; Fig. 3.25). Most of the settlement appears to have been uncovered, yet the phasing of occupation remains uncertain due to the scarcity of closely datable pottery and lack of stratigraphic relationships between buildings (ibid. 195–7, figs. 114–16). A two-celled building with a possible tower (Buildings 1 and 1a; see Chapter 2) appears to belong to the earliest phase, as does the east–west aligned hall (Building 3) and a small square structure identified as a possible kitchen (Building 2). A D-shaped ditched enclosure, only the southern part of which survived, appears to belong to the second phase of settlement, as does the large hall (Building 18), and another possible kitchen, although both of these lay outside the enclosure. Within it lay a relatively modest post-built structure, Building 14, although it is possible that Building 1 also continued in use into this phase. In the third phase of occupation at least part of the enclosure ditch was backfilled. Two buildings cut the ditch and a number of other buildings could belong to this phase. A short stretch of an enclosure ditch uncovered some 30m to the east of the settlement has been interpreted as marking the boundary between the settlement and its associated fields (ibid. 198).

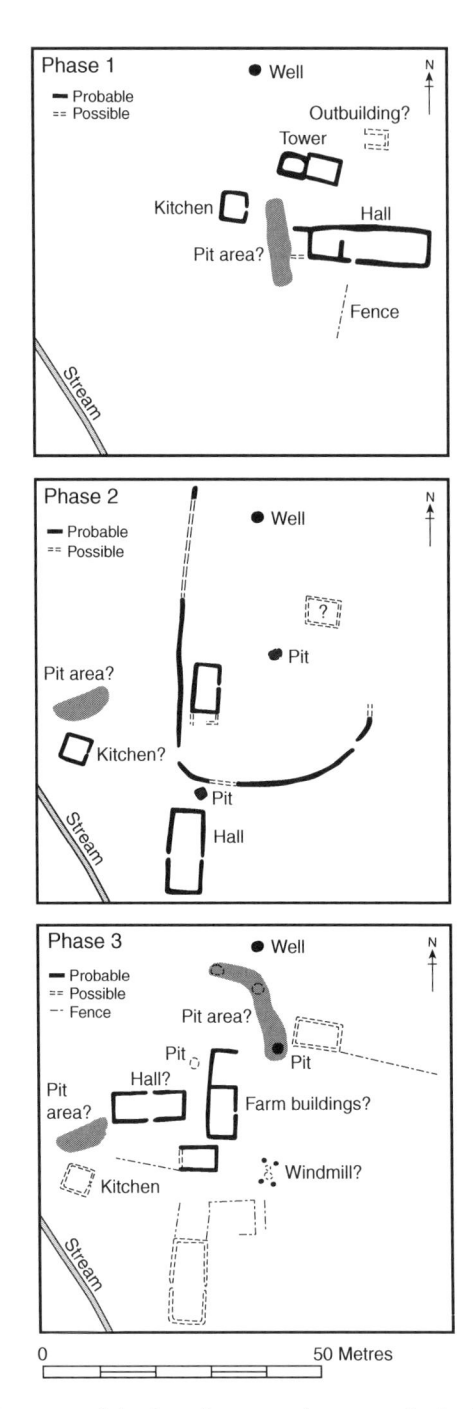

Fig. 3.25. The development of the Late Saxon settlement at Springfield Lyons (after Tyler and Major 2005).

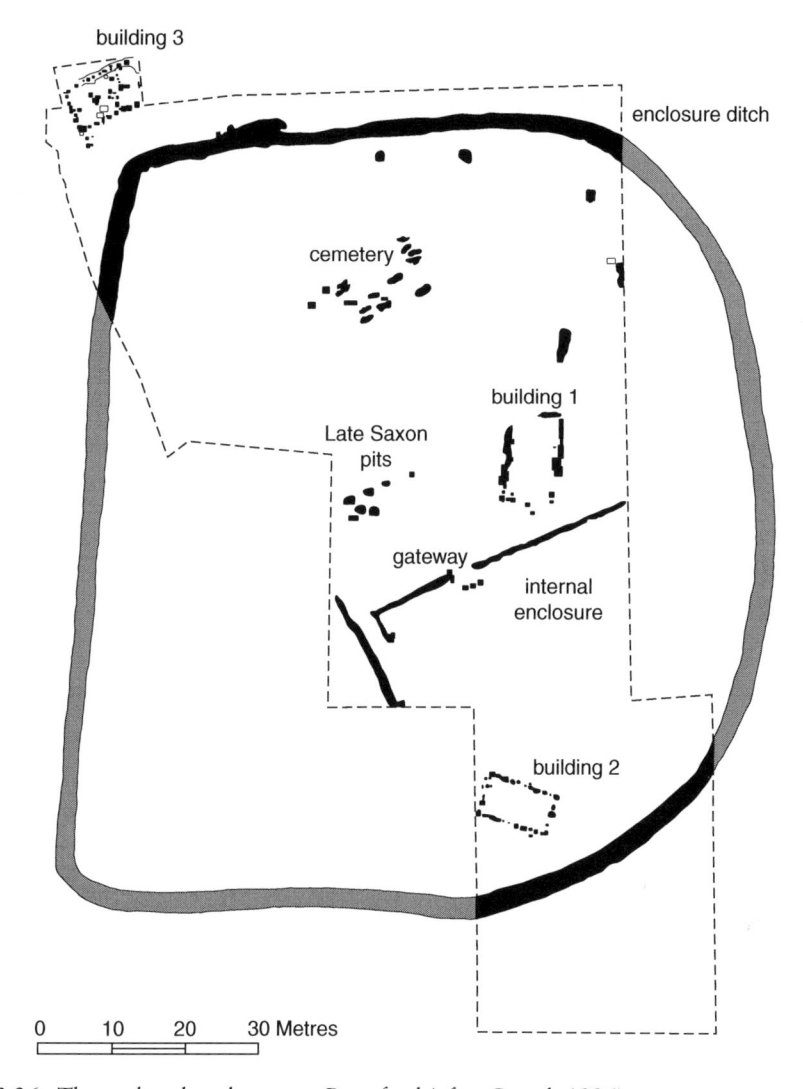

Fig. 3.26. The enclosed settlement at Bramford (after Caruth 1996).

At Bramford, near Ipswich in Suffolk, another roughly D-shaped ditched enclosure contained several buildings of Mid Saxon date, a small cemetery, and other features; at least one further building lay outside the enclosure. The settlement continued into the Late Saxon period and was at some point subdivided by internal ditches into at least three zones, one of which was entered via a gate (Fig. 3.26; Caruth 1996). Bramford appears to have eighth-century origins, as does the impressive enclosed settlement at Higham Ferrers, plausibly interpreted by the excavators as an estate centre associated with the royal centre at Irthlingborough (Hardy et al. 2007). It was laid out on a 'green-field' site in the late seventh or early eighth century and was dismantled around the

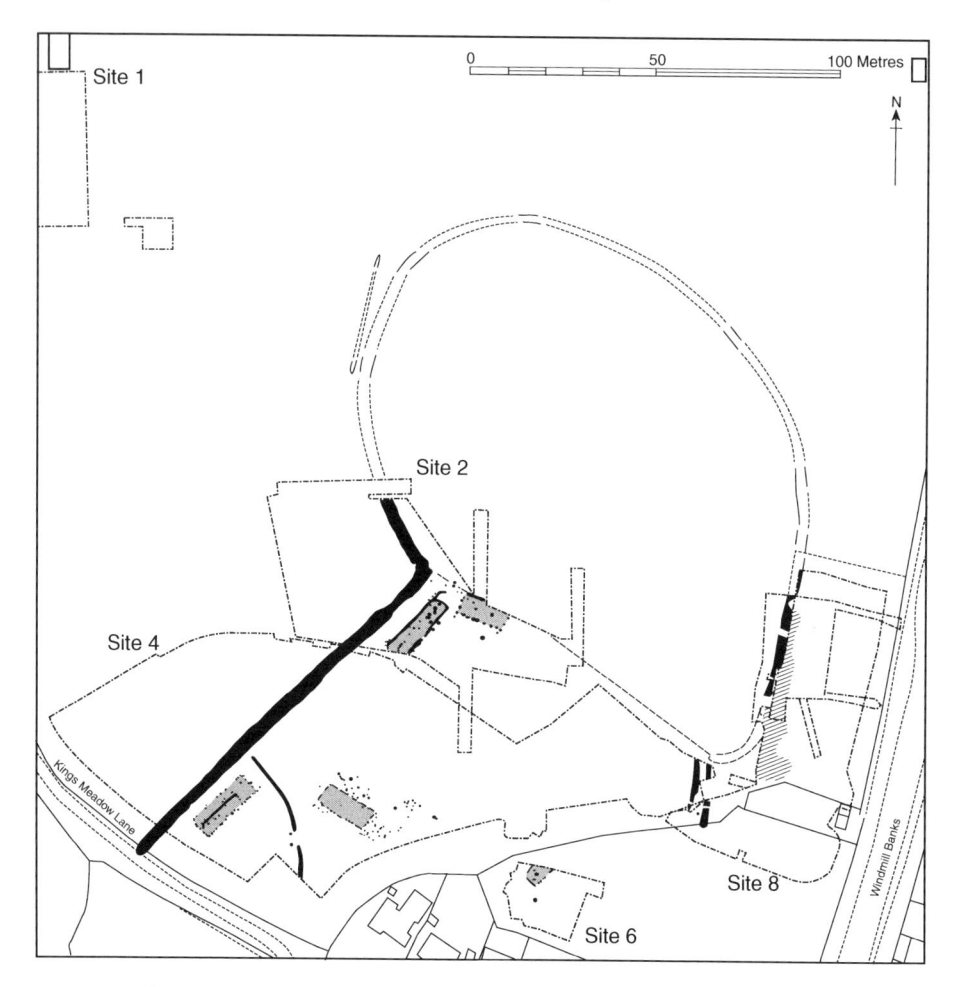

Fig. 3.27. The Mid Saxon settlement at Higham Ferrers, Phase 2b (after Hardy et al. 2007).

beginning of the ninth, after which occupation appears to have shifted, first slightly to the north and, by the twelfth century, to the south, to the site of the medieval village. Its chief element was a large horseshoe-shaped ditch with arms extending to the south, enclosing some 0.8 ha, with several barns and other timber buildings set within, and in several cases aligned along, the western extension ditch. The ditch was only around 2 metres wide, although the enclosure was probably augmented by a bank. During Phase 2b, the enclosure was re-cut and made somewhat more elaborate, notably by the construction of a 'private' enclosure against the south-west end of the western extension ditch (Fig. 3.27). The entrance into this enclosure appears to have been fitted with a gate, although it lacks a central catch-post (ibid., fig. 3.21 and p. 44). Within it lay a large timber building, measuring some 19m x 6.5m (Fig. 3.28). In the

Fig. 3.28. Reconstruction of the Mid Saxon settlement at Higham Ferrers. (Illustrated by P. Lorimer; Copyright Oxford Archaeology Ltd.)

following phase (Phase 2c), the horseshoe-shaped enclosure was abandoned and the south-west extension re-cut to extend eastwards before curving southwards to form a more rectilinear enclosure (Fig. 3.29).

The scale of the enclosure at Higham Ferrers would have been beyond both the means and the needs of a single household. The presence, furthermore, of buildings interpreted as barns (on the basis both of their form and of significant quantities of charred grain in their postholes; see Chapter 2), a possible corral, and a stone malting oven are further indicators that this was a specialized centre for managing agricultural produce (Hardy et al. 2007, 163–7).

Goltho, whose buildings have already been discussed, remains one of the most extensively excavated enclosed settlements. The earliest phase of early medieval occupation, only part of which was excavated, apparently took a rectilinear form (Beresford 1987, 22–3). Within the excavated area lay two rectangular plots containing posthole buildings separated by a ditched boundary, with another ditched boundary defining a probable trackway running to the east of the plots. One of the buildings—probably a dwelling—had a small, enclosed yard containing a stone-built hearth used for iron-smithing. Originally dated by the excavator to *c*.800–50, this phase has been convincingly re-dated by Andrew Reynolds to no earlier than the late ninth century, based on the pottery assemblage associated with it. He has also observed that at least two of the boundary ditches of this first phase are aligned with later medieval linear earthworks, the implication being 'that the Deserted Medieval Village preserves in essence its Anglo-Saxon plan' (Reynolds 2003, 123). The later, enclosed manorial settlement thus replaced an earlier settlement, elements of

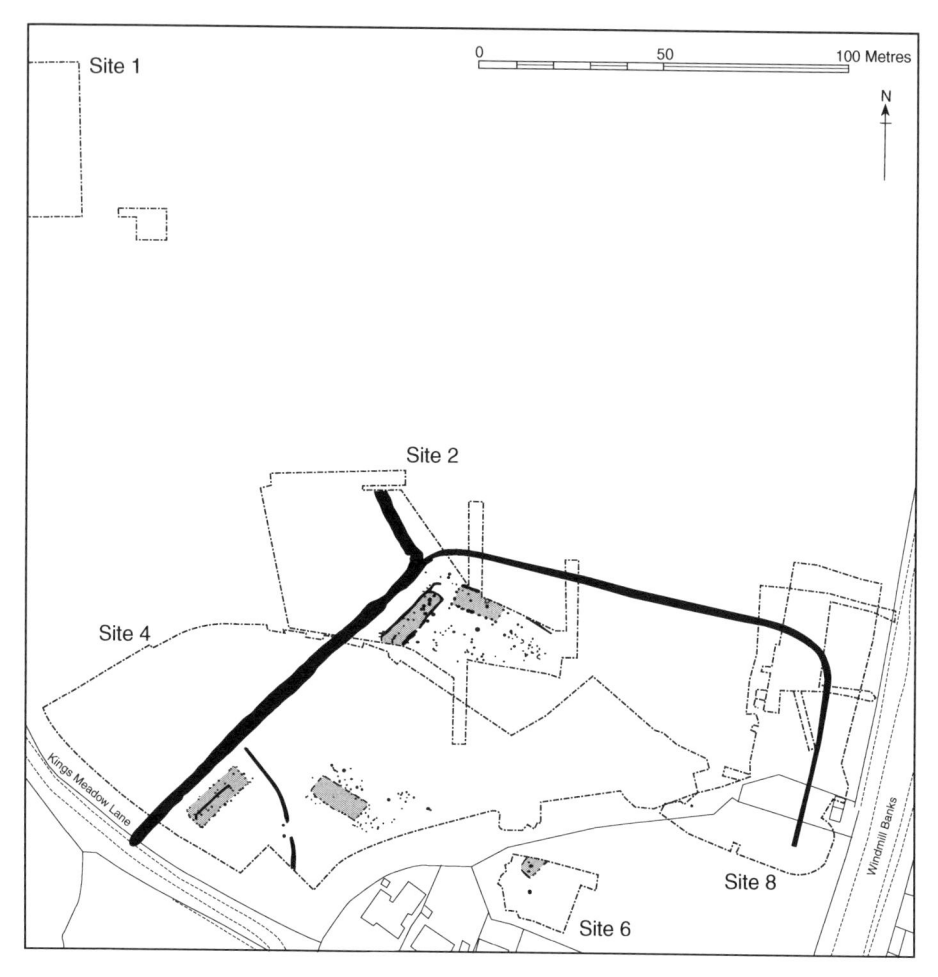

116   *Settlement forms and community structures*

Fig. 3.29. The Mid Saxon settlement at Higham Ferrers, Phase 2c (after Hardy et al. 2007).

which became fossilized in the later medieval landscape (ibid., fig. 14).[37] The settlement took on a more obviously high-status character in the following period, when a long hall and a number of special-purpose buildings 'stood round three sides of a courtyard and were enclosed by substantial fortifications', the earthwork ramparts of which were still clearly visible at the time of the excavation (Beresford 1987, 29–30). The later tenth century saw the construction of a new aisled hall arranged as part of a so-called 'long range' with a contiguous chamber, although the general layout remained much the

---

[37] At Catholme too, an excavated trackway leading into one of the enclosed farmsteads can be traced in post-medieval field boundaries (Fig. 3.15). It should be noted, however, that the survival of routeways and the survival of early enclosures associated with farmsteads are distinct phenomena.

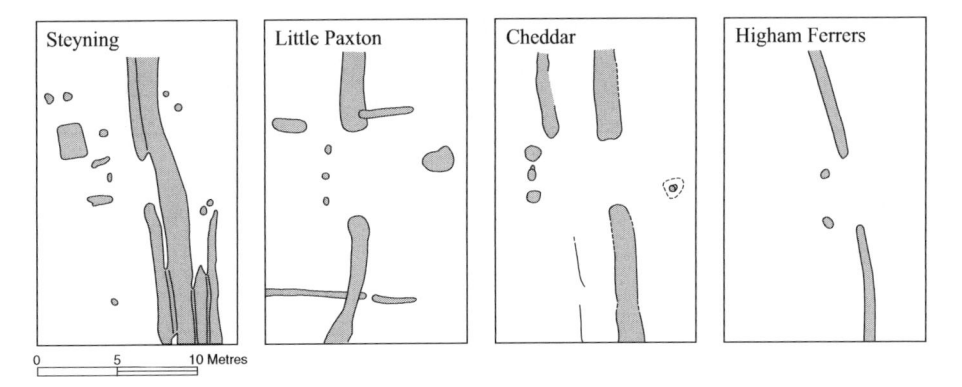

Fig. 3.30. Anglo-Saxon gated entrances (after Gardiner 1993 and Hardy et al. 2007).

same.[38] During the last eighty or so years of occupation, the buildings were 'rebuilt around a larger courtyard' (ibid. 71).[39]

A number of Late Saxon 'minor halls' or manors—dependent holdings of locally based minor lords—have also been investigated archaeologically. Such lords could own their own halls and have dependent peasants in nearby hamlets (Faith 1997, 156–7). An example of such a 'minor hall' has been identified at Ketton (Northamptonshire), where a mostly tenth-century enclosed settlement containing a small, narrow-aisled hall, chapel, and small cemetery has been excavated (Meadows, forthcoming; Fig. 3.31). At West Cotton (Northamptonshire), which was probably dependent on the manor of Raunds Furnells, a 'long range' similar to those found at Raunds Furnells (Fig. 3.32) and Goltho, as well as at least one other building, were identified within a ditched enclosure and associated with a watermill (Audouy and Chapman 2009).

It should be noted, however, that not all enclosed settlements have produced independent evidence of high status. The proliferation of early to mid Anglo-Saxon settlements on the western side of Thetford has already been mentioned (see Chapter 1). One of these, at Brandon Road, contained six early Anglo-Saxon *Grubenhäuser* as well as two possible post-built buildings which had gone out of use by around 700, when the site is believed to have reverted to fields. Soon thereafter, however, an irregular ditched enclosure measuring some 80m x 70m was established. Inside the enclosure, though not certainly contemporary

---

[38] Directly comparable 'long ranges'—which appear to hark back to the axiality seen in the earliest princely settlements such as Yeavering—have been identified at Raunds Furnells, West Cotton, Faccombe Netherton, and Sulgrave (Boddington 1996; Audouy and Chapman 2009; Fairbrother 1990; Davison 1977). Gardiner is surely correct in arguing that a continuous hall and chamber was an innovation intended to impress the visitor by displaying 'an extended façade' (2011, 206).

[39] The courtyard plan, usually regarded as emerging during the late tenth century, was in fact first used in high-status settlements of the early seventh century, for example at Yeavering, Cowdery's Down, and Chalton (see above).

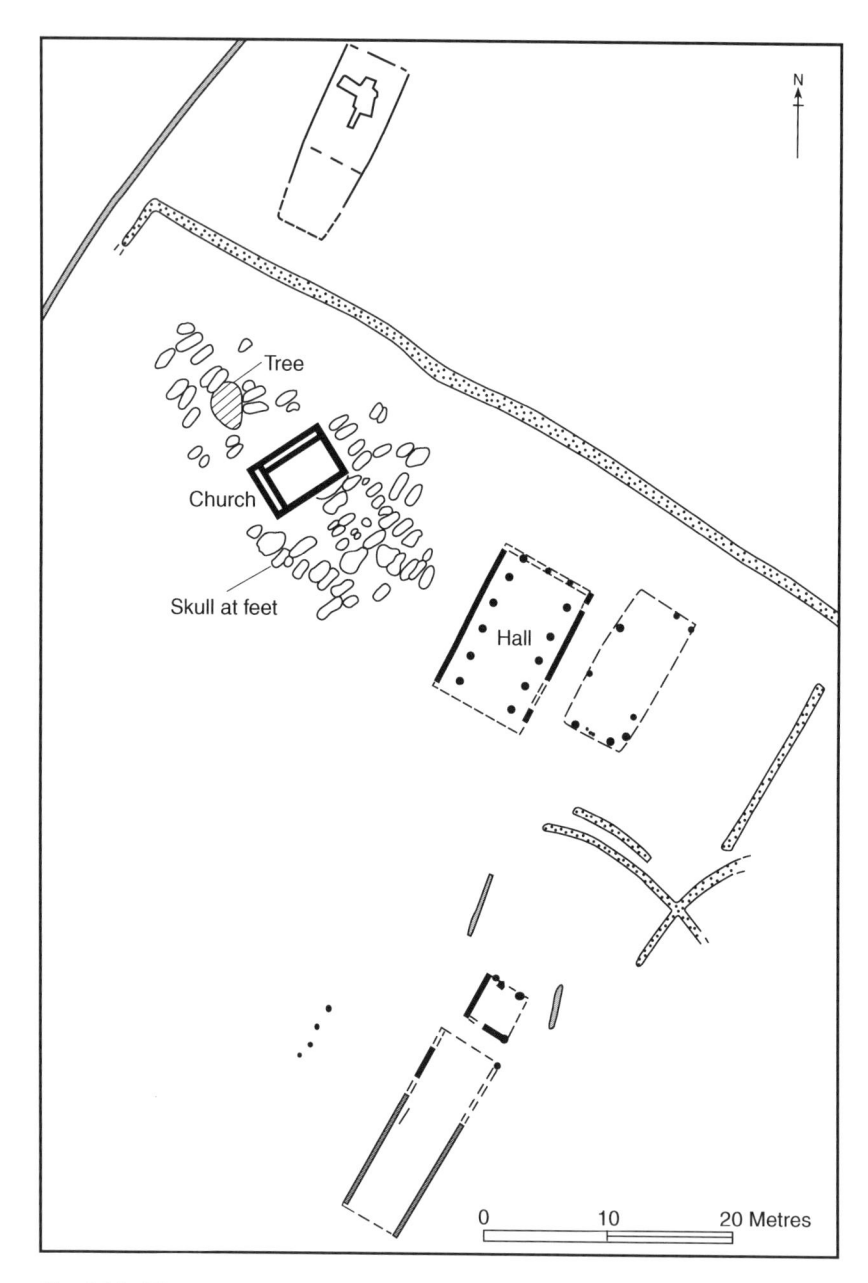

Fig. 3.31. The Late Saxon settlement at Ketton (after Blair 2005).

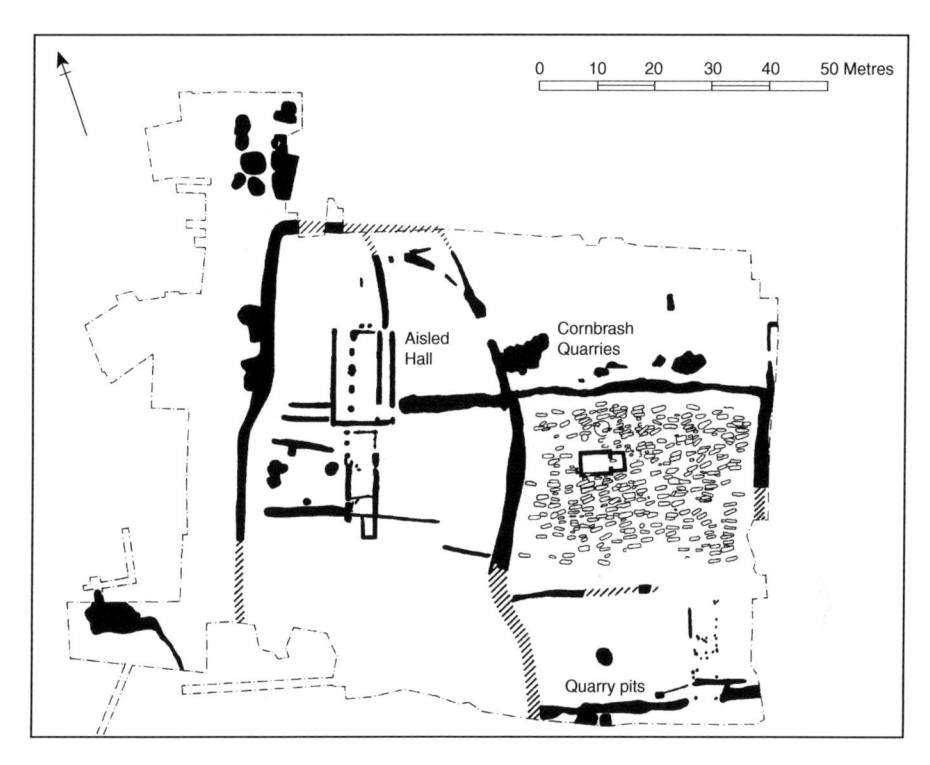

Fig. 3.32. The Late Saxon settlement at Raunds Furnells (after Boddington 1996).

with it, lay two possible earth-fast timber buildings, one *Grubenhaus*, several ovens and a midden. The enclosure was extensively re-cut along its outer edge, implying some longevity and perhaps an internal bank. The site—which appears to have been abandoned by the mid ninth century—produced iron tools and some 1.75 kg of ironworking debris including off-cuts and scrap, probably from a smithy, but otherwise no finds indicative of high status (Atkins and Connor 2010). Thus, while there can be little doubt that buildings, enclosures, and settlement form were a means of conveying formal power from the seventh century onwards, the attribution of status to excavated reality remains fraught with difficulty.

4

The ritualization of domestic life

Archaeologists have, perhaps understandably, tended to focus their attentions on the socio-economic aspects of life in Anglo-Saxon communities, and in particular on subsistence activities; the role of ritualized behaviour in daily life has been largely overlooked. More recently, however, changing perspectives within archaeology generally have led to a growing awareness that, as in prehistoric Britain, no strict division between 'sacred' and 'profane', or 'ritual' and 'economic' actions, existed in early medieval cosmologies. Furthermore, evidence for ritualized behaviour is not restricted to cemeteries, but instead pervades the archaeological record (Bradley 2005; Chester Kadwell 2009, 29). This idea has already been touched upon in the preceding chapter in relation to the association between certain settlements and prehistoric monuments. This chapter returns to this theme by exploring the relationship of settlements to mortuary landscapes (both Anglo-Saxon and ancient), the phenomenon of 'placed deposits', and the evidence for special-purpose ritual structures in settlements, and considers what these reveal about the role of ritual and the supernatural in the daily life of Anglo-Saxon communities.

Communities of the living and the dead

In a paper published in 1980, Richard Bradley observed that the failure to integrate settlement and cemetery studies was 'a real weakness of Anglo-Saxon archaeology' and argued that such integration was necessary if archaeologists were to assess whether the treatment of the dead reflected, in his words, 'the actual relations of the living' (Bradley 1980, 172). In the last ten years or so, the complex topography of Anglo-Saxon burial sites has been the subject of systematic study,[1] yet, despite its importance, the relationship—spatial and symbolic—of rural settlements to cemeteries has still to receive extended treatment.[2] Despite the small numbers of settlements that have been excavated in tandem with associated cemeteries, enough evidence exists (albeit

---

[1] See for example Williams 2006.
[2] Chester-Kadwell and Hadley have, however, recently considered aspects of this relationship in, respectively, early and later Anglo-Saxon England (Chester Kadwell 2009; Hadley 2007).

primarily from southern and eastern England) to examine the development of this relationship from the fifth to the mid ninth centuries, after which the increasing prevalence of burial in churchyards fundamentally and permanently altered it.

Early Anglo-Saxon England

Most of the inhabitants of Anglo-Saxon England during the fifth to mid seventh centuries were buried in ancestral cemeteries which remained in use for a century or more and which lay near—sometimes immediately adjacent to—a settlement. The relationship between such cemeteries and the settlements of the contributing populations varied widely, however, and the ratio was not always 1:1; an early Anglo-Saxon cemetery cannot, therefore, necessarily be used as a proxy for a single settlement. At Mucking, for example, two cemeteries, both in use during the fifth and sixth centuries, lay immediately next to the settlement (Fig. 3.1; Hirst and Clark 2009).[3] They do not correspond neatly to a 'northern' and a 'southern' settlement, however, and it remains unclear how these two burial communities related to the settlement and to each other. Cemetery I appears to have been relatively small, with 63 regularly oriented inhumation burials (believed to represent around one third of the original number), while Cemetery II contained some 463 cremations and 276 inhumation graves containing around 282 individuals (Hirst and Clark 2009). Cemetery I lay well to the west of the main settlement area while Cemetery II was largely contained within an area defined by two Roman ditches, which contained few buildings. It nevertheless appears likely that at least one *Grubenhaus* sited within Cemetery II was in use at the same time as the cemetery, and this has been tentatively identified as a mortuary structure, as has another such structure found within the remarkable cemetery at Street House (North Yorkshire) (Hirst and Clark 2009, 454–5; Sherlock and Simmons 2008). Indeed, the interpretation of the Street House example is all the more convincing as no other settlement features have been found in the vicinity. At the settlement complex excavated at Lakenheath (Suffolk), no fewer than three cemeteries containing in total over 400 burials dating mostly to the sixth century lay some 250m to the south of an area of dispersed occupation consisting of *Grubenhäuser*, ditches, and pits (Caruth 2005 and pers. comm. 2009). One of the cemeteries was laid out in rows, while another was arranged around a Bronze Age barrow. Cremations (including a relatively high proportion of animal cremations) were found in only one of the cemeteries.

What determined who was buried in which burial ground at Mucking and Lakenheath remains a matter for speculation. Variations in burial rite and

---

[3] Cemetery II continued in use into the early seventh century, although few burials could be dated to this period. Cemetery I was incompletely excavated and it is therefore not possible to be sure how long it remained in use.

cemetery layout, however, coupled with the fact that the ratios of male to female burials and of adults to children appear to have been broadly similar in all three cemeteries at Lakenheath and both cemeteries at Mucking, suggest that cult, and perhaps membership of certain moieties, played at least some role (J. Caruth, pers. comm. 2009).[4]

While some early Anglo-Saxon settlements lay adjacent to their burial grounds, cemeteries have also been found at a distance of several hundred metres from contemporary settlements: far enough to make it impossible to prove an association, but close enough to make it likely.[5] The cemetery at West Heslerton, in use from the late fifth to early seventh centuries and originally containing some 300 burials, lies *c.*450m from a settlement which continued to be occupied for a considerable time after the cemetery went out of use (Haughton and Powlesland 1999). A similar relationship can be seen at Flixton, Suffolk, where a cemetery was identified some 600m from a settlement (Boulter 2006).

In contrast to arrangements such as those just described, where the occupants of what appears to be a single settlement made use of one or more contemporary burial grounds, the large cremation cemetery at Spong Hill, Norfolk, where over 2,000 cremation burials have been excavated, is estimated to have served a population of between 450 and 750 individuals (McKinley 1994, 70). This is much larger than even the largest known settlements of this period. It, and several other large cremation cemeteries found in East Anglia and the East Midlands, must therefore have acted as the central burial ground for a number of surrounding settlements, including one which lay immediately adjacent to the cemetery, a small part of which has been excavated (Rickett 1995).

If meaningful comparisons between the size and composition of populations in settlements and associated cemeteries are to be made, high-quality data relating to the chronology, gender, and age of the burials are required, yet these, for the most part, are lacking.[6] In addition, most or all of both the settlement and cemetery (or cemeteries) must have been excavated. At the time of writing, only two sites—Mucking and West Heslerton—meet the latter criterion (though see the discussion of Bloodmoor Hill below). The poor bone preservation at Mucking has made it still more difficult to calculate the size of the contributing population, which in any case would have fluctuated throughout the

---

[4] No fewer than five early Anglo-Saxon cemeteries have been identified in the area of the royal centre at Eastry, in Kent, but as yet no significant traces of occupation have been found (Welch 2008; Dickinson and Richards 2011). Similarly, four closely-spaced, contemporary, yet clearly separate, cemeteries have been uncovered at Saltwood, also in Kent (Glass et al., forthcoming).

[5] A recent study has shown that the distance between early Anglo-Saxon settlements and what excavators consider to be 'associated' cemeteries can be as great as 1,800m (Chester-Kadwell 2009, 23).

[6] There is, furthermore, no generally agreed method for calculating population size from numbers of burials, although see Brugmann 2007, 94–5 and Hirst and Clark 2009, 763–4 for recent attempts at such calculations.

period of use. Nevertheless, using the revised cemetery data, Hirst and Clark suggest 'an average reproductive generation of 38–46 individuals forming 8–10 households (based on posthole buildings), with an average of 4–5 adolescent and adult individuals in each household with perhaps an average of 3–4 surviving children per family' (Hirst and Clark 2009, 763–4). The revised average total population size is somewhat larger, 'suggesting that a household might have contained an average total of 13–16 or 15–19 individuals' (ibid.); this is largely because the revised calculations have taken seventh-century buildings out of the equation, in light of the small number of burials which could be dated to that century. In either case, however, there is a reasonably close correlation between the estimated number of burials and the number of buildings.

At West Heslerton, where the demographic information recovered from the cemetery is better due to good skeletal preservation, it should be possible to make more accurate comparisons once the settlement has been fully analysed and published. It is possible to suggest, based on an original number of between 300 and 350 individuals buried over a period of between 125 and 175 years, that the cemetery represents a relatively small contributing population equivalent to only a few households (Haughton and Powlesland 1999, 93).

It seems clear, therefore, that notions of what constituted an early Anglo-Saxon 'burial community' varied widely and did not always correspond neatly to a group of households living together in the same settlement. We can nevertheless suggest that, for the most part, the same communal burial grounds were used over many generations by members of several households.

The Mid and Late Saxon periods

The pre-Christian communal cemeteries described above had for the most part been abandoned by the early eighth century, although exactly what replaced them is still unclear. The number of what are conventionally referred to as 'Final Phase' cemeteries—namely, those characterized by aligned inhumations, a high proportion of unfurnished burials, and certain characteristic artefact types—is far smaller than the number of early Anglo-Saxon cemeteries (Boddington 1990). Where and how the majority of the population of eighth- and ninth-century England was buried therefore remains a mystery, although John Blair has suggested that many may lie hidden among the substantial number of unfurnished inhumations which have been recorded as undated, or have been misdated to the Late Roman or post-medieval periods (Blair 2005, 243–4; see also Hadley 2007). Despite these uncertainties, it is clear that settlement and burial space began to become more integrated, even to merge, from around the mid seventh century onward: it is quite common for Mid and Late Saxon settlements to yield at least a few burials. This indicates that the relationship between the communities of the living and the dead was changing well before churchyard burial became the norm from the late ninth century onwards. A few well-documented examples of rural settlements with associated groups of burials serve to illustrate this trend.

Two groups of burials were associated with the Mid Saxon settlement at Yarnton, Oxfordshire. Six west–east aligned adult inhumations including four males and one female lay some 100m to the west of the settlement (Hey 2004, 163–5 and fig. 7.1). A further three inhumations were found in grave-like scoops cut into the fills of ditches. Two of these were children, while the third was aged between 13 and 19. Radiocarbon dating of three of the skeletons—two from the first group and one from the second—indicate that they date to the ninth century.

A larger and more highly structured burial ground of 26 west–east aligned graves, as well as two outlying burials, lay within the settlement at Bloodmoor Hill, Carlton Colville (Suffolk), where some thirty-eight *Grubenhäuser*, at least nine earth-fast timber buildings, several extensive surface middens, and over 250 pits were excavated (Lucy et al. 2009; Fig. 4.1). A substantial radiocarbon dating programme indicates that the settlement was probably established in the sixth century and occupied until the late seventh or early eighth century. The cemetery is, however, unlikely to have been established much before the mid seventh century and had ceased to be used by *c*.700. Radiocarbon dates and grave goods suggest that it was in use for at most fifty years, whereas the settlement was occupied for three or even four times as long. The burials (not all of which could be aged or sexed, due to poor bone preservation) included eleven adults, a further three sub-adults or adults, and four juveniles or sub-adults. A further five small graves where bone did not survive are likely to have contained juveniles. Five of the burials were male and four female, based on skeletal evidence, while a further six are likely to have been female, based on their grave goods. The total size of the contributing population represented by the cemetery is estimated to have been between around twelve and twenty-nine individuals (Scull 2009, 422).

This estimate appears to correspond relatively well to the number of dwellings likely to have been in use at any one time. Yet, while it is certainly possible that the cemetery was 'the main or single burial ground for those living in buildings nearby' (Scull 2009, 424), the fact that five of the burials—all female—stand out as richly furnished cast some doubt on this interpretation. The excavation uncovered no exceptionally large buildings which might be regarded as having housed a leading family, nor did it recover high-status material culture dating to this period, despite having preserved midden deposits. The fact that the cemetery was divided into zones according to status and gender—the well-furnished females lay in the same part of the cemetery, while juveniles were similarly clustered—further militates against the interpretation of this as the burial place of several equally ranked households whose heads

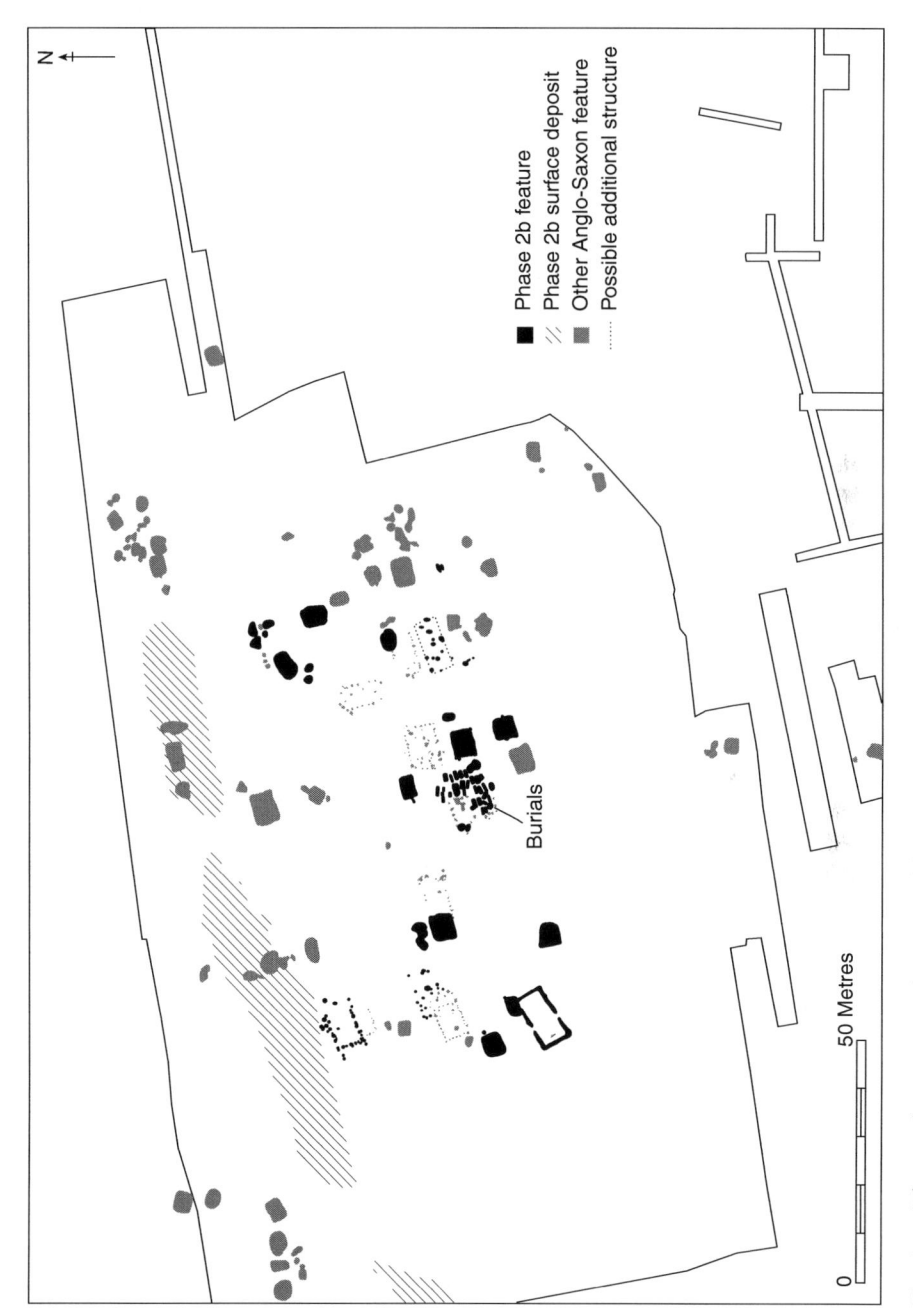

Fig. 4.1. The Anglo-Saxon settlement and burial ground at Bloodmoor Hill (after Lucy et al. 2009).

were given an ostentatious burial rite.[7] Chris Scull offers an alternative possibility, namely that the cemetery was the burial ground 'of a single establishment, perhaps a large farm or small estate centre' (ibid. 425) and, further, that this establishment housed a female religious community. The cemetery dates to a time when Christianity was well established in East Anglia. Certainly, as Scull observes, 'the decision to establish a new cemetery also implies abandonment, at least by those burying here, of an earlier burial site', a reconfiguration that is likely to signal 'an ideological or social realignment' (ibid. 424). The fact that the establishment of the cemetery around the middle of the seventh century does not appear to have been marked by any obvious changes in the buildings or material culture of the settlement suggests a further possibility, namely that some of those buried in the Bloodmoor Hill cemetery—notably the high-ranking females at least—had lived elsewhere.

A further example of a small, formal cemetery associated with a settlement was uncovered at Gamlingay, where a sequence of ditched enclosures, trackways, and buildings was uncovered as discussed in Chapter 3 (Fig. 3.11; Murray with McDonald 2006). Dating evidence is extremely limited, but occupation probably began in the sixth or seventh century, while the latest phase probably dates to the ninth. The cemetery consisted of over 110 west–east aligned inhumations, most of which were laid out in seven rows, and contained a remarkably high percentage (around one quarter) of infant burials (ibid. 265–68). A few inter-cutting graves suggest the cemetery could have remained in use for some time. The near-complete absence of dress items and grave goods, and the apparent use in a few cases of shrouds, suggest that it was probably contemporary with the last phase of occupation. A second group of around half a dozen inhumations lay some 30m to the north-east of the main cemetery and adjacent to a small timber building, although one of the burials clearly post-dates it. It seems unlikely that this structure was a church or chapel as originally suggested; in any event, the phasing of the enclosures suggests that the main burial ground probably post-dated it. The number of burials at Gamlingay seems large, given that only one or at most two potential dwellings were identified within the excavated area. The clustering of some burials, as well as the distribution of male, female, juvenile, and infant burials is suggestive of family groups.

A less formal arrangement of burials was found at the Mid to Late Saxon settlement at Flixborough, where exceptional preservation conditions enabled radical changes in the character of the settlement to be traced, as described in Chapter 3. Two groups of burials were identified: eleven poorly preserved west–east inhumations, all adults, were found some 60m south of the main

---

[7] This has become the most widely accepted explanation for richly furnished fifth- and sixth-century burials associated with settlements comprised of relatively small, similarly sized buildings, as found, for example, at Mucking (Hamerow 1993, 89; Härke 1997, 147; Scull 1993, 73).

excavation area, while a further six lay adjacent to one of the buildings within the excavated area.[8] Dating evidence for the southern group was lacking, although iron coffin fittings point to an eighth- to tenth-century date and suggest the presence of at least some burials of high status.

The northern group of burials was much better preserved and comprised one adult female along with one perinatal infant and four children, all apparently eighth-century in date. Four of the graves were clearly associated with Building 1, whose unusual construction (notably the use of gravel footings) together with the associated burials has led to the suggestion that it was some kind of mortuary chapel, although the fact that it contained a hearth and domestic debris militates against this interpretation.

Even after 850, small groups of burials were occasionally established within settlements which lacked chapels or churches. At Bramford, a ditched enclosure containing several buildings of Mid and Late Saxon date also contained a small cemetery containing as many as nineteen individuals, of whom at least seven were female and six were male (Fig. 3.26). Radiocarbon dates from two of the skeletons indicate that both were probably tenth-century in date (Caruth 1996 and pers. comm. 2009).

Bringing the ancestors home

The establishment between the seventh and ninth centuries of small, short-lived burial grounds within pre-existing settlements implies the abandonment of relatively large, long-lived cemeteries which had been established in the fifth or sixth century, and a new emphasis on affiliation with a particular settlement. As Richard Morris—one of the first archaeologists to consider this question—wrote in 1983, 'the act of gathering the dead within or close to the living rather than consigning them to the perimeter...gives the impression of a definite change of practice' (1983, 53). While one might now question whether most early Anglo-Saxon cemeteries were 'on the perimeter' in the sense of occupying marginal locations, this change of practice suggests that ancestors took on a new significance as 'the dead were no longer "out there,"' but were instead incorporated into the settlements of the living (Parker-Pearson 2003, 129).

The examples cited above suggest an intriguing diversity of practice. At Yarnton, the number of contemporary dwellings suggests that the settlement was small but long-lived. The small number of burials could therefore correspond to one generation of a single household. The cemetery at Bloodmoor Hill was in use for at most two generations, and included a group of high-ranking females who may have lived elsewhere. At Gamlingay, the relatively large number of burials compared to the number of potential dwellings in the settlement suggests that the cemetery must have included individuals

---

[8] It is possible, however, that both groups formed part of the same cemetery (Geake 2007).

whose dwellings lay at some distance from the cemetery, although there is no obvious reason to think that any of them was of high status. When viewed against the wider background of seventh- to ninth-century burial grounds, the demographic composition, size, and layout of those established within settlements do not immediately suggest that they contained only or primarily 'special' individuals. The key question may therefore be, not *who* was buried within settlements, but rather, *why* were burial grounds established within settlements in the first place?

The establishment of cemeteries within settlements is one aspect of a more general dislocation of burial during the seventh to ninth centuries. It reflects the changing structure of Anglo-Saxon communities and, as Helen Geake has observed, a degree of choice (or uncertainty) regarding where the dead should be buried (Geake 2007, 119). It is part of a wider picture which indicates that attitudes towards the dead and their proximity to the living were changing. Explanations for why members of certain communities were buried within settlements understandably tend to emphasize religious ideology. Some see the introduction of groups of burials into settlements as a kind of precursor to the later establishment of churches and churchyards within settlements (ibid. 118). Dawn Hadley has argued, conversely, that some families may have deliberately avoided cemeteries associated with minsters as a means of resisting 'the centralizing forces of kings, religious communities and the secular elite' and 'to keep the dead…within the settlement rather than taking them to the churchyards of the elite' (Hadley 2007, 200).[9] Christianity of course encouraged a closer relationship between the communities of the living and the dead, yet adaptation to, or resistance against, a new religious ideology may not account for the whole picture.

An alternative possibility hinted at by Richard Bradley deserves closer consideration. If communal cemeteries were a means of establishing and legitimizing group rights over restricted resources by demonstrating descent from important ancestors, then it may follow that 'the closest spatial relationship between the living and the dead may be found in periods of intensification of competition', notably in periods of agricultural expansion or intensification (Bradley 1980, 172–3).[10] The 'long eighth century'—when new farming regimes emerged which were geared towards producing regular surpluses (see Chapter 5)—was just such a period and the changes in burial practice described above should be viewed against the backdrop of contemporary changes in the configuration of settlements. These include, as we have seen, the introduction of complexes of enclosures and droveways, often maintained over long periods, as well as the

---

[9] She also raises the alternative possibility, however, that these were individuals who had for some reason been 'excluded from burial in consecrated ground' at a time when churchyard burial was something to be aspired to rather than a requirement (Hadley 2007, 199).

[10] While Parker-Pearson has more recently warned that this view verges on the deterministic, he nevertheless asserts that 'the fixing of the dead in the land is a social and political act which ensures access and rights over natural resources' (Parker-Pearson 2003, 141).

establishment of hay meadows, developments which seem to be associated with new, more intensive animal and crop husbandry regimes.

If settlements—and in some cases particular buildings, as at Gamlingay and Flixborough—became associated with ancestors and provided a focus for their veneration, the possibility that burial within settlements was used as a means of strengthening and legitimizing claims to landed resources must at least be considered.[11] The link between land and ancestors would in one sense have been reinforced by the building of churches associated with the burials of landowning founders; paradoxically, however, like their contemporaries in Ireland, once the majority of the Anglo-Saxon dead had been 'relegated to the graveyards of churches, [they] lost their power to defend the land which they left to their heirs' (Charles-Edwards 1976, 86).

Deviant burials in settlements

A further aspect of the relationship between the living and the dead is illuminated by so-called 'deviant burials' (Reynolds 2009). These appear for the most part to represent execution burials, and date mostly to the seventh to ninth centuries. A few such 'deviant' burials have been found in direct association with settlements. This was the case at Yarnton, where a shallow scoop cut into a partly backfilled enclosure ditch contained the remains of a female placed face-down with the legs folded backwards. Beneath the body were found the remains of at least four sub-adults (Hey 2004, 163–5; Boyle 2004). Another adult female, radiocarbon dated to the eighth or ninth century, was found buried in the final backfill of the main enclosure ditch surrounding the Mid Saxon estate centre at Higham Ferrers. The position of the body suggested that it may have been bound and placed in a sack; much of the upper part of the body was missing (Hardy et al. 2007, 140–5, 206–8). Examination of the skeletal material has led to the suggestion that the woman had been hanged. In the same backfill and within a few metres of this first burial were found the mandibles of two adult males, and 'it is difficult to avoid the conclusion that the bodies or body parts were collected from a...formal execution site...' (ibid. 207). It appears that these remains were deposited just at the time when the settlement as a whole was being dismantled and 'closed', and therefore do not represent burials within an occupied settlement. Not all isolated inhumations found in settlements were 'deviant', however (ibid. 218–19); as will be seen in the following section, some were associated with entrances to enclosures and buildings and may be more appropriately regarded as 'placed deposits'.

---

[11] Theuws has argued that the burial of 'founders' in newly established farmsteads in northern Austrasia was a means of emphasizing claims on the land; in England, however, burial grounds appear to have been added to pre-existing settlements, suggesting that these were not the burials of founders (Theuws 1991). A better parallel may be found in the law codes of early medieval Ireland, where burial mounds sited on boundaries appear to have served a similar purpose (Charles-Edwards 1976).

'Placed deposits' in rural settlements

The burial of animals, humans, and 'special' objects in settlements of the late Germanic Iron Age and Migration Period (fourth to seventh centuries AD) has long been recognized as a distinctive phenomenon in north-west Europe as well as in Iron Age and Roman Britain (van Giffen 1963).[12] Comparable deposits found in Anglo-Saxon settlements, however, have received little attention and have often been dismissed as refuse.[13] It is, in fact, far more difficult to distinguish 'ritual deposits' from 'waste' in archaeological sites than is usually assumed, especially as even the deposition of waste followed cultural rules and could be symbolically structured (Hill 1995).[14] The identification of placed deposits in Anglo-Saxon settlements is further hampered by the difficulty of dating such deposits and establishing their association with other settlement features; the poor preservation conditions on a number of settlements (including some of the most extensively excavated, such as Mucking), where bone survives poorly if at all; and the possibility that post-depositional processes may be responsible for the completeness and apparently 'special' character of some deposits.[15] Nevertheless, animal or human remains deposited in pits, ditches, buildings, but also graves, in a manner which indicates careful placement, can reasonably be interpreted as deliberately 'placed'.

The small number of placed deposits in rural settlements identified by the present writer in an earlier study (Hamerow 2006) has been more than trebled by recent work to around 150 (Sofield, forthcoming). It is, however, still possible to characterize them broadly according to the following categories: complete and near-complete skeletons that were certainly, or probably, originally articulated; skulls or parts of skulls; articulated limbs or a trunk; and disarticu-

---

[12] Recent work by Roberta Gilchrist draws attention to placed deposition in later medieval contexts in England (Gilchrist, forthcoming).

[13] The description of what sounds very much like a placed deposit at Wykeham (North Yorkshire) is fairly typical of early accounts. One *Grubenhaus* had 'evidently seen the use of the larger bones of domestic animals, particularly the jawbones and crania, as paving material…At any rate, whoever it was that lived here did not possess very delicate sensibilities' (Moore 1963–6). Even in recent reports, potential examples of placed deposits are overlooked. Thus an Anglo-Saxon pit at Market Lavington (Wiltshire) is described in the animal bone report as having contained the 'back half of a cattle skull with both cores in place…and with complex, careful butchery.…There was a major insertion hole right of centre on the forehead, then two parallel forward through-cuts.…It seems that some special need or special occasion had called for such careful preparation of this head' (Bourdillon 2006, 151). The deposit is neither mentioned nor the context illustrated in the main report. A possible analogy for this find was uncovered in 1949 at Butley (Suffolk), where a *Grubenhaus* was found containing an ox skull 'in which was fixed an iron spear head' (Maynard 1952, 208).

[14] Morris and Jervis have recently argued that all deposits in pits, ditches, and *Grubenhäuser* should be regarded as part of a continuous spectrum ranging from 'rubbish' to 'ritual' (2011, 72); nevertheless, they acknowledge that it is possible to distinguish between those that 'are more deeply rooted in the superstitious or spiritual domain and [those] which are more functional' (ibid. 74).

[15] The term 'placed deposits' is used here in preference to 'special deposits' as used by the author in a preliminary survey of such material published in 2006 as it avoids assumptions about the 'special' nature of deposits that may merely appear unusual due to post-depositional processes.

lated bone apparently deposited en masse. It should be noted, however, that the last category is especially difficult to identify with certainty as such deposits are particularly prone to be regarded as 'rubbish' by excavators who may only have recorded that a particular pit or *Grubenhaus* contained a large quantity of animal bone.[16] Two examples of a fifth type of placed deposit have been uncovered at Friars Oak, near Hassocks in West Sussex, where relatively small-scale excavation revealed traces of several Mid Saxon pits and structures, although not enough to establish the character of occupation or indeed whether these represent part of a larger settlement (Butler 2000). The fill of a probable *Grubenhaus* contained a large piece of fire-fractured flint within a deposit of charcoal and ash. Within this were two concentrations of burnt animal and human bone that have been interpreted as re-deposited material from a cremation pyre. A pit sited 29m to the north-east contained a similar deposit. An unusual, square timber building which had been destroyed by fire was uncovered lying some 200m from the *Grubenhaus*. Although no placed deposits were found in association with it, its unusual form and construction have led the excavator to postulate that it was a ritual structure or shrine.

The most common species represented in these deposits is cattle, present in around one third of all deposits; humans were present in just under one third; dogs and horses occurred in between 12–16 per cent of all deposits; sheep/goats in around 10 per cent, while pigs and other species were represented in fewer than 5 per cent of deposits.[17] What is striking about these figures is that the percentage of dogs and horses is disproportionately high compared with animal bone assemblages for Anglo-Saxon settlements as a whole. It is particularly notable that dogs and horses actually outnumber pigs and sheep/goats in placed deposits, whereas in animal bone assemblages generally, the latter greatly outnumber the former.

More than half of the 'placed' deposits identified in the 2006 survey were found in *Grubenhäuser* (Fig. 4.2.).[18] While a small number were placed in the postholes of these buildings, over half were placed on the base of the sunken hollow, or on the basal or primary fill; two had either been dug into the infill of an abandoned building or been placed in the *Grubenhaus* as part of the process of backfilling, while a further two contained one placed deposit on the base and another higher up in the fill. Most of these deposits appear to have

---

[16] At Sutton Courtenay, for example, a *Grubenhaus* and pit are both recorded as having contained large quantities of disarticulated bones, but little further detail is provided (Leeds 1927, 63–4, fig. 2; Leeds 1923, 163–5, fig. 8). More recently, SFB 44 at West Stow was described as having contained 'a heap of animal bones, mainly ox...half-way down the fill in the South East corner' (West 1986, 37).

[17] I am grateful to Clifford Sofield for making available to me the results of his statistical analysis in advance of publication.

[18] The majority of 'associated animal bone groups' identified in a more recent study (Morris and Jervis 2011) were, in contrast, found in pits. This appears to be the result of the inclusion in the latter study of a higher proportion of Mid and Late Saxon settlements, since few if any rural *Grubenhäuser* post-date c.750.

Fig. 4.2. A placed deposit in a *Grubenhaus* at Horcott (Gloucestershire) consisting of animal bones and an inverted human cranium (Photo: J. Blair).

been associated with the abandonment or dismantling of the buildings, suggesting that they were associated with important points in the 'life-cycle' of the building in which they were found (see Chapter 2).

A relatively small number were isolated inhumation burials of the kind normally found in cemeteries (as distinct from the small groups of burials discussed in the preceding section). In one highly unusual case at Wharram Percy (North Yorkshire), an infant had apparently been carefully laid in the centre of a partly backfilled ditch, close to a *Grubenhaus* and the partly butchered remains of a sheep (Milne and Richards 1992, 84–5). A boulder with 'an unusual veined appearance' found nearby may have been used to mark the deposit.

Most of these placed deposits could not be associated with specific locations within settlements, although where only a small proportion of the settlement was uncovered, it is difficult to be certain. There is, however, a direct association in several cases with entrances and boundaries.[19] In these cases at least, not only were the deposited items being ritually treated, but the placed deposits themselves acted to reinforce the liminal, transitional nature of the locations where they were buried. At the settlement of Catholme, Staffordshire, all three placed deposits (two human and one bovine) were placed near the entrances to

---

[19] Placed deposits, often of fragments of quern stones, are also associated with entrances in early medieval Ireland (O'Sullivan 2008).

ditched enclosures, at least some of which appear to have defined ancestral properties (Fig. 4.3.; Losco-Bradley and Kinsely 2002, 40–1; Hamerow, ibid. 26). At Cheddar, an inhumation burial was positioned just inside the entrance to a ditched enclosure (Rahtz 1979, figs. 10, 12, 29). Although the burial has been assigned to Period 1 and the enclosure to Period 2, there are no clear stratigraphic grounds for doing so and the phasing of the ditch is described by the excavator as 'indecisive' (Rahtz 1979, 55); it seems unlikely that the positioning of the burial was coincidental. An inhumation of probable Anglo-Saxon date at West Stow lay immediately adjacent to a boundary ditch (and possible entrance), while Grave 2 lay just a few metres away (West 1986, 58 and fig. 7). Three out of the four deposits associated with ground-level buildings were also positioned at entrances. The cow burial at Cowdery's Down immediately next to the west entrance of Building C13, and Grave AX at Yeavering, have already been mentioned (see Chapter 3), as has the pit filled with cattle skulls next to the entrance into Yeavering Building D2. At the probable (but undocumented) monastery at Brandon, Suffolk, a horse skull was placed into a post-pit at the entrance between the chancel and nave of a timber church, probably in the eighth century, testifying to the persistence of such practices not only into the Christian period, but in explicitly Christian contexts (A. Tester, pers. comm.).

Placed deposits are thus found in a wide range of features and there appears to be no strong correlation between species type and context (apart from that between humans and graves). Recent statistical analysis is, however, beginning to reveal some correlations between species and type of deposit: there is, for example, a strong correlation between cattle and deposits of skulls, while humans and dogs, in contrast, were most likely to be buried whole (Sofield, forthcoming).

While exact stratigraphic position is not always recorded, most placed deposits lie on, or just above, the base of the feature in which they were placed. Furthermore, of the human placed deposits, one third were infants, a much higher proportion than is normally found in Anglo-Saxon cemeteries (less than 6 per cent of burials in most cemeteries are of individuals under the age of 3; Crawford 1993, 84). The disposal of the remains of infants outside of cemeteries and separate from the rest of the community has been interpreted in various ways. Sally Crawford, in her study of childhood in Anglo-Saxon England, has, for example, suggested that infants were not considered to 'be full persons' (Crawford 1999, 77–84).

Several of the human burials also exhibited unusual traits. The position of Human Burial 2 from Cheddar suggested to the excavator a 'hasty burial': 'The left arm was sharply bent at the elbow; the right arm was under the torso, slightly bent at the elbow with the right hand under the left radius' (Rahtz 1979, 96). An adult male buried in, or abutting, a *Grubenhaus* at Sutton Courtenay was covered with 'a blanket of clay' (Leeds 1923, 169). Another burial at Sutton Courtenay was deposited in a large pit nearly 2 metres in diameter. In it, the body of an adult female lay at a sharp angle, head downwards, with

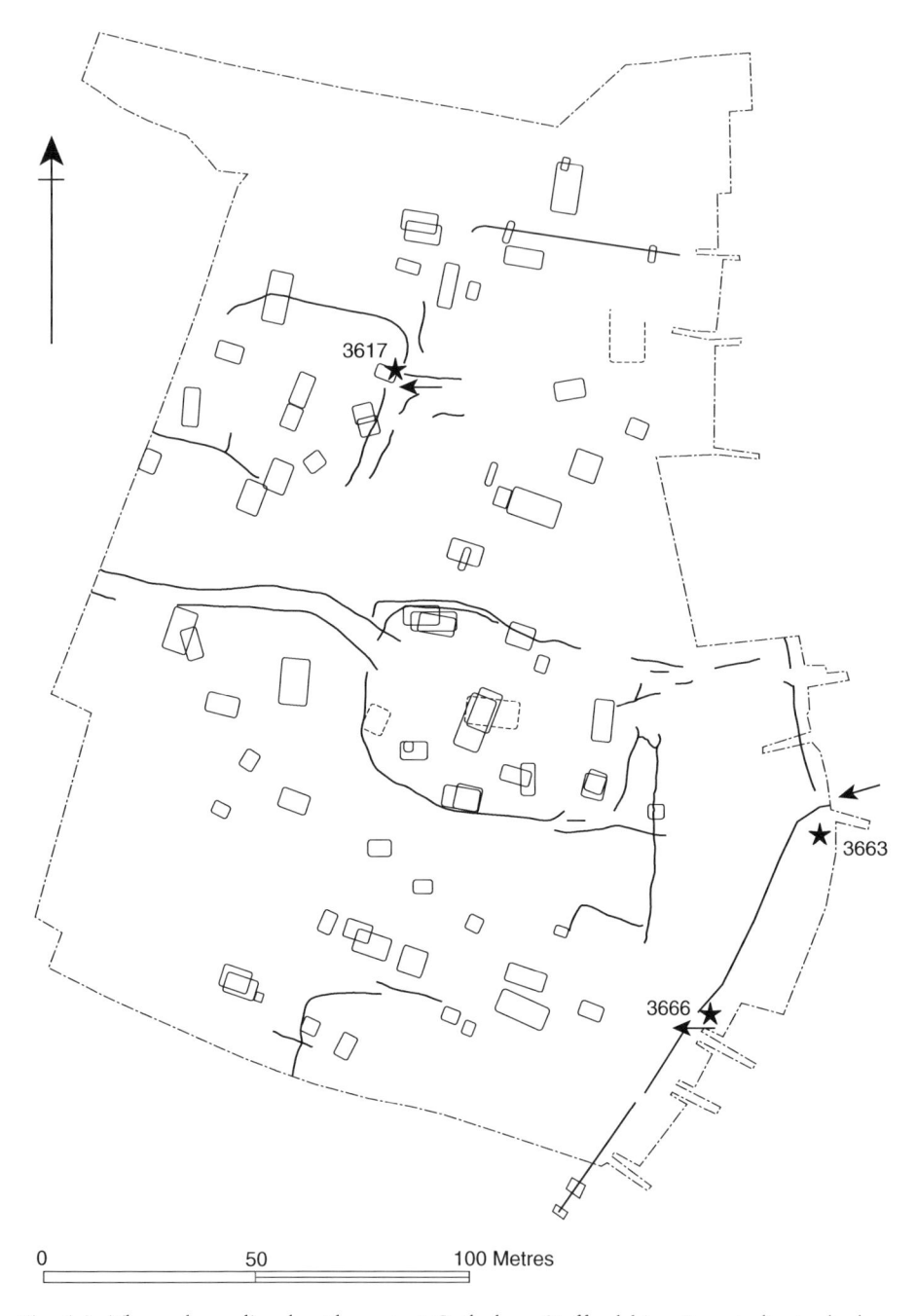

Fig. 4.3. The early medieval settlement at Catholme, Staffordshire. Stars indicate the location of placed deposits; arrows indicate entrances (after Losco-Bradley and Kinsley 2002).

'arms half-outstretched...towards the remains...of an infant....Behind the woman's head and over the body of the child there was a layer about six inches thick of earth and gravel which must have been stamped hard....Behind the woman's head were three animal skulls, two oxen and a horse' (Leeds 1947, 86). The partial skull of an adult female found buried halfway down a pit at the settlement of Cottam in Yorkshire may be interpreted as both a deviant burial and a 'placed deposit'. A block of chalk had been placed next to the skull and the overlying fill contained significant quantities of animal bone and several metal and other objects (Richards 2000, 86 and 92). The skull—radiocarbon-dated to the second half of the seventh or the eighth century—appears already to have been old when (re-)buried and may derive from an execution burial.

Deposits of large quantities of disarticulated bone that can reasonably be interpreted as the remains of large-scale food preparation and feasting are comparatively rare. Perhaps the most striking early example comes from Yeavering: the deposit of ox bones, mostly skulls, in Structure D2 and the long bone fragments associated with Structure D3 have already been described in Chapter 3. Another example comes from the site of Eynsham Abbey, in Oxfordshire. A pit over 2 metres in diameter and nearly 3 metres deep and coin-dated to the early/mid eighth century contained substantial quantities of animal bone (Hardy et al. 2003, 45–6, 357–9, 471–2, fig. 3.8, plate 3.3). The faunal assemblages from the upper and lower fills were quite distinct, with the lower layers containing primary butchery waste including skulls, limb and foot bones, while the upper layers, which contained the majority of the animal bone and small finds and seem to represent rapid infilling, also included kitchen and table waste. The pit contained thirteen complete skulls and an exceptionally wide range of species, including prime meat bones of red and roe deer, as well as fish, oyster, and various types of bird, including crane and partridge, all of which point to high-status consumption. The pit appears to have stood open for some time and the large number of individual animals represented (including 12 cattle, 45 sheep, and 22 pigs) suggests either 'a collection of material over a significant period of time, or from a substantial group of people', or indeed both (ibid. 357–8). The pit was filled at a time of 'intense activity' on the site as evidenced by 'numerous hearths, burnt areas and pits', although no buildings were found within the excavated area (ibid. 357). It nevertheless seems likely that the site of the later minster was already a high-status centre by this time (ibid. 7).

Most of the deposits described in the preceding sections cannot be closely dated and no clear chronological trends have emerged thus far, apart from a general decline in frequency after the seventh century, a development which is probably largely due to the decline in the use of *Grubenhäuser*. The earliest deposits probably date to the fifth or early sixth century, while the latest well-dated examples include the partial skull at Cottam, the eighth-century pit at

Eynsham, and the burial at Cheddar, which is presumably ninth- or early tenth-century in date. The eighth- or ninth-century deposits at Friars Oak are not only amongst the latest placed deposits so far identified, but may also provide evidence for cremation at an exceptionally late date, unless the re-deposited pyre material derives from a much earlier cemetery.

Other forms of placed deposit

Although this discussion has so far focused on deposits of animal and human remains, other forms of placed deposit are also found in Anglo-Saxon settlements. The artefacts included in such deposits were for the most part ordinary objects associated with daily life and as such are often interpreted as waste or casual losses and receive little if any detailed treatment in excavation reports.[20] Where, however, complete or semi-complete objects are found lying on the base or primary fill of a feature, against a background of an otherwise highly fragmented finds assemblage, this is strongly suggestive of formal placement (cf. Fulford 2001). For example, a *Grubenhaus* at Eye Kettleby contained both the remains of an infant and a small, complete, lugged pot; as the infant remains were only recognized during post-excavation analysis, it is impossible to know whether there was an association between the two (N. Finn, pers. comm.). A semi-complete jar placed on the base of a *Grubenhaus* excavated at Brooklands, Milton Keynes appears to have been deliberately perforated in antiquity. The same remarkable feature contained the remains of semi-articulated piglets and ten pike heads (Stansbie 2008). Mucking produced a number of probable placed deposits: *Grubenhäuser* 42, 93, and 105 all contained substantial quantities of pottery resting on or just above the base of the hollow, in the case of GH 42 and 105 representing assemblages of at least seven complete or semi-complete vessels, clearly deposited at the same time (Hamerow 1993, 17, figs. 73, 77, 105, 106). In GH 42, the layer containing the pottery was recorded as black and charcoal-rich and also contained two complete seventh-century brooches, one lying on the base of the hollow, the other just above the base; several large pieces of iron, subsequently identified as hearth bottoms, were found higher in the fill (ibid., fig. 73; Mucking excavation notebooks). The black layer overlay one of the postholes, leading the excavators to conclude that it was formed after the building had been dismantled. GH 93 also contained a large quantity of pottery in one corner, including a semi-complete bowl lying on the base of the hollow beneath a number of clay loomweights (ibid., fig. 135 and Mucking excavation notebooks). The plan of GH 105 suggests that a number of complete and/or semi-complete vessels had been placed on the base of the

---

[20] Several of the *Grubenhäuser* excavated at Puddlehill (Bedfordshire), for example, contained complete objects described as lying on or just above the floor, including a coin, four dress pins, an amber bead, and a weaving-beater, all of which are interpreted as accidental losses (Hawkes and Matthews 1985, 67, 99).

feature and then broken *in situ*; also on the base were found *c.*30 unfired clay loomweights (ibid., fig. 77). The three sceattas found on the floor of GH 168 might also be regarded as a placed deposit (ibid., fig. 79). All of these deposits are likely to date to the seventh century and could reasonably be interpreted as associated with termination or closure rituals. Finally, a pit containing two near-complete vessels above a layer of burnt bone lay within the 'footprint' of a ground-level timber building although it cannot be established whether the two were contemporary (ibid., table 4, 20; Tipper 2004, in n. 7, 28).

The latest example of what appears to be a 'closure deposit' comes from the high-status Late Saxon settlement at Bishopstone, where a remarkable group of iron artefacts was found carefully placed in the cellar of the probable tower described in Chapter 2. The assemblage included door furniture consisting of several suites of decorative hinges and locks, as well as tools, agricultural implements, a wool comb, and horseshoes. The excavator has argued that the items may have been selected to symbolize what is needed to manage an estate (Thomas 2009), such a 'material metaphor' deriving power from its allusion to the domestic world (Tilley 1999; Bradley 2005, 194).

Gibson has considered whether the presence of articulated animals and complete or semi-complete objects in *Grubenhaus* fills at the Anglo-Saxon settlement at Godmanchester could indicate that the backfilling of these buildings involved 'a ritual component' (Gibson 2003, 210–11). She notes in particular the prevalence in such deposits of artefacts associated with textile production, above all spindle whorls and clay loomweights, including extremely fragile unfired loomweights. The rows of loomweights found lying on the base of some *Grubenhäuser* have generally been interpreted as the result of the burning down or abandonment of a building with a warp-weighted loom *in situ*. Gibson notes, however, that it is difficult to understand why such objects would not be retrieved for re-use. She cites the evidence from a *Grubenhaus* at Upton, Northamptonshire, in which, despite the destruction of a loom and apparently the entire building by fire, many of the weights remained unfired, suggesting that they had been placed there as part of a closure ritual after the conflagration (ibid. 210).[21] A still more striking example of such a deposit comes from Posthole Building 2 at Spong Hill, Norfolk. Just inside the south doorway were two postholes, interpreted by the excavator as emplacements for a loom; one of these contained thirteen complete and twelve incomplete loomweights, as well as 'other smaller fragments' (Rickett 1995, 135–6 and plate VIII). Some of these were clearly stacked and must have been deliberately placed in the posthole when the building, or at least the loom, went out of use. Spinning and weaving were not only essential economic activities, but were intimately

---

[21] Chapman has also found evidence from prehistoric settlements in south-east Europe that objects were sometimes placed in houses prior to deliberate firing of the structures, perhaps to 'form an idealised set specific to the mortuary house' (Chapman 2000, 106).

connected with female identity in Anglo-Saxon society; indeed there are many semantic links in Old English between women and cloth production (Fell 1984, 39–40). The discovery at West Heslerton of several placed deposits which include girdle-hangers—normally found uniquely in female-gendered graves—also appears to connect such deposits with women (Powlesland 1998). A final intriguing, if poorly recorded, example of such a deposit was found in a *Grubenhaus* excavated in the 1920s at Car Dyke (Cambridgeshire), which contained not only an articulated dog skeleton on top of which had been placed a sherd of Romano-British pottery, but also a 'female' assemblage: five glass beads, three needles (one bronze, two bone), three spindle whorls, and what appears to have been a fragment of an ivory bag ring, as well as a silvered disc which could derive from a square-headed brooch (Lethbridge 1927, 141–6). Further research into this question would undoubtedly yield more examples of this kind of 'female' deposit, which appear to be a further illustration of 'how inseparable the [Anglo-Saxon] domestic experience was from a mind-set that also encompassed metaphysical ideas about human life' (Hines 2011, 39).

Placed deposits and domestic life

It would appear from the surveys undertaken to date that true foundation deposits—indeed all forms of placed deposit directly associated with dwellings—were less common in England than elsewhere in early medieval northwest Europe or in Roman Britain (although even on the other side of the North Sea, such deposits were more common in the Iron Age than in the post-Roman period: Hamerow 2006). The few unambiguous examples of Anglo-Saxon foundation deposits—at Yeavering and Cowdery's Down—do, however, follow a north-west European tradition (ibid.). The practice of depositing precious, high-status artefacts within buildings—as seen at elite Scandinavian settlements like Gudme and Uppåkra—is so far unattested in Anglo-Saxon England, although the gold coin and a tiny ring of beaded gold wire associated with Buildings A3(b) and A4 at Yeavering could conceivably fall into this category (see above; Hope-Taylor 1977, 57, 182; Nielsen et al. 1993; Larsson 2002). Although many ritualized activities will have left no archaeological trace, true foundation deposits are likely by their very nature to have been placed in the ground, whether in building foundations or associated pits, so that their rarity in Anglo-Saxon England is probably genuine and not merely the result of poor preservation or inadequate recording.

Another clear trend is that 'closure deposits' consisting of animals, humans, ceramic vessels, and other items are relatively widespread in early Anglo-Saxon rural settlements, particularly in *Grubenhäuser*. Thirdly, infants, dogs, and horses are particularly prominent in Anglo-Saxon placed deposits, as they are across the whole of the North Sea Zone, as well as in Roman and Iron Age Britain; indeed, their prominence can be traced back to the Bronze Age

(Hamerow 2006). Finally, there is an association of human and animal burials with entrances and boundaries. The wide-ranging chronological and geographical affinities of these latter characteristics should warn us, however, against invoking 'cultural continuity' to explain them.

As we have seen, a number of placed deposits can be shown to post-date AD 700. It is, therefore, interesting to consider what the attitude of the Church would have been to the rituals that lay behind such deposits. There are no specific references in Anglo-Saxon sources such as law-codes and penitential handbooks to such rituals, beyond specifying penalties for those who 'sacrificed to devils' (e.g. *EHD* 31.12, 13); indeed, very few surviving Anglo-Saxon texts of any kind preserve elements of pagan practices. A letter from Pope Gregory to the Abbot Mellitus preserved in Bede's *Historia Ecclesiastica* refers to the pagan Anglo-Saxons' 'habit of slaughtering much cattle as sacrifices to devils'—a description which is not inconsistent with the evidence for ritual consumption at Yeavering— and urges Mellitus to replace such practices with religious feasts on Christian holy days (*HE* I.30; Colegrave and Mynors 1969). Also of possible relevance is an Anglo-Saxon charm dating to the late tenth or early eleventh century, known as the *Æcerbot* ('Field Remedy'), which was meant to 'heal' land that had been subjected to harmful magic or which was unproductive (Hill 1977). The charm involves a fertility ritual that, while Christianized and requiring the participation of a priest, clearly preserves elements of pagan practice which may be distantly related to placed deposits. The relevant passage instructs that four turves should be cut, one from each side of the field, that a wooden cross should then be placed in the bottom of each cut and the turves replaced. In general, however, written sources for the period (as well as finds such as the horse skull buried in the church at Brandon) suggest that the Church for the most part tolerated, or was even indifferent to, popular 'religious' practices.

It thus appears that, while settlements in certain periods and places were 'permeated by ritual activity' (for example, Neolithic Central Europe; Bradley 2002, 20), Anglo-Saxon settlements have produced comparatively few placed deposits and, as yet, none containing obviously 'cultic' objects; even deposits of deliberately broken pottery or animal/human burials in direct association with dwellings are rare in comparison with either contemporary Continental settlements or with Iron Age and Roman Britain. It remains to be considered whether this could indicate differences in the role of the house generally as a locus for at least certain kinds of ritualized activity.

As already noted, closure deposits are comparatively widespread in Anglo-Saxon settlements.[22] The purpose(s) served by such deposits and their symbol-

---

[22] It could be argued that the dumping of midden material to backfill an abandoned *Grubenhaus* should be regarded as part of the closure 'rite' just as much as the placing, for example, of a group of complete pots or the head of an ox on the base of the feature (see Morris and Jervis 2011). The two forms of deposit are very unlikely, however, to have played the same role or have served the same 'function' in such rites; the argument, therefore, that 'none of these deposits is special' is unconvincing (ibid. 74).

ism are unlikely ever to be understood through archaeological evidence alone, although there are exceptions, such as the deposit placed in the cellared building at Bishopstone, described above. If, however, some *Grubenhäuser* were used for the storage of agricultural produce (as suggested in Chapter 2), the concentration of early Anglo-Saxon placed deposits in these structures could point to a fertility ideology in which such sacrifices were a means of offering thanks to chthonic powers and calling on them to ensure future fertility. This is no more than an intriguing possibility, although one strengthened by the well-attested link between death, fertility, and regeneration in earlier periods, illustrated, for example, by the association of infant burials and other placed deposits with grain processing and storage facilities in Iron Age and Roman Britain (Cunliffe and Poole 1985; Scott 1991).

The fact that placed deposits were rarely if ever associated with ordinary dwellings in Anglo-Saxon England raises interesting questions, though not ones which can be readily answered. The absence in early Anglo-Saxon England of the longhouse and enclosed farm complexes of the kind seen elsewhere in the North Sea Zone implies important differences in the organization of social and resource-controlling groups (Hamerow 2002). The lack of an association between placed deposits and dwellings may be a further indication that early Anglo-Saxon social groups were structured differently both from those in the 'longhouse zone' of north-west Europe and in Roman Britain. These differences are expressed in certain functional changes: unlike the Continental longhouse, for example, the Anglo-Saxon house did not accommodate cattle—the chief form of wealth throughout the North Sea Zone. There were also differences in the way grain was stored: whereas on the Continent storage took place in post-built granaries as well as in the rafters of houses, few examples of the former have been identified in Anglo-Saxon settlements (see Chapter 2). If, instead, *Grubenhäuser* began to be used more widely for grain storage, one may speculate that the need to associate dwellings with the fertility of the earth was diminished. The fact that the clearest examples of placed deposits associated with Anglo-Saxon timber buildings relate to high-status buildings—i.e. 'Great Halls'—is also suggestive. The Great Hall was not strictly a dwelling, but rather a piece of 'competitive architecture', distinct from, albeit related to, ordinary houses (Herschend 1998, 37–43). The situation at Yeavering and Cowdery's Down may in this way be akin to that seen in Scandinavia, where placed deposits were yet another means of emphasizing the exceptional status of buildings associated with leading families.

Ritual structures in settlements

Place-name scholars and historians have long been aware of the evidence for the use of mounds, holy trees, groves, and other natural places in pre-Christian Anglo-Saxon worship, evidence which indicates that certain rituals were performed in special settings separate from the domestic sphere (Blair 1995; Meaney 1995; Semple 2007). Nevertheless, Anglo-Saxon clerics such as Bede and Aldhelm clearly believed that in the early seventh century, special-purpose religious structures—'temples'—had existed in England (Blair 1995, 2). In a seminal survey of the inevitably elusive archaeological evidence for such structures, John Blair has identified a number of potential ritual structures within settlements. The best-known of these is Building D2, which lay at the western end of the complex at Yeavering and was identified by Hope-Taylor as a temple (see Chapter 3). Also at the western end of the site lay a prehistoric stone circle with a central monolith which was apparently removed in the post-Roman period; the circle not only served to define the alignment of the main Anglo-Saxon buildings, but also acted as a focus for human burials. Furthermore, as Blair describes, 'the post-Roman occupants...built a square fenced enclosure within the circle, and bedded a round post...into the pit of the central monolith....By this stage graves were being dug within the square enclosure' (Blair 1995, 16; Hope-Taylor 1977, 95–118). Other square structures with central posts could also represent 'domestic shrines'. One such example was excavated at New Wintles Farm (Oxfordshire) and comprised a post-built structure some 5m square with a central post (Blair 1995, fig. 11). Another is the annexe attached to Cowdery's Down Building A1, which measured 4.4m square and was lightly built in comparison to the main building (Fig. 2.2). The annexe projected into an adjoining fenced enclosure, and so would have been hidden from external view, yet the absence of a doorway indicates that it did not provide access into the enclosure (Millett 1984, 201–2). Blair has suggested that both examples may have been unroofed, rather like the fenced enclosure projecting from the southern gable end of Yeavering D2, which 'acted as a focus for burials' (Blair 1995, 19, fig. 11). He sees a possible connection between these structures and the small, square, ditched enclosures around some Anglo-Saxon inhumation burials, to which could be added the square four-post structures, some with central cremations, found in cemeteries such as Apple Down, and interpreted as mortuary 'houses' (Down and Welch 1990, 25–33).[23]

More recent discoveries add to this picture. A fascinating settlement-cemetery complex has been excavated at Flixton Park Quarry, Suffolk, on a gravel terrace of the River Waveney. Part of a settlement dating mostly to the sixth to early seventh centuries and comprising six earth-fast timber buildings, eight *Grubenhäuser*, and one 'hybrid' building (see Chapter 2), was uncovered some 500m from a sixth-century cemetery. The settlement would have been

---

[23] The seventh-century settlement at Chalton (Hampshire) produced a unique post-built structure over 24m long and consisting of four unequal sections, slightly misaligned. The plan suggests that they were not erected as a single building, but rather as separate units (Champion 1977, 368). One element of this composite structure measured 6m square and had a central post, potentially providing a further analogy.

dominated by a large Bronze Age barrow (Boulter 2006, 283). Most intriguingly, however, in the middle of a large rectangular ditched enclosure[24] lay a much smaller enclosure, measuring some 9m square. Into the centre of this smaller enclosure had been dug a circular pit some 2m in diameter, 'with a box-shaped cutting...in its base and a single line of flint cobbles on the ledge of soil above the box' (ibid.). Its similarity to the 'circle-in-square' structures has led the excavator to suggest that this was a ritual complex. Five lightly built structures, each measuring approximately 5m square, also lay near the square enclosure. Other buildings lay both inside and outside the large ditched enclosure, and it is not yet possible to say which features were contemporary.

More ambiguous are two circular post-built structures measuring 3–4m in diameter and associated with several *Grubenhäuser* of Mid Saxon date recently excavated at Black Bourton (Oxfordshire) (Gilbert 2006). The first of these consisted of a central, oval pit surrounded by an irregular circle of seven postholes, while the second consisted of six postholes surrounding three small, oval pits. The buildings lay near a later medieval church, and the presence of Ipswich Ware—a rarity in this region—could be an indicator of high-status occupation. It has been suggested that the circular structures could be shrines, although their similarity to three circular structures interpreted as roundhouses (admittedly larger and lacking central pits) at Quarrington illustrates the difficulty of distinguishing between 'shrines' and other kinds of domestic structures (ibid.; Taylor 2003b, 237 and fig. 7; see Chapter 2 and Fig. 3.15).

A final intriguing example of a ritual focus within an Anglo-Saxon settlement is a possible 'holy tree' which appears to have attracted a small group of burials at the Late Saxon settlement at Ketton. A small church and associated cemetery immediately adjacent to the tree may represent the successors to this earlier ritual focus, although the lack of closely datable artefacts means that it is not possible to be certain that the settlement and tree were contemporary (Fig. 3.30; Blair 2005, 381).

Settlements within 'remembered landscapes'

Recent years have seen a growing awareness of the degree to which early Anglo-Saxon cemeteries and assembly places were sited with reference to pre-existing mortuary landscapes and monuments, above all prehistoric burial mounds (Williams 1997; 2006; Semple 2004). Such associations became particularly pronounced during the seventh century, when, for example, more than half of the known cemeteries in the Upper Thames valley lay adjacent to earlier monuments. Howard Williams has argued that this reflects a 'ritual appropriation of the past' achieved by associating dead family members with

---

[24] A placed deposit in the form of an articulated horse spine lay on the base of the enclosure ditch (Boulter 2006 and pers. comm. 2009).

much more ancient 'ancestors' (Williams 1997).[25] It has already been observed in Chapter 3 that high-status settlements and assembly places also appear to have been attracted to, in particular, Bronze Age barrows. A systematic survey currently being undertaken across the midland counties of England suggests that monument re-use may in fact have been relatively widespread and was not restricted to 'special' settlements (Crewe 2009).

It is not, of course, always possible to establish with certainty whether earlier monuments were still visible in the Anglo-Saxon period and some apparent associations appear likely, on closer inspection, to have been merely coincidental. At Mucking, for example, the large Late Bronze Age earthwork enclosure known as the 'South Rings' was no longer an upstanding feature by the late Iron Age, and—despite appearances to the contrary—could not have acted as a focus for the early Anglo-Saxon settlement (Etté 1993, 18–19). Similarly, the impressive Late Bronze Age enclosure at Springfield Lyons may not have been visible when an early Anglo-Saxon cemetery and Late Saxon settlement were established around and across it (Tyler and Major 2005).

It is, nevertheless, striking how many Anglo-Saxon settlements lie adjacent to earlier monuments. The case of Flixton Park Quarry, where Bronze Age barrows attracted both burials and settlement in the early Anglo-Saxon period, has already been mentioned. At Cossington, near Leicester, a Bronze Age barrow was the focus of a small inhumation cemetery in the late sixth and early seventh centuries, following a period of placed deposition in and around the barrow in the Iron Age and Roman periods (Thomas 2007; 2008). A *Grubenhaus* lay some 50m to the north along with several pits and a ditch, although whether this represents part of a more extensive settlement is impossible to judge given the limited scale of the excavation. At Radley, Barrow Hills, a Neolithic oval barrow and at least three Bronze Age round barrows were still substantial features when the Anglo-Saxon settlement was established, although several ring ditches were deliberately filled in by the new occupants (Chambers and McAdam 2007, 84 and 303). Finally, at the remarkable settlement complex at Thwing, in East Yorkshire, a major Bronze Age circular earthwork was re-used (and ditched enclosures added to it) between *c*.700 and 950, for both burial and occupation (Manby 1985, 1986, 1987; Reynolds 2003, 128–9). Such associations, along with placed deposits and ritual structures, demonstrate that Bradley's compelling observation regarding prehistoric Britain applies equally to Anglo-Saxon England: 'Ritual and domestic life went together throughout the prehistoric sequence and it is wrong and—more than that—it is impossible to separate them now' (2005, 210).

---

[25] It is possible, however, that in exceptional cases such as Yeavering, such re-use may point to the continuing significance of certain places in the 'social memory' of communities over very long timespans (Waddington 2005, 84).

5

Farming systems and settlement forms

Post-Roman land use and farming systems

While it is rare, as we saw in Chapter 1, to find evidence of direct continuity from Romano-British to Anglo-Saxon occupation at the level of individual settlements, evidence for the continuity of Romano-British territorial units into the Anglo-Saxon period can be identified at several levels. At a macro scale, we see the survival of some *Civitates* names, even in the south-east of Britain, where the Brittonic name *Cantium* became the supposedly 'Jutish' kingdom of Kent (Brooks 1989, 57). Indeed, a range of linguistic and place-name evidence points to the survival of Romano-British and older land units into the post-Roman period. At a more local scale, there is considerable evidence to support the idea that Anglo-Saxon leaders took over contiguous Romano-British estates, creating in the process miniature kingdoms by the late sixth century; it has even been suggested that the most basic unit of Anglo-Saxon landed assessment, the hide, may have Roman origins (Bassett 1989; Barnwell 1996; see also Charles-Edwards 1972). What remains unclear, however, is the extent to which the Late Roman agricultural system survived beyond the early fifth century, and it is the continuity of such systems, and of land use more generally, that is considered briefly here.

The conventional view, developed primarily by W. G. Hoskins, was that there was widespread abandonment of farmland after the end of Roman rule (Hoskins 1955). The most easily identifiable effect of such abandonment would be the regeneration of scrub and woodland, and for this reason pollen studies play a key role in understanding what happened to farmland during the fifth century. These studies have largely quashed the view that the Anglo-Saxons carved their settlements and fields out of re-afforested land (e.g. Dark 2000, 140 ff.). Instead, a growing number of pollen sequences from within the 'villa zone' indicates that Roman fields were, by and large, maintained as open, cleared land throughout the Anglo-Saxon period.[1] Extensive and closely dated environmental evidence from palaeochannel sediments in

---

[1] The picture is, of course, mixed: in some areas, for example around Bignor villa in Sussex, a good deal of farmland did revert to woodland in the late or post-Roman period (Dark 2000, 140).

Wiltshire, for example, produced 'no evidence of a post-Roman recovery of woodland' (Williams and Newman 2006, 123). The south-west also appears to have seen little change in land use between the fourth and sixth centuries, 'suggesting continuity at the end of the Roman period in an essentially pastoral landscape' (Rippon 2010, 59). Plant and animal remains from Anglo-Saxon wells at Barton Court Farm, Dorchester-on-Thames, and elsewhere, indicate that in the upper and middle Thames valley too, the post-Roman period saw relatively little change in the general character of the surrounding landscape (Miles 1986; Dark 2000 141; Booth et al. 2007). Rippon's observation regarding the situation in Essex could in fact be applied to large parts of southern Britain: 'The overall picture appears to be one of partial survival of Romano-British landscapes...and partial discontinuity that suggests a decrease in the intensity with which the landscape was exploited, but not its abandonment' (2008, 166).

Post-Roman farming systems were of course less intensive: with no urban populations or armies to provision, there was neither the need for the intensive production of cereals, nor the labour forces previously associated with villas to sustain it. Roman drainage systems fell into disuse and, in many regions—including the upper Thames valley, North Yorkshire, and parts of East Anglia—light soils that were easy to cultivate, such as river gravels, were favoured over heavier soils (Hamerow 1992). Again taking the Oxford region as an example, there was a retreat of settlement from previously drained land on the first gravel terrace of the River Thames by the late fourth century. Early Anglo-Saxon settlements instead occupied the lighter soils on the second terrace. This does not necessarily point to discontinuity, but does suggest a partial reversion or retreat to a pre-Roman pattern of land use. There is, furthermore, evidence from several regions, including East Anglia and Staffordshire, which points to a general increase in pastoral over arable farming during the fifth and sixth centuries (Moffett 1994; Murphy 1994; Williams and Newman 2006, 123–31).

Excavation and fieldwork have yielded a significant number of cases where Roman field systems appear to have become fossilized in the Anglo-Saxon landscape, suggesting a degree of territorial, and maybe even tenurial, continuity. A striking example comes from southern Cambridgeshire, at the Roman villa at Godmanchester (Green 1978, 116). Here, the furlong boundaries of an area of medieval ridge-and-furrow respected the boundaries of Roman 'lazy beds'—ridges produced by spade cultivation—as well as a Roman droveway, providing remarkable evidence that a minor Roman land division was maintained into the Anglo-Saxon period and beyond. Small areas of medieval furlongs in Northamptonshire and Cambridgeshire also appear to represent the 'fossilization' of Roman fields, to judge from correlations between areas of Late Roman and Anglo-Saxon pottery scatters and later medieval small furlongs; excavation has also revealed Roman boundaries running parallel to several later medieval headlands (Upex 2003b).

Evidence like this of course remains open to interpretation. The re-use of Roman field boundaries does not necessarily imply continuity of land use. Instances where Roman ditches and banks underlie medieval field boundaries may merely indicate use of a convenient pre-existing earthwork after several generations of disuse. This is what makes Godmanchester so remarkable: the lazy beds were *not* major elements in the Roman field system; their boundaries could easily have been erased or ignored. The fact that they were not is therefore a powerful indicator of continuous cultivation. Rippon's observations of abandoned modern fields in south-east Essex, furthermore, suggest that infestation with brambles and scrub would rapidly have rendered former field boundaries 'practically invisible' (2008, 166–7). The process of clearing such fields would contribute still further to the destruction of earthen banks. The implication of this kind of evidence is that the opportunistic re-use of Romano-British field boundaries decades or even centuries after they were abandoned seems less likely, while continuous usage appears increasingly plausible.

We should not be surprised, therefore, to find that Late Roman 'fieldscapes' were often maintained rather than dismantled. The inhabitants of post-Roman Britain are unlikely to have been pioneers where farming was concerned and the evidence suggests that, for the most part, they took over farmland that was still in reasonable working order. Indeed, the farming practices of early Anglo-Saxon communities probably differed little from those of Romano-British small farms (Hamerow 2002a, 152–3). The range of crops grown remained largely unchanged, apart from the virtual disappearance of emmer and of 'cash crops' such as lentils and grapes. There is even growing evidence that spelt—the main crop of Roman Britain, conventionally assumed to have been replaced by free-threshing wheat during the early Anglo-Saxon period—continued to be cultivated in some places well beyond the end of the Roman period (Murphy 1994, 37; Pelling 2001, 422; Ballantyne 2010, 175).[2] Evidence which hints at some small-scale continuity of agricultural production in Late Roman settlements comes from the Roman town of Alchester (Oxfordshire) (Booth et al. 2001). A dump of charred grains, similar in composition to a deposit found in a nearby corn dryer and presumably derived from it, contained abundant examples of characteristic Romano-British crops, notably spelt and hulled six-row barley. Yet beneath this charred deposit were found sherds of early Anglo-Saxon pottery, indicating that the corn dryer remained in use well into the fifth century and perhaps beyond.

---

[2] Spelt, for example, was the dominant cereal in a charred deposit found in a *Grubenhaus* in East Molesey (Surrey), although the material may have derived from a nearby Roman corn dryer (Andrews 1996, 98).

We must take care not to exaggerate the extent of continuity; we do not know whether the few examples of preserved Roman field systems and the Alchester corn dryer are exceptions to the rule or accidental survivals of a wider phenomenon that is archaeologically extremely difficult to identify. Pollen sequences nevertheless provide good grounds for accepting that there were broad, underlying continuities in many regions. Thus, despite the fact that the collapse of the villa system in Britain was undoubtedly more dramatic than in Gaul and Iberia, post-Roman land use here displays certain similarities to the 'Late Antique' landscapes of the other western provinces (Dark 2004). This still leaves us with something of a paradox, however: on the one hand, we see an apparently sudden and near-complete disjunction between Romano-British and Anglo-Saxon settlements, cemeteries, and material cultures—not merely pottery and metalwork, but also architecture, mortuary rituals, and settlement forms; on the other, we see a much more subtle and gradual evolution in land use, which in some cases appears to have changed relatively little in the transition from Roman Britain to Anglo-Saxon England.

Perhaps these two seemingly contradictory perspectives are not entirely incompatible, however. Most of that part of the archaeological record which is distinctively 'Roman' reflects the activities of only a small proportion of the population of Roman Britain (Esmonde Cleary 2011). In a similar way, archaeology has revealed the settlements and cemeteries of only one segment of the population of post-Roman Britain, namely immigrants, their descendants, and those indigenous inhabitants who most readily embraced the new culture that these immigrants introduced. The material culture and practices associated with this group is thus largely to do with issues of power and identity. The evidence for land use, in contrast, reflects decisions made by farming communities as they responded to local demographic and environmental conditions as well as tenurial arrangements, in some regions adopting new strategies of production following the collapse of the villa system, but in many others making few changes to existing practices. It is inevitable that such different forms of evidence reveal different, but equally 'real', aspects of life in post-Roman Britain.

Innovation and investment: crop husbandry, processing, and storage in Mid Saxon England

Expansion of arable

The Mid Saxon period witnessed a number of important developments in agricultural production, reflected first and foremost by an increased emphasis on arable farming. Increasing alluviation apparent along the Thames valley, together with pollen sequences indicating a marked increase in cereal cultivation around the eighth and ninth centuries, point to an expansion of arable in the Mid Saxon period; comparable evidence comes from the Nene valley around Raunds and

West Cotton (Robinson 1991 and unpublished). At Yarnton, cereal remains associated with the Mid Saxon settlement were considerably more abundant than for the early Saxon phase, and it is evident that part of the floodplain, abandoned since the Late Roman period, was once again being cultivated (Hey 2004, 48–9). The area around Stafford saw an increase in cultivation in the Late Saxon period following a period of scrub regeneration, while at Market Lavington (Wiltshire), a marked increase in pollen from cereals and other crops was apparent from *c*.900 onwards (Moffett 1994, 55; Williams and Newman 2006, 136–7).

The greater frequency of certain arable weeds indicates, furthermore, that heavier soils were increasingly being brought under cultivation in the Mid to Late Saxon period, something which could not have been readily achieved without the use of heavy ploughs pulled by teams of oxen (Robinson 2007, 30–1; see also Williams 1993, 96; Williamson 2003, 120–2).[3] This implies the use of mouldboards and strip fields, direct evidence for which is slowly but surely increasing. At Drayton (Oxfordshire), 'broad, parallel stripes of clayey material'—dated archaeomagnetically to the Late Saxon period—were recognized as representing furrows created by a mouldboard plough, producing in section 'a very distinctive sandwich of inverted alluvial clay, gravel and re-deposited soil' (Booth et al. 2007, 333). The very recent discovery on the base of a *Grubenhaus* of a coulter—an iron bar mounted in front of the ploughshare and mouldboard which cuts through the soil—at the probable monastic settlement at Lyminge (Kent) demonstrates the use of this technology in England as early as the seventh century, and suggests that Kent was at the forefront of agricultural innovation, as of so much else (Pitts 2011). The numbers of oxen needed to pull such ploughs would have increased even as the grazing land needed to sustain these animals was being encroached upon by fields.[4] One response to the need to feed large numbers of hard-working traction animals on high-quality fodder was to establish hay meadows. At West Cotton, values for grass pollen in the Mid Saxon period were very high, while macroscopic plant remains show the grassland to have been a managed hay meadow, possibly on seasonally flooded land (Robinson, unpublished). Insect remains from Oxey Mead near Yarnton, radiocarbon dated to between AD 650 and 850, indicate that here too, the floodplain grassland changed from pasture to hay meadow (Hey 2004, 47; Robinson 2007, 31). Elsewhere in the upper Thames valley, and at Market Lavington in Wiltshire, pollen sequences suggest that the transition from pasture to hay meadow probably occurred in the Late Saxon period

---

[3] The ard, or scratch-plough, nevertheless remained in use throughout the Mid and Late Saxon periods, as indicated both by weed seed assemblages (e.g. Bateman et al. 2003) and finds of plough shares (e.g. Thomas 2009, 373–4, illus. 13, 5).

[4] To give some idea of the numbers of animals involved, 10 ploughs were recorded at Yarnton in Domesday Book, suggesting that fodder would have been needed for somewhere between 40 and 80 oxen (Booth et al. 2007, 333).

(Williams and Newman 2006, 136; Robinson 2007, 31). Bede's observation, already noted in Chapter 2, that in Ireland the mild climate meant that 'there is no need to store hay in summer for winter use' suggests that, by the eighth century, hay-making was the norm in Northumbria (*HE* I.i). The establishment of hay meadows would have required keeping animals off the meadow in the spring—which may account for some of the complexes of paddocks and droveways associated with Mid Saxon settlements discussed in Chapter 3—mowing in the summer, and grazing from late summer onwards (Booth et al. 2007, 333). Indeed, so important were hay meadows to the expansion of arable that Tom Williamson has argued for an association between nucleated villages with open fields, and those regions with abundant meadowland (Williamson 2003, 169 and fig. 52).[5]

Crop husbandry and 'new foods'

After the collapse of Roman Britain, the cultivation of cash crops such as dill, lentils, and grapes appears to have ceased (Jones 1982, 103; Hamerow 2002a, 152). Spelt was soon largely replaced by bread wheat, which had been comparatively rare in Roman Britain. Emmer, as already noted, also declined greatly in importance.[6] As on the Continent, bread cereals had replaced barley as the dominant cereal by the ninth century, but whereas the emphasis elsewhere in northern Europe was on rye, in England, bread wheat predominated, this dominance becoming particularly marked from the eighth century onward (Hagen 1995, 21; Banham 2010, 188; Moffett 2011). Late Saxon written sources indicate that wheat was considered more palatable than barley: barley bread, for example, was the preferred food of saints as a mark of their self-denial (Hagen 1995, 19). An apparent expansion of wheat cultivation in Anglo-Saxon England has been argued by Debby Banham to be the result of preference and the desire 'for that prestigious dietary item, light, white wheat bread' (Banham 2010, 192).[7] It is likely that barley was primarily used for brewing, and possibly fodder, by the Mid Saxon period. This can be inferred from the fact that,

---

[5] Even marginal land at the fen-edge was brought under cultivation in the Mid Saxon period, as remarkable evidence from the siltland of eastern England demonstrates. Communities such as the one at Walpole St Andrews (Norfolk) occupied 'roddons' (raised riverbeds) that were still tidal, and adapted to these difficult conditions by growing barley, which is salt-tolerant relative to other crops; a sea bank must have been constructed during the Late Saxon period, as evidenced by the fact that the environment ceased to be tidal (Crowson et al. 2005).

[6] It must be remembered, however, that the abundance of particular types of plant remains in preserved assemblages is a reflection of how likely they were to be exposed to charring or waterlogging, and not necessarily of their economic importance. Some agricultural products, furthermore (e.g. pulses), are consistently under-represented because processing them leaves little behind in the way of waste product.

[7] It should be noted that Banham's 1990 study undertaken as part of her doctoral thesis was based on 'presence/absence' figures (2012, n. 23). Very recent work based on a larger sample of sites suggests that the expansion of bread wheat in the Mid Saxon period may not have been so marked, at least in some regions (M. McKerracher, pers. comm.).

while 'naked' varieties of wheat which did not need to be parched prior to threshing became more widespread, naked varieties of barley did not, with hulled barley remaining prevalent. Barley used for malting did not need to be threshed (Hagen 1995, 28).

Plant remains from settlements also indicate that the Mid to Late Saxon periods saw the introduction of a wider range of crops, including rye and legumes, and a new emphasis on horticulture, a development which was presumably linked to the emergence of formal markets (Hey 2004, 351–60). At Market Lavington, a sharp increase in pollen from both cereals and other crops is apparent from *c.*900 onwards, when the community appears to 'have been engaged in much larger-scale and diverse agriculture and horticulture' (Williams and Newman 2006, 136–7). Market Lavington also yielded evidence for viticulture, as have Yarnton and Scole, in Essex (Williams and Newman 2006, 136–7; Hey 2004, 351; Rippon 2010). Oil and fibre crops such as flax and hemp were also more widely grown (Williams 1993, 96; Campbell 1994, 81; Murphy 1994, 34; Hey 2004; Booth et al. 2007, 337–8) and there appears to have been a new emphasis on oats, which would have been used both for fodder and human consumption (Green 1994, 85; Moffett 1994, 62).

Farming techniques: weeding, manuring, and field systems

A growing dominance of bread wheat would have had implications for ploughing, weeding, and manuring regimes, as free-threshing wheat is more vulnerable to fungi, less able to compete with weeds, and requires greater soil fertility. It thus demands a greater investment of labour in order to achieve the potentially high yields. Weed seeds are again one of the best indicators of changing cultivation regimes. The samples taken from the later eighth- and ninth-century phases at Yarnton, for example, indicate an increase in annual weeds at the expense of less plough-tolerant biennial and perennial weeds, in marked contrast to the earlier phases. This suggests either more frequent ploughing and shorter fallow periods, which would naturally act to suppress perennial weeds, and/or the use of a mouldboard, which would be better tolerated by annual species (Stevens 2004, 361–4; cf. evidence for deep cultivation from Mid Saxon Pennyland: Williams 1993, 96). Evidence for manuring in the form of pottery scatters comes from a number of sites including Yarnton, where henbane—a plant associated with middens—was also found (Hey 2004, 48–9); indeed some of the paddocks seen in settlements might have served, at least in part, to facilitate the collection of manure.

These new weeding and manuring regimes, together with the increased use of the heavy plough, would of course have required a considerable investment of labour. There thus appears to be a strong case for linking the increasing use of the heavy plough on the one hand, and the introduction of strip fields and settlement nucleation on the other (Banham 2010; although see also Oosthuizen

2010 for a more cautious perspective on the link between open fields and settlement nucleation). The date for the widespread adoption of open fields has been much debated, but the tenth-century date often posited is based on the earliest written references to such fields described in charter bounds (Rippon 2010); as we have seen, the palaeobotanical and environmental evidence suggests that open fields were established somewhat earlier than this.[8]

Crop processing and storage

The Mid Saxon period also saw the construction of the first centralized crop processing and storage facilities seen in lowland Britain since the Roman period. The lack of purpose-built corn dryers during the fifth to seventh centuries may be partly explained by the fact that spelt wheat—which must be heated before it can be husked—was largely replaced by free-threshing (primarily bread) wheat. Nevertheless, heating bread wheat extends its storage life by reducing moisture content, which also enables it to be more easily ground to flour and improves its flavour (van der Veen 1989; Moffett 1994, 61). These benefits would presumably have been achieved in the early Anglo-Saxon period by individual households roasting their cereal grains over ordinary domestic hearths or ovens, both of which are relatively common features in settlements of that period. The construction of corn dryers which could hold large quantities of grain implies a new need for centralized cereal processing on a large scale. Their context is therefore significant. A few are known from towns, notably Hereford, London, and Stafford (Moffett 1994). Rural examples include two Mid or Late Saxon L-shaped corn dryers, consisting of a flue and drying chamber, at Chalton Manor Farm, Hampshire (Hughes 1984, 72–6) and another of probable Mid Saxon date, with a drying chamber measuring some 3m x 2.5m, from Feltham, Middlesex (Cowie and Blackmore 2008, 105–8). The Feltham example contained a large charred plant assemblage, a sample of which proved to consist of nearly 80 per cent fully cleaned bread wheat. At Ebbsfleet, in Kent, one or possibly two Mid to Late Saxon corn dryers were found lying at some distance from a contemporary settlement. The function of one of these remains uncertain, but the second example—an oval pit with a sloping base measuring some 3m x 1.5m—was lined with a thick layer of clay, showed signs of burning, and contained burnt daub from the collapsed superstructure. The pit contained large quantities of grain, again mostly bread wheat (Andrews et al. 2011). Further evidence for Late Saxon corn dryers comes from Renhold, Water End West and Springfield Lyons. At the latter settlement, nearly two kilos of fired clay was found in the foundation trench of

---

[8] A study of early maps and landscape features in the Bourn Valley (Cambridgeshire) has revealed a system of 'proto-open fields' which must pre-date the early tenth century, and probably originated between the eighth and mid ninth centuries, exactly at the time when rectilinear settlements were becoming widespread in eastern England (Oosthuizen 2005).

Building 1 together with a semi-cleaned assemblage of, primarily, wheat and oats, while archaeomagnetic dating demonstrates that the last use of a corn dryer found at Wolverton Mill was between 970 and 1020 (Tyler and Major 2005, 162; Timby et al. 2007, 175; A. Chapman, pers. comm.). A remarkable complex of structures used for corn drying was also uncovered at the Northumbrian ecclesiastical site at Hoddom in south-west Scotland, with some of these potentially dating as early as the mid seventh century (Lowe 2006).[9]

A well-preserved example of another kind of grain-processing facility—a malting oven, used to make ale from germinated barley—was found some 100m south-west of the main settlement at Higham Ferrers. Radiocarbon dates indicate a period of use sometime between the mid eighth and mid ninth centuries. The oven consisted of a large, rectangular, flat-bottomed pit, c.2.7m x 3.1m, the sides of which were lined with coursed rubble walling; the base was covered with stone slabs and a long flue extended from one end of the pit. The feature showed signs of intense burning and the primary fill contained a high concentration of charred cereals, some 90 per cent of which was barley, much of it germinated (Hardy et al. 2007; Fig. 5.1).

The evidence for Anglo-Saxon barns and granaries remains fairly limited (see Chapter 2), yet the appearance of at least some purpose-built grain-storage facilities in the Mid Saxon period, following their apparent absence during the fifth to seventh centuries, may well reflect a new need to store large quantities of threshed grain extracted from tenants, presumably prior to redistribution and/or marketing. The considerable capacity of the two barns at Higham Ferrers, for example, implies that the quantity of grain stored greatly exceeded that produced by an individual household (Fig. 2.12).

The appearance of watermills also points to an increase in the scale of agricultural operations in the Mid Saxon period.[10] While over 5,000 watermills are listed in Domesday Book, and references to mills in charters and place-names were relatively common by the ninth century, a small number of archaeologically identified mills indicate that they were already a feature of the Anglo-Saxon landscape well before this (Hagen 1992, 5; Snape 2003, 38, 62).[11] The earliest and most extensively preserved of these is a tidal mill found at Ebbsfleet, constructed towards the end of the seventh century and demolished after a short period of use, probably because of rising water levels (Andrews et al. 2011; Fig. 5.2). Radiocarbon dates from another mill at a strategic river crossing in the Tyne valley at Corbridge suggest that it, in contrast, was operational

---

[9] Other possible examples include two large stone and clay ovens dating to the late seventh or early eighth century found at Gillingham, Dorset, although these could equally have been used for roasting iron ore (Heaton 1993).

[10] Grain also, of course, continued to be ground by hand by individual households, as testified by the frequent finds of rotary quernstones in settlements of the Mid and Late Saxon periods.

[11] The earliest written reference to an Anglo-Saxon watermill is contained in a charter issued by the King of Kent in 762 (Watts 2002, 72).

Fig. 5.1. A reconstruction of the Mid Saxon malting oven at Higham Ferrers. (Illustrated by P. Lorimer; Copyright Oxford Archaeology Ltd.)

for a long time, between the mid eighth and early eleventh centuries (Snape 2003). Two well-preserved vertical-wheeled watermills found at Wellington (Worcestershire), probably associated with a Mercian royal estate, were constructed in the late seventh or early eighth century, to judge from radiocarbon and dendrochronological dates; a similar mill was constructed around the same time near Wareham (Dorset) (R. Jackson, pers. comm.; Watts 2002, 81). A mill with three vertical wheels excavated at the Saxon royal residence at Old Windsor (Berkshire) may have been in existence by the late seventh century and was fed by a leat over 1 km long and 6m wide (Wilson and Hurst 1958, 183–5; Rahtz and Meeson 1992, 156). Excavations at Barking Abbey uncovered not only evidence of high-status Anglo-Saxon occupation, but also the backfilled course of the headrace of a leat. Timbers from the leat have been dendrochronologically dated to just after AD 705, and evidence for substantial repairs dated to some eighty years later (MacGowan 1996, 175). The well-preserved horizontal watermill constructed around the middle of the ninth century at Tamworth was probably part of the historically attested royal residence, although it could have served the town (Rahtz and Meeson 1992). Finally, a mid tenth-century mill—possibly an undershot vertical-wheeled watermill—lay adjacent to the manorial complex at West Cotton, Raunds (Windell et al. 1990; Chapman 2010).

Most of the archaeological evidence for large-scale, centralized crop storage and processing thus comes, unsurprisingly, from monastic and secular estate

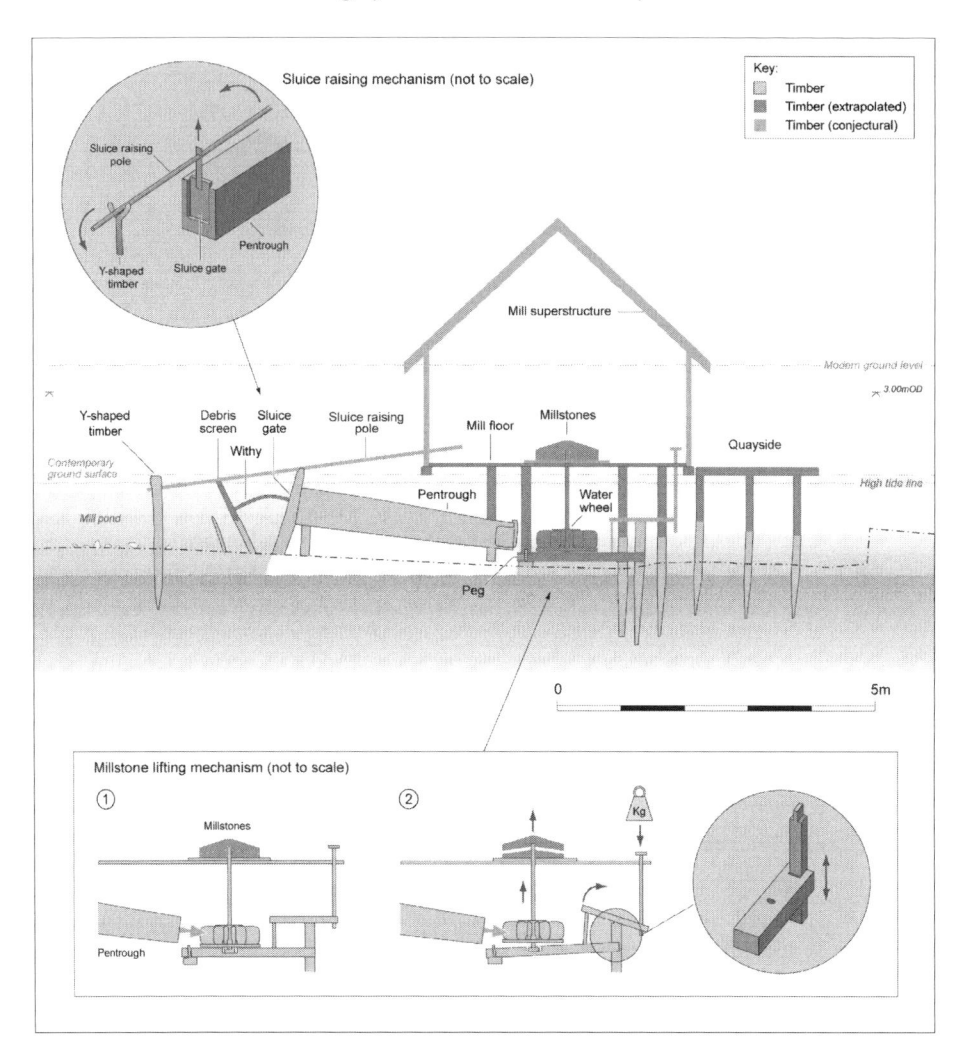

Fig. 5.2. A reconstruction of the Mid Saxon watermill at Ebbsfleet (reproduced with kind permission of Wessex Archaeology).

centres as well as from towns, although there is no conclusive evidence for the existence of such estates at either Corbridge or Ebbsfleet. References to watermills in charters also relate mostly to royal residences and estates, or to royal grants to churches or laymen. Indeed, Alcock described the mill as a 'self-evidently essential element of an estate centre' (1988, 27).

Despite the fact that the archaeological evidence related to grain processing is steadily increasing, we still know comparatively little about how milling was organized and the scale of outputs. It is likely, for example, that while bread wheat would have been dried close to where milling took place, oats and other hulled grains would have been heated to aid de-husking; thus, *Gerefa* lists making a kiln for 'the threshing floor' as one of the duties undertaken by the estate manager. It is therefore useful to know whether cereals were processed within a settlement, or were brought to it cleaned and ready for consumption. At Gamlingay, for example, cereal processing appears to have occurred on-site, 'with chaff, weed seeds and spoiled grains being dumped in pits or other available open features' (Murray 2006, 251). The absence of such material, however, does not necessarily mean that the initial stages of cleaning the crop took place away from the settlement, since debris such as straw and chaff only rarely survive as charred remains (Cowie and Blackmore 2008, 160).

The number of archaeologically recorded Anglo-Saxon mills, barns, corn dryers, and related structures remains undeniably small, due both to poor preservation conditions and, in the case of corn dryers, the need to place them at a safe distance from dwellings in order to minimize the risk of fire.[12] Nevertheless, the surviving examples are sufficient to indicate that the Mid Saxon period marked a real turning point in terms of the scale at which agricultural produce was extracted from producers, processed, and distributed, at least in certain regions.

Animal husbandry

While crops, above all bread cereals, would always have been more significant than meat to Anglo-Saxon communities in strictly dietary terms, animal products remained important, not only for subsistence, but also for their social value, notably in gift exchange. Yet the differences between animal bone assemblages within the same region—even from neighbouring settlements—should warn us against drawing generalizations about the economic importance of different species on the basis of isolated cases. For example, despite the fact that the Early Anglo-Saxon settlements of Melford Meadows and West Stow in Suffolk occupied similar Breckland environments, cattle clearly predominated at the former, sheep at the latter (Mudd 2002). Bone frequency, furthermore, is not always a reliable guide to the economic importance of different species. Even when the number of sheep bones far exceeds that of cattle, for example, the latter may nevertheless have provided most of the meat consumed by the community (Gibson 2003, 197).[13] The complex processes which led to the deposition of animal bone within settlements mean, furthermore, that only a small percentage of the total number of animals slaughtered and

---

[12] This is attested by written sources, including the early Irish laws, which require that drying kilns not be built within a specified distance from the dwelling (Lowe 2006, 102).

[13] In most reports on faunal remains, bones are quantified according to 'number of identified specimens' (NISP). This can create distortions, however, not least because the skeletons of some species have more parts than others, or are more robust and therefore more likely to be preserved (e.g. Sykes 2006, 57). On the other hand, bones which are easily fragmented may also be disproportionately represented. Ideally, the 'minimum number of individuals' (MNI) represented by a group of animal bones should be considered alongside NISP to provide a more meaningful form of quantification.

consumed is ever recovered archaeologically. Animal bones should, therefore, not be regarded as a direct guide to livestock rearing and consumption in Anglo-Saxon communities. It is, nevertheless, possible to evaluate the economic importance of the main domesticates and to gain some sense of how animal husbandry developed over time through the careful study of age and sex profiles, species ratios, and body-parts represented.

Early Anglo-Saxon animal husbandry practices are well attested at a number of settlements, notably at West Stow, whose large, well-preserved faunal assemblage was one of the first to receive detailed study and publication (Crabtree 1990). The broad, unstructured slaughter patterns indicated by the faunal assemblage of the fifth to seventh centuries point towards 'extensive' livestock management geared towards self-sufficiency. Animal husbandry was, furthermore, 'unfocused', that is, not geared towards producing a single commodity (Crabtree 2010). This is unsurprising, given the absence in that period of both a market for meat and of landowners requiring regular food rents. This meant that, in some respects, animal husbandry practices during the early Anglo-Saxon period had more in common with those of the Iron Age than of Roman Britain, although there were also some significant continuities with the Roman period (Crabtree 1990, 68, 107).

There are signs that this picture began to change in the Mid to Late Saxon periods, although characterizing those changes and drawing generalizations remains problematic. Added to the difficulties already noted is the fact that the introduction of markets and food rents would have resulted in the increased movement of animals on the hoof, adding a further layer of complexity to the already complex pattern of animal bone deposition within settlements. There is, nevertheless, clear evidence that, from the Mid Saxon period onwards, some farmers were beginning to manage livestock in new ways.

Sheep

Sheep, together with cattle, dominate the animal bone record for the whole of the Anglo-Saxon period, indeed the whole of the Middle Ages. The fact that most survived to maturity indicates that they were kept primarily for wool and dairying, rather than meat.[14] The proportion of sheep appears to have increased at least somewhat during the Mid to Late Saxon periods, and it is generally assumed that the production of wool and textiles gained in importance in this period. Much of the evidence for this comes from *emporia* such as *Hamwic*, but it is also possible to discern a trend in favour of sheep—often at the expense of cattle—in some rural animal bone assemblages (Crabtree 1994, 41; Taylor 2003b; Loveluck 2007, 96–7; K. Poole, pers. comm.). At Wolverton Turn, for example, cattle represented only 32 per cent of the major domesticates (calcu-

---

[14] There are, however, exceptions: the cull-patterns at Wolverton Turn 'suggest a concentration on prime meat', as do those from the Mid Saxon settlement at Cadley Road, Collingbourne Ducis (Preston 2004; Pine 2001).

lated according to NISP), with sheep being the dominant species. At Yarnton, the proportion of cattle decreased slightly in relation to sheep from the Mid to Late Saxon periods, while the high proportion of mature sheep has been interpreted as reflecting a growing emphasis on wool production (Mulville and Ayres 2004, 345, 350). At the high-status settlement of Bishopstone, sheep and pigs, rather than cattle, dominated the animal bone assemblage (Poole 2010). A growing emphasis on sheep rearing may also explain the function of at least some of the enclosures seen at settlements such as Cardinal Park, Godmanchester, where 59 per cent of the bone fragments were of sheep in a part of the country where cattle normally dominated. Indeed, the occurrence of a pathology found on sheep bones known as 'penning elbow' peaked during the ninth century at Flixborough,[15] a period which also saw the highest percentage of sheep and greatest quantity of textile working equipment, evidence which, viewed together, does seem to point to a new strategy for sheep husbandry (Loveluck 2007, 97). The age structure at many sites also points to a greater emphasis on wool production in the Mid to Late Saxon periods, as a comparison of the age profiles for sheep from Mid Saxon Brandon and the nearby early Anglo-Saxon settlement of West Stow demonstrates (Fig. 5.3; see also Gibson 2003, 192 and fig. 40; Hardy et al. 2003, fig. 10.4). Not only the age, but also the sex profile of sheep at Brandon— the site of a probable monastery—is suggestive of specialized wool production, a theory further supported by evidence for cloth production and dyeing from the settlement (Crabtree 1996a; 1996b; 2010).[16]

What Bourdillon has called 'a new and serious emphasis on wool' in the Mid Saxon period, particularly in East Anglia, thus finds substantial support in the archaeological record (1998, 182). It has, nevertheless, recently been argued that the economic importance of wool in Anglo-Saxon England has been exaggerated, especially for the early period, thanks to the disproportionate survival of spinning and weaving equipment and later references to textile production in written sources (Tipper 2004, 177 ff.). While it is possible to question whether there was a steady increase in the overall proportion of sheep on Anglo-Saxon farms, it is difficult to avoid the conclusion that sheep rearing by the Late Saxon period was in many cases clearly managed to maximize wool production, and that such evidence is lacking in early Anglo-Saxon assemblages. It is interesting, therefore, to consider how the evidence for sheep rearing compares with the evidence for textile production in rural settlements.

Textile production
As already noted in Chapter 2, artefacts associated with spinning and weaving are amongst the most abundant found in early Anglo-Saxon settlements and

---

[15] Such pathologies, however, are not exclusively caused by 'penning' (D. Serjeantson, pers. comm.).
[16] As Tipper has pointed out, however, the actual proportion of sheep/goats (based on NISP) at Brandon is roughly the same as that at West Stow (2004, 181).

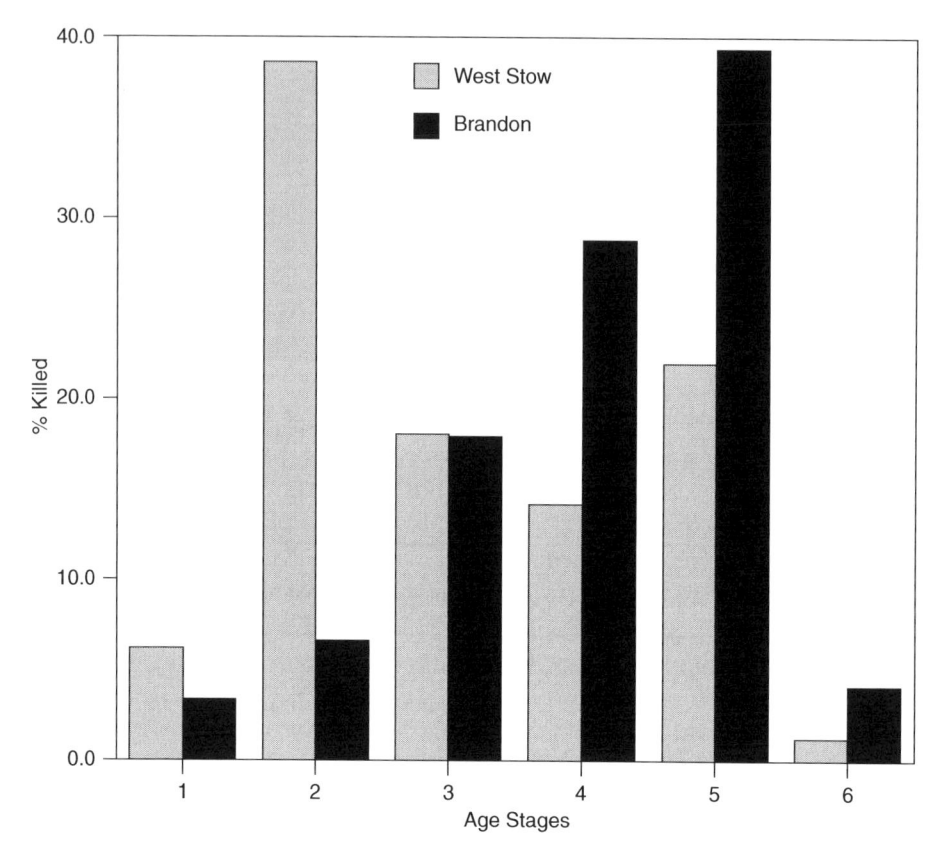

Fig. 5.3. Age profiles for sheep from Brandon (Mid Saxon) and West Stow (early Anglo-Saxon). The age categories, based on tooth wear, are as follows: 1–3 = unworn; 4 = in wear; 5 = full wear; 6 = heavily worn. After Crabtree 1996b, fig. 9.3.

are generally assumed to relate to small-scale cloth production by individual households. There is some evidence, however, that workshops for specialized cloth production were operating as early as the seventh century. This is suggested in part by an admittedly small number of finds of loomweights found lying in rows on the bases of unusually large *Grubenhäuser*. At Pakenham, Suffolk, rows of loomweights, which appear to indicate the presence of two exceptionally large looms (Brown et al. 1954), have been argued to represent 'organized production workshops making large textiles of standardized character and quality, probably for commercial as well as domestic purposes' (Plunkett 1999, 295). The date of this find (which was incompletely excavated under difficult conditions) is uncertain, although the form of the loomweights and some of the metal finds from the feature suggest a later sixth- or seventh-century date. Comparable finds have been made at Upton (see Chapter 2) and Old Erringham (West Sussex), both of which can be more certainly dated to the seventh century or later (Holden 1976; Jackson et al. 1969).

Due to the limited scale of the excavations, little can be said about the wider settlement contexts of the finds from Old Erringham, Upton, and Pakenham. Analysis of the large quantity of textile production equipment recovered from Flixborough, however, indicates that the community included specialist weavers who produced fine cloth—both linen and wool—during the later eighth to mid ninth centuries, when the settlement was probably monastic (see Chapter 3). While little if any of this material could be associated with specific buildings, when considered together with the animal bone evidence, it 'suggests production...of a fine textile on a larger scale than seen previously', possibly for export (Loveluck and Walton Rogers 2007, 102). It should be noted that at this same period, Frisian cloth was being widely traded and high-quality textiles have been recovered from a number of settlements along the Frisian coast (for example, at Hessens, Wulf 1991).

Nevertheless, less spinning and weaving equipment is recovered from Mid and Late Saxon rural settlements than from those of the earlier period, despite the fact that the age and sex profiles of sheep bones from these sites point to the increasing importance of wool production precisely in these later centuries. It appears, however, that artefacts from rural settlements relating to non-agrarian production in general declines somewhat during the same period. Changes in the patterns of deposition of archaeological material and, in particular, the gradual disappearance of *Grubenhäuser* and their artefact-rich fills may account for some of this apparent trend. Nevertheless, the development of formal markets, together with a shift of non-agrarian production away from ordinary farms to monasteries, *emporia*, and towns, where crafts became increasingly the preserve of specialists, must also be part of the explanation (Thomas 2011a).

Cattle

As with sheep, the overall age profile for cattle in animal bone assemblages from Mid Saxon settlements points to a greater emphasis on mature animals, i.e. those three years and over (Sykes 2006, 58). This pattern would be consistent with an increasing demand for plough oxen. Some limited evidence also exists, however, for specialist cattle rearing; the age profile of the cattle bones from Pennyland, for example, suggests that farmers here were at least partly engaged in rearing cattle for beef and hides. Unlike the cattle consumed in the *emporia* and estate centres—the overwhelming majority of which had served out a full working life in the countryside—some 70 per cent of those at Pennyland had been culled by the age of three, that is, on reaching their full weight (Bourdillon 1988; Williams 1993). A similar pattern may be apparent at West Fen Road, Ely, where many cattle were again slaughtered at the optimum age for beef (Mortimer et al. 2005). The Mid Saxon faunal assemblage from Quarrington indicates that at least 40 per cent of cattle were culled in their third year, as 'prime' beef animals, in contrast to the less structured slaughter patterns apparent for the early Saxon phase at the same site (Taylor 2003b, 263–5). The age profile of the animals slaughtered and the large quantity of cattle 'waste' bones recovered from a ninth-century site at the Treasury in London indicate that this too was a farm where some slaughter and marketing of dressed meat took place (probably to provision the inhabitants of the *emporium* of *Lundenwic*), as well as the rearing of animals for marketing on the hoof (Cowie and Blackmore 2008, 90–100). An alternative view of this material which illustrates the complexities of interpreting such data sees the Treasury site as a royal vill which both collected and redistributed food renders (Cowie 2004).

In addition to their obvious economic importance, it should also be remembered that written sources and linguistic evidence demonstrate that cattle possessed a particularly high social value and played an important role in the political economy of Anglo-Saxon England, notably in feasting (as the deposit of ox skulls and long bones at Yeavering appears to confirm; see Chapter 4).[17] Indeed, cattle were widely used as a unit of account and medium of payment in the Roman and Germanic Iron Age in north-west Europe, as well as in early medieval Ireland (Hamerow 2002a, 129; Tipper 2004, 151; McCormick 2008).

Pigs

Despite the large numbers of pigs which, to judge from contemporary written sources, roamed the Anglo-Saxon countryside, pig generally makes up a relatively small proportion of the animal bones recovered from settlements, and recent isotopic analyses suggest that pigs were 'not the major animal resource' for most Anglo-Saxon communities (Clutton Brock 1976, 378; Hull and O'Connell 2011, 673). It is likely, however, that pigs are under-represented in archaeological deposits due to the fact that they were generally killed off for meat as soon as they reached their full size and the bones of young animals do not survive as well as those of fully mature ones. There is also evidence to suggest that pig meat was sometimes processed off-site (Taylor 2003b, 271). There are, nevertheless, indications that pork may have become at least somewhat more important in the Mid to Late Saxon period. At Cottenham, the proportion of pig increased sharply from 9 per cent during the Mid Saxon period to 22 per cent during the Late Saxon phases (Mortimer 2000, 16–17); pigs were roughly as numerous as sheep at both Wolverton Turn and West Cotton (Preston 2004; Robinson, unpublished), while at Late Saxon Wraysbury (Berkshire) pig was the second most important meat animal after cattle (Astill and Lobb 1989). At Late Saxon Portchester, pig bones were actually more numerous than cattle bones, and it has been estimated that pigs would have supplied around

---

[17] A further indication of this may be the fact that they are the most common species found in placed deposits in rural settlements (see Chapter 4; Hamerow 2006).

20 per cent of the meat consumed (Grant 1976, 284). At Wicken Bonhunt, over 100,000 animal bones dating to the Mid Saxon period revealed an exceptionally high proportion of pig—around 70 per cent of the identifiable large domestic animals (based on NISP).[18] This, combined with a high percentage of cranial elements, has led to the suggestion that the occupants of the settlement specialized in pork production and that the dressed carcasses of pigs slaughtered at Wicken Bonhunt were consumed elsewhere (Crabtree 1996a, 63; Crabtree 2010). The mortality profiles at both Wicken Bonhunt and Flixborough point, furthermore, to a highly structured cull of pigs, in the case of Flixborough at around 20 and 32 months (Loveluck 2007, 89).

The evidence for more focused, closely managed animal husbandry, geared towards producing both primary and secondary products, is thus clear.[19] It seems unlikely that this can be entirely accounted for by the need to provision the populations of the *emporia*; indeed, there is as yet relatively little evidence for intensification, specialization, or expansion of crop and animal husbandry in the immediate hinterlands of these trading settlements (Hamerow 2007). High-status secular and religious communities such as those at Yeavering, Eynsham, and Flixborough would also have drawn upon a system of tribute which probably encouraged a degree of specialization or intensification, evidence for which comes not only from animal bones, but also indirectly from the creation of hay meadows and the increasing importance of oats (see above; Hooke 1998, 133). Monastic estates could, furthermore, support very large herds of cattle. The Lindisfarne Gospels, produced in Northumbria *c.*700, famously required 127 calf-skins to complete, while the *Codex Amiatinus*, one of three complete Bibles produced slightly earlier at the twinned monasteries of Monkwearmouth and Jarrow, required over 500 (Bruce-Mitford 1969, 2; Brown 1991, 47).[20] Such communities—unlike those in the *emporia*—would have been in direct contact with meat producers and thus have had access to a greater variety of foods and more palatable meat, as the faunal assemblages from settlements such as Eynsham, Brandon, and Flixborough attest.

Animal bones and status

The debate regarding whether settlements of high status can be recognized by means of a distinctive material culture (see Chapter 3) is paralleled by disagree-

---

[18] Anglo-Saxon faunal remains found beneath the medieval chapter house at St Albans Abbey also contained a very high proportion of pig (Crabtree 2010).

[19] A small number of settlements may even have specialized in horse breeding. At Yarnton, horse bones accounted for 10% of the bones from the Late Saxon phase, while at Wolverton Turn they made up over 11% of the main domesticates calculated by NISP, significantly higher than on most settlements of this period (Preston 2004; Mulville and Ayres 2004, table 18.16). The fact that the remains from Wolverton Turn derive from very young as well as mature animals indicates that horses were actually reared at the settlement.

[20] Gameson, however, warns against over-estimating the cost of producing such manuscripts (1992).

ment over whether a distinctively high-status faunal assemblage can be identified. A high proportion of pork consumption, for example, is regarded by some specialists, but by no means all, as an indicator of wealth and status since pigs are reared purely for meat (e.g. Hardy et al. 2003, 360; Albarella 2006; Loveluck 2007, 89). Less contentious is the argument that a higher than average percentage of wild animals—above all, deer—is an indicator of high status. The percentage of game in Anglo-Saxon animal bone assemblages is usually tiny, and hunting, as elsewhere in north-west Europe, played only a small role in early medieval subsistence strategies. The social value of wild animals such as red deer, boar, beaver, and bear, as attested by their appearance in the literature, images, and amulets of the period, was nevertheless considerable. Already by the Mid Saxon period, a higher than average percentage of game together with a generally varied meat diet appears to have been a marker of privilege, with high-status settlements producing around 2.5 per cent game bones, compared with around 0.5 per cent from ordinary rural settlements and towns (Hardy et al. 2003, 359–60; Sykes 2007; Sykes 2010).[21] By the Late Saxon period, the community at Bishopstone enjoyed a diet which included not only mutton, pork, and beef—much of it from young animals—but also chicken, goose, fish, deer, hare, boar, and even whale (Poole 2010).

A near-complete skeleton of the earliest peregrine falcon found in Britain comes from Brandon, and is broadly contemporary with the earliest written evidence for falconry in England (Crabtree, forthcoming). The same site also yielded the remains of a range of wild birds, including species such as crane which could have been hunted using falcons, although Crabtree has concluded that the presence of wild birds is not necessarily 'a signature of a high-status site'. She makes the further important point that species diversity is closely related to sample size, i.e. the larger the assemblage, the greater the identified diversity is likely to be (ibid.). Sykes has also argued that the exploitation of wild birds per se was not an indicator of status prior to the mid ninth century, although hawking was (Sykes 2004, 99).

---

[21] Naomi Sykes has also suggested that some communities may have signalled their high status by consuming more sheep in regions where cattle predominated, and vice versa (2006, 65).

6

Production, exchange, and the shape of rural communities

A theme which has been central to this volume is the changing relationship between production and exchange—in short, who produced what for whom—and the impact of this changing relationship on Anglo-Saxon settlements and the material culture associated with them. Indeed, as the preceding chapters have sought to illustrate, once communities emerged which consumed foodstuffs and goods produced by the labour of others and, conversely, once many ordinary households no longer produced solely for their own consumption, the archaeological signature associated with rural settlements changed in a number of important ways.

Perhaps the most obvious of these changes is the growing prominence, from broadly the mid seventh century onwards, of enclosures and boundaries. These developed in tandem with new crop and animal husbandry regimes, as greater political stability brought with it a growing emphasis on arable over pastoral farming and hence more stable settlements. These changes point to an increasingly specialized use of the landscape, particularly in eastern and southern England, regions which were, for much of the Anglo-Saxon period, wealthier and more commercially active than the rest of the country.[1] The increased investment by farming communities in the construction of extensive systems of enclosures and droveways needs, furthermore, to be seen against a wider backdrop of growing investment by elites—perhaps initially by monasteries, whose wealth peaked between the mid seventh and mid eighth centuries—in new technologies and 'capital projects' such as watermills, river canalization, and causeways from the Mid Saxon period onwards (Blair 2007; Brunning 2010).[2] The considerable effort devoted to the construction and maintenance of

---

[1] While much of the evidence cited in Chapter 5 comes from southern and eastern England, it can be argued, based on palaeoenvironmental evidence, that the south-west too saw a 'significant and widespread intensification in land use' around the eighth century (Rippon 2010).

[2] Increased investment in the exploitation of natural resources generally is also evident from the large-scale construction in eastern England, perhaps by monastic communities, of fish traps from the Mid Saxon period onwards (Murphy 2010).

droveways and enclosures is, of course, also linked to the expansion of arable, the introduction of hay meadows, and the increasing use of the heavy plough and of open fields, all of which would have required the movement of livestock to be more closely controlled.

As Stephen Rippon has recently pointed out, such investment in agrarian production may have been encouraged by the introduction of 'bookland', whereby land was granted by the king to religious institutions from the later seventh century, and to secular lords from the later eighth, essentially unburdened and in perpetuity, to be passed on to whomever the owner chose (Rippon 2010).[3] While not all estates were held as 'bookland', the security and stability afforded by the perpetual, unrestricted ownership of estates must have encouraged investment in landed production; the planting of vines and orchards, for example, suggests investment in future productivity, while the construction of watermills, and even of malting ovens of the kind seen at Higham Ferrers, represented major capital investments that the owners would presumably want to keep 'in the family'. The fragmentation of estates in the later Saxon period would, furthermore, have encouraged more intensive use of ever smaller units of land (Rippon 2010; Faith 1997, 153–9).[4]

At least some of the enclosures and boundaries within and around settlements must also reflect new social relations between lords and peasants, with some enclosed plots being associated with the holding of land in return for rent. Settlements such as Cottenham and Ely could, indeed, be early examples of settlements that were divided into measured units to facilitate assessment, although it is of course impossible to be certain of this. Indeed, the rise of secular and religious landowning elites—who remained rural for most of the Anglo-Saxon period—is one of the key forces that can be seen to have shaped settlements. One question which requires not only further research but also a new conceptual approach is why seemingly 'high-status' settlements so dominate the archaeological record of the Mid and Late Saxon periods, and why the farms and dwellings of ordinary farmers appear to have lacked the kind of complex, durable, and visually distinctive material culture which makes their fifth- to seventh-century predecessors so readily recognizable to archaeologists.

---

[3] Another possible factor, though not one hitherto considered in this volume, is the possibility that more stable climatic conditions post c.700—i.e. mild, humid summers—may have helped to make arable agriculture more profitable, as appears to have been the case elsewhere in north-west Europe, to judge from tree-ring evidence and eye-witness accounts of climatic conditions (Büntgen et al. 2011).

[4] The fact that much of the evidence for innovation and intensification of agricultural production comes from settlements either known or presumed to be of high status, raises the question of whether these developments should be regarded as essentially a 'top–down' process, whereby monastic and secular estate centres were the source of such innovation. It could be argued that only such communities would have had the resources, power, and contacts to undertake initiatives and implement new technologies (cf. van der Veen 2010, 6). Nevertheless, a 'bottom–up' process may also have been at work, and we cannot assume that settlements with extensive networks of enclosures such as Cardinal Park, Cottenham, Warmington, and Wolverton Turn were, for example, parts of monastic estates.

A degree of stabilization and nucleation of settlement also appears to be a feature of the Mid Saxon period, although again, this is a process more readily identifiable in some regions than others. In a paper published in 1991, I argued that a widespread shift and nucleation in settlement as early as the seventh century was unlikely. Instead, evidence (deriving mostly from field surveys and investigations into Deserted Medieval Villages) appeared to indicate that any widespread nucleation and stabilization of settlement associated with open-field farming was unlikely to have begun earlier than the late eighth or ninth century (Hamerow 1991, 16–17). More recently, however, archaeology has yielded clear evidence for a horizon of settlement reorganization during what has been referred to as the 'long eighth century', namely the period between c.670 and 830. This period—traditionally conceptualized as a 'dark age' but now seen as exceptionally dynamic in both economic and political terms across much of Europe (Hansen and Wickham 2000)—appears to have been pivotal in village formation. Mid Saxon settlements such as Cottenham, Warmington, and West Fen Road, Ely, may not always have occupied exactly the same footprints or have adopted the same layouts as their Saxo-Norman successors, but they can nonetheless reasonably be described as 'nucleated'.

Increased stabilization is also reflected in the changing life-cycles of timber buildings. Following a pattern familiar from later prehistory, early Anglo-Saxon houses appear to have been abandoned or dismantled after roughly one generation, perhaps upon the death of a key member of the household, with relatively little effort made to extend the life of organic, earth-fast structures whose main supporting posts were prone to rotting. Many of the structures associated with Mid Saxon settlements such as Cottenham and Ely also appear to have been ephemeral, even by the standards of the earlier period; yet some buildings were, from the seventh century onwards, clearly multi-generational, with the increased effort invested in repairing and rebuilding them, transforming them into quasi-permanent 'monuments' which could evoke links with important ancestors.

Changing relations with the ancestors are also apparent in the evolving spatial relationship between the communities of the living and the dead. The mortuary landscape of Mid to Late Saxon England was highly variable and remains relatively poorly understood. It is nevertheless clear that in some cases, the dead were buried in close association with particular settlements and sometimes—as at Flixborough and Gamlingay—with particular buildings. Bloodmoor Hill and Yarnton provide excellent examples of what future research into such burials could potentially reveal about the changing dynamics between settlements and cemeteries and about the definition of 'community' in this period. The possibility that the closer spatial relationship between settlement and burials is related to the more intensive and specialized use of the farmed landscape already alluded to also demands further investigation; so too does the suggestion that there was a growing tension between traditional belief systems concerning the relationship between kin groups and the local landscape on the one hand, and Christian ideology on the other.

Local and extended kin groups remained, of course, the essential unit of production throughout the Anglo-Saxon period. Indeed, it could be argued that, in some respects, the archaeology of rural settlements points to a growing 'localism' in the later Saxon period, with regional variation in building styles, settlement forms, and land use emerging more clearly and in tandem with other localized practices, for example, the development of regionally distinctive pottery wares. The large-scale, co-operative enterprises being undertaken by farmers in many parts of the country from the late seventh century onwards—whatever the driving forces behind them—must, furthermore, have reshaped relationships and contributed to the formation of a distinct social identity (Astill 2009, 227). Community identity would, first and foremost, naturally have been associated with a particular settlement and its fields—indeed, it is not always easy to distinguish settlement boundaries from field enclosures in the complex rectilinear systems so characteristic of this period. Nevertheless, as production became increasingly geared towards those living in other communities, a growing awareness of more distant markets and centres, both secular and religious, must also have developed.

In this way, not only did the internal structures of peasant communities begin to change, but so too did their relationship to the wider world. This brings us to another central feature of the Mid and Late Saxon periods, namely the rising power of market-based exchange. Such exchange was, of course, underpinned by the agricultural surpluses yielded by the wide-ranging developments in crop and animal husbandry reviewed in Chapter 5. The substantially increased investment of labour and material capital that these developments imply would have been in response to a variety of factors, including the need to supply rents in kind—*feorm*—to monastic and secular landlords (Faith 1999) and to feed the populations of the *emporia*, as well as, in all likelihood, a growing population generally.

At least as important, however, were the new opportunities presented by emerging markets, not only in the coastal *emporia* but also in secondary inland markets of a kind that is being recognized in ever increasing numbers (Pestell and Ulmschneider 2003). More specialized land use, in turn, would have encouraged and perhaps even necessitated increased exchange between communities. It enabled the first post-Roman mass-production of certain commodities, reflected in the presence in Mid and Late Saxon settlements of exotic, if mundane, items such as pottery and quernstones imported from the Rhineland and the growing access to medium- and long-distance trade networks that these imply. Such networks come much more clearly into focus from the late seventh century onwards, thanks to the widespread circulation across much of England of the small silver coins known as sceattas, estimated to have been minted in their millions, as well as the mass-produced, wheel-turned pottery known as Ipswich Ware; the latter must have been distributed by a highly efficient marketing system, to judge from its near-ubiquity in East Anglian settlements, particularly in Norfolk (Wade 1988, 95–6; Metcalf 1993–4; Scull 1997, 277–8; Blinkhorn 1999; Palmer 2003). The fact that sceattas were being used and lost by members of so many different communities clearly indicates that, in large parts of Mid Saxon England, coinage was thoroughly integrated into the rural economy, in contrast to Scandinavia and Frisia, where it was used almost exclusively by those engaged in long-distance trade (Metcalf 1996, 406–7).[5]

It will be all too apparent that the tentative attempts made here to link the archaeological remains of settlements and buildings with the realities of household and community dynamics leave many questions unanswered. If future research is to move beyond these first steps, a number of methodological challenges in addition to those already mentioned need to be addressed. There is a pressing need for the results of site-based settlement archaeology, of the kind which forms the focus of this volume, to be more fully integrated with studies of the wider farmed landscape in order to gain a holistic view of the Anglo-Saxon agrarian system. Important steps in this direction have recently been taken (Rippon 2008; Banham and Faith, forthcoming).

More work also needs to be done to clarify the distinction between 'rural' and 'urban' settlement forms in the ninth to eleventh centuries, a period which saw what could be described as a manorial landscape emerge in parallel with towns. The difficulties of distinguishing between urban and rural have already been touched upon in Chapter 3 in relation to settlements such as Steyning and West Fen Road, Ely. The question also arises, however, in relation to certain building types: what, if any, link existed between the kind of *Grubenhäuser* found in rural settlements, virtually none of which can be securely dated to after *c*.750, and those—generally rectangular, deep, and with perpendicular sides—which date primarily to the tenth and eleventh centuries and are found exclusively in towns and a small number of settlements which have been described as 'incipient minster towns' such as Bampton (Oxfordshire) and, again, Steyning (Blair 2005, 337; Tipper 2004, 11–14)? Might even the type and density of pits found within a 'rural' settlement point to some elements of an 'urban' lifestyle (Thomas 2010, 208–9)?

Regional variation in settlement form remains poorly understood. In particular, we need to understand why it remains so difficult to identify rural settlements for so much of this period in the south-west and north-west of England, regions which appear to lack pre-Conquest nucleated villages. The underlying cause probably lies in the Roman period, for it is striking how closely the dis-

---

[5] It has, for example, been suggested that concentrations in Oxfordshire and Dorset of a type of sceatta probably minted in Frisia might reflect direct purchases of wool by merchants using Frisian money in the middle of the eighth century (Metcalf 2003, 41–7 in Pestell and Ulmschneider).

tribution of early and mid Anglo-Saxon settlements mirrors that of Romano-British villas, and contrasts with that of the roundhouse settlements of the same period (see Taylor 2007, fig. 4.7). But how should we explain this? Could the near-absence of settlements readily datable to the Anglo-Saxon period in the north-west and south-west be due to the continuing persistence in these regions of 'essentially Iron Age architectural forms' well into the post-Roman centuries (ibid. 31)? It is certainly possible that the small, dispersed farmsteads and settlements of these regions reflect many centuries of less specialized, more autarkic, forms of land management.

Finally, although the pace of change in rural production and exchange from *c.*650 onwards was truly remarkable, the chronology of these changes still requires closer calibration. Only with a more precise chronology will it be possible, for example, to demonstrate (or disprove) Moreland's contention that increased investment in agrarian production began *before* the establishment of the first Anglo-Saxon *emporia* (Moreland 2000, 97). All we can say at the moment is that the first signs of increased production coincide broadly with the period of the foundation of specialized trading settlements, as appears to have been the case elsewhere within the North Sea Zone (Hamerow 2002a). In this respect and many others it is now clear, despite differences of detail, that the broad pattern of intensification and innovation in land use seen in England during the 'long eighth century' fits within a wider pattern apparent in north-west Europe, extending from southern Scandinavia to the northern Frankish world.

Questions such as those posed here will not be easily answered. Yet, as this volume has tried to show, settlement archaeology offers a unique window onto the lives of the rural communities of Anglo-Saxon England. There is every reason to hope that, as the settlement record grows in variety and richness, it will offer new perspectives on, and new understandings of, these lost communities.

Bibliography

Addyman, P. (1964), 'A Dark Age settlement at Maxey, Northants', *Medieval Archaeology*, 8: 20–73.
——(1972), 'The Anglo-Saxon house: a new review', *Anglo-Saxon England*, 1: 273–308.
——and Leigh, D. (1973), 'The Anglo-Saxon village at Chalton, Hampshire: second interim report', *Medieval Archaeology*, 17: 1–25.
—— Leigh, D., and Hughes, M. (1972), 'Anglo-Saxon houses at Chalton, Hampshire', *Medieval Archaeology*, 16: 13–32.
Albarella, U. (2006), 'Pig husbandry and pork consumption in medieval England', in C. Woolgar, D. Serjeantson, and T. Waldron (eds), *Food in Medieval England: Diet and Nutrition* (Oxford: Oxford University Press), 72–87.
Alcock, L. (1982), 'Cadbury-Camelot: a fifteen-year perspective', *Proc. British Academy*, LXVIII: 355–88.
——(1988), *Bede, Eddius and the Forts of the North Britons* (Jarrow Lecture, Jarrow: St Paul's Church).
Andrews, P. (1996), 'Hurst Park, East Molesey, Surrey: riverside settlement and burial from the Neolithic to the Early Saxon periods', in P. Andrews and A. Crockett, *Three Excavations Along the Thames and its Tributaries* (Salisbury: Wessex Archaeology).
——(1997), *Excavations at Hamwic*. Volume 2: *Excavations at Six Dials* (York: Council for British Archaeology).
——Biddulph, E., and Hardy, A. (2011), *Settling the Ebbsfleet Valley: CTRL Excavations at Springhead and Northfleet, Kent*. Volume 1: *The Sites* (Salisbury: Wessex Archaeology).
Astill, G. (2009), 'Anglo-Saxon attitudes: how should post-AD 700 burials be interpreted?', in D. Sayer and H. Williams (eds), *Mortuary Practices and Social Identities in the Middle Ages* (Exeter: Exeter University Press), 222–35.
——and Lobb, S. (1989), 'Excavations of prehistoric, Roman and Saxon deposits at Wraysbury, Berkshire', *The Archaeological Journal*, 146: 68–134.
Atkins, R., and Connor, A. (2010), *Farmers and Ironsmiths: Prehistoric, Roman and Anglo-Saxon settlement beside Brandon Road, Thetford, Norfolk* (Bar Hill: Oxford Archaeology East).
Audouy, M., and Chapman, A. (2009), *Raunds: The Origin and Growth of a Midland Village AD 450–1500* (Oxford: Oxbow).
——Dix, B., and Parsons, D. (1995), 'The tower of All Saints' Church, Earls Barton, Northamptonshire: its construction and context', *The Archaeological Journal*, 152: 73–94.
Ballantyne, R. (2010), 'Charred and mineralized biota', in G. Thomas, *The Later Anglo-Saxon Settlement at Bishopstone* (York: Council for British Archaeology), 164–76.
Banham, D. (2010), '"In the sweat of thy brow shalt thou eat bread": cereals and cereal production in the Anglo-Saxon landscape', in N. Higham and M. Ryan (eds), *The Landscape Archaeology of Anglo-Saxon England* (Woodbridge: The Boydell Press), 174–92.

Banham, D. and Faith, R. (forthcoming), *Anglo-Saxon Farms and Farmers* (Oxford: Oxford University Press).

Barber, A., and Watts, M. (2006), 'Excavations at Saxon's Lode Farm, Ryall Quarry, Ripple, 2002: Romano-British and Anglo-Saxon rural settlement in the Severn Valley', Unpublished Report, Cotswold Archaeology.

Barford, P. (2002), *Excavations at Little Oakley, Essex 1951–78: Roman Villa and Saxon Settlement*, East Anglian Archaeology 98 (Chelmsford: Essex County Council, Heritage Conservation Planning Division).

Barker, P. (1977), *The Technique of Archaeological Excavation* (New York: Universe Books).

Barnwell, P. (1996), '"Hlafeata, ceorl, hid and scir": Celtic, Roman or Germanic?', *Anglo-Saxon Studies in Archaeology and History*, 9: 53–62.

Barton, K. (1962), 'Settlements of the Iron Age and Pagan Saxon periods at Linford, Essex', *Transactions of the Essex Archaeological Society*, 3rd ser. 1: 57–102.

Bassett, S. (1989), 'In search of the origins of Anglo-Saxon kingdoms', in S. Bassett (ed.), *The Origins of Anglo-Saxon Kingdoms* (Leicester: Leicester University Press), 3–27.

Bateman, C., Enright, D., and Oakey, N. (2003), 'Prehistoric and Anglo-Saxon settlements to the rear of Sherborne House, Lechlade: excavations in 1997', *Transactions of the Bristol and Gloucestershire Archaeological Society*, 121: 64–5.

Beresford, G. (1987), *Goltho: The Development of an Early Medieval Manor, c 850–1150* (London: Historic Buildings and Monuments Commission).

Bettess, F. (1991), 'The Anglo-Saxon foot: a computerized assessment', *Medieval Archaeology*, 35: 44–50.

Blair, J. (1993), 'Hall and chamber: English domestic planning, 1000–1250', in G. Meirion-Jones and M. Jones (eds), *Manorial Domestic Buildings in England and Northern France* (London: Society of Antiquaries), 1–20.

——(1994), *Anglo-Saxon Oxfordshire* (Stroud: Alan Sutton).

——(1995), 'Anglo-Saxon pagan shrines and their prototypes', *Anglo-Saxon Studies in Archaeology and History*, 8: 1–28.

——(1996), 'Palaces or minsters? Northampton and Cheddar reconsidered', *Anglo-Saxon England*, 25: 97–121.

——(2005), *The Church in Anglo-Saxon Society* (Oxford: Oxford University Press).

——(2007), 'Introduction', in J. Blair (ed.), *Waterways and Canal-Building in Medieval England* (Oxford: Oxford University Press), 1–20.

——(2011), 'Flixborough revisited', *Anglo-Saxon Studies in Archaeology and History*, 17: 101-108.

Blinkhorn, P. (1999), 'Of cabbages and kings: production, trade and consumption in middle-Saxon England', in M. Anderton (ed.), *Anglo-Saxon Trading Centres: Beyond the Emporia* (Glasgow: Cruithne Press), 4–23.

Blockley, K., Blockley, M., Blockley, P., Frere, S. S., and Stow, S. (1995), *Excavations in the Marlowe Car Park and Surrounding Areas* (Canterbury: Canterbury Archaeological Trust).

Boddington, A. (1990), 'Models of burial, settlement and worship: the Final Phase reviewed', in E. Southworth (ed.), *Anglo-Saxon Cemeteries: A Reappraisal* (Stroud: Alan Sutton Publishing), 177–99.

——(1996), *Raunds Furnells: The Anglo-Saxon Church and Churchyard* (London: English Heritage).

Böhme, H. W. (ed.) (1991), *Siedlungen und Landesausbau zur Salierzeit Teil 1* (Sigmaringen: Thorbecke Verlag).

Booth, P., Evans J., and Hiller, J. (2001), *Excavations in the Extramural Settlement of Roman Alchester, Oxfordshire, 1991* (Oxford: Oxford Archaeology).

——Dodd, A., Robinson, M., and Smith, A. (2007), *Thames Through Time: The Archaeology of the Gravel Terraces of the Upper and Middle Thames, The Early Historical Period* (Oxford: Oxford Archaeology).

Boulter, S. (2003), 'Flixton Park Quarry: a royal estate of the first Anglo-Saxon kings?', *Current Archaeology*, 187: 280–5.

——(2006), *An Assessment of the Archaeology Recorded in Flixton Park Quarry*, Unpublished assessment report of the Suffolk County Council Archaeological Service.

Bourdieu, P. (1990), *The Logic of Practice* (Cambridge: Polity Press).

Bourdillon, J. (1988), 'Countryside and town: the animal resources of Saxon Southampton', in D. Hooke (ed.), *Anglo-Saxon Settlements* (Oxford: Blackwell), 176–96.

——(2006), 'The animal bones', in Williams and Newman, *Market Lavington*, 150–69.

Boyle, A. (2004), 'The Human Burials', in Hey (ed.), *Yarnton*, 317–21.

Bradley, R. (1980), 'Anglo-Saxon cemeteries: some suggestions for research', in P. Rahtz, T. Dickinson, and L. Watts (eds), *Anglo-Saxon Cemeteries*, BAR British Series 82 (Oxford: British Archaeological Reports), 171–8.

——(1987), 'Time regained: the creation of continuity', *Journal of the British Archaeological Association*, 140: 1–17.

——(1992), 'The excavation of an oval barrow beside the Abingdon Causewayed Enclosures, Oxfordshire', *Proc. of the Prehistoric Society*, 58: 127–42.

——(2002), *The Past in Prehistoric Societies* (London: Routledge).

——(2005), *Ritual and Domestic Life in Prehistoric Europe* (London and New York: Routledge).

——(2006), 'Bridging two cultures—commercial archaeology and the study of prehistoric Britain', *The Antiquaries Journal*, 86: 1–13.

Brodribb, A. (1968), *Excavations at Shakenoak Farm, near Wilcote, Oxfordshire* (Oxford: A. R. Hands).

——Hands, A., and Walker, D. (1972), *Excavations at Shakenoak III* (Oxford: privately printed).

————(1973), *Excavations at Shakenoak IV* (Oxford: privately printed).

————(1978), *Excavations at Shakenoak V* (Oxford: British Archaeological Reports).

Brooks, N. (1989), 'The creation and early structure of the kingdom of Kent', in Bassett (ed.), *Origins of Anglo-Saxon Kingdoms*, 55–74.

Brown, B., Knocker, G., Smedley, N., and West, S. (1954), 'Excavations at Grimstone End, Pakenham', *Proc. Suffolk Institute of Archaeology*, XXVI/3: 188–207.

Brown, M. (1991), *Anglo-Saxon Manuscripts* (London: The British Library).

Bruce-Mitford, R. (1969), 'The art of the Codex Amiatinus', *Journal of the British Archaeol. Assoc.*, 3rd ser. 32: 1–25.

Bruce-Mitford, R. (1997), *Mawgan Porth: A Settlement of the Late Saxon Period on the North Cornish Coast* (London: English Heritage).

Brück, J. (1999), 'Houses, lifecycles and deposition on Middle Bronze Age settlements in southern England', *Proc. of the Prehistoric Society*, 65: 1–22.

Brugmann, B. (2007), *Aspects of Anglo-Saxon Inhumation Burial: Morning Thorpe, Spong Hill, Bergh Apton and Westgarth Gardens, East Anglian Archaeology*, 119 (Dereham: Norfolk Museums Service).

Brunning, R. (2010), 'Taming the floodplain: river canalisation and causeway formation in the Middle Anglo-Saxon period at Glastonbury, Somerset', *Medieval Archaeology*, 54: 319–29.

Büntgen, U., Tegel, W., Nicolussi, K., McCormick, M., Frank, D., Trouet, V., Kaplan, J., Herzig, F., and Heussner, K.-U. (2011), '2500 years of European climate variability and human susceptibility', *Sciencexpress*, hwww.sciencexpress.org/13 January 2011.

Butler, C. (2000), *Saxon Settlement and Earlier Remains at Friars Oak, Hassocks, West Sussex*, BAR British Series 295 (Oxford: British Archaeological Reports).

Campbell, G. (1994), 'The preliminary archaeobotanical results from Anglo-Saxon West Cotton and Raunds', in J. Rackham (ed.), *Environment and Economy in Anglo-Saxon England* (York: Council for British Archaeology), 65–82.

Carr, R., Tester, A., and Murphy, P. (1988), 'The Middle-Saxon settlement at Staunch Meadow, Brandon', *Antiquity*, 62/235: 371–6.

Caruth, J. (1996), 'Hewlett Packard, Whitehouse Industrial Estate', *Proc. Suffolk Institute of Archaeology and History*, XXXVIII/4: 476–9.

——(2005), 'RAF Lakenheath: excavations 1987–2005: assessment report', Unpublished report of the Suffolk Archaeological Unit.

Carver, M., Hills, C., and Scheschkewitz, J. (2009), *Wasperton: A Roman, British and Anglo-Saxon Community in Central England* (Woodbridge: Boydell).

Chambers, R. (1988), 'The late- and sub-Roman cemetery at Queenford Farm, Dorchester-on-Thames, Oxon.', *Oxoniensia*, 52: 35–70.

——and McAdam, E. (2007), *Excavations at Radley Barrow Hills, Oxfordshire. Volume 2: The Romano-British Cemetery and Anglo-Saxon Settlement* (Oxford: Oxford Archaeology).

Champion, T. (1977), 'Chalton', *Current Archaeology*, 59: 364–9.

Chapman, A. (2010), *West Cotton, Raunds: A Study of Medieval Settlement Dynamics, AD 450–1450: Excavation of a Deserted Medieval Hamlet in Northamptonshire, 1985–89* (Oxford: Oxbow Books; Oakville, Conn.: David Brown Book Co.).

Chapman, J. (2000), *Fragmentation in Archaeology: People, Places and Broken Objects in the Prehistory of South Eastern Europe* (London: Routledge).

Charles-Edwards, T. (1972), 'Kinship, status and the origins of the Hide', *Past and Present*, 56: 3–33.

——(1976), 'Boundaries in Irish law', in P. Sawyer (ed.), *Medieval Settlement: Continuity and Change* (London: Edward Arnold), 83–7.

Chester-Kadwell, M. (2009), *Early Anglo-Saxon Communities in the Landscape of Norfolk*, BAR British Series 481 (Oxford: British Archaeological Reports).

Clutton-Brock, J. (1976), 'The animal resources', in D. Wilson (ed.), *The Archaeology of Anglo-Saxon England* (Cambridge: Cambridge University Press), 373–92.

Coggins, D. (2004), 'Simy Folds: twenty years on', in Hines et al. (eds), *Land, Sea and Home*, 324–34.

Colgrave, B., and Mynors, R. (1969), *Bede's Ecclesiastical History of the English People* (Oxford: Clarendon Press).

Cowie, R. (2004), 'The evidence for royal sites in Middle Anglo-Saxon London', *Medieval Archaeology*, 48: 201–8.

——and Blackmore, L. (2008), *Early and Middle Saxon Rural Settlement in the London Region* (London: Museum of London Archaeology Service).

Crabtree, P. (1990), *West Stow: Early Anglo-Saxon Animal Husbandry,East Anglian Archaeology* 47 (Ipswich: Suffolk County Planning Department).

——(1994), 'Animal exploitation in East Anglian villages', in Rackham (ed.), *Environment and Economy*, 40–54.

——(1996a), 'Production and consumption in an early complex society: animal use in Middle Saxon East Anglia', *World Archaeology*, 28: 58–75.

——(1996b), 'The wool trade and the rise of urbanism in Middle Saxon England', in B. Wailes (ed.), *Craft Specialization and Social Evolution* (Philadelphia: University Museum Publications), 99–105.

——(2010), 'Agricultural innovation and socio-economic change in early medieval Europe: evidence from Britain and France', *World Archaeology*, 42/1: 122–36.

——(forthcoming), 'Hunting in early and middle Anglo-Saxon East Anglia'.

Cramp, R. (1957), 'Beowulf and archaeology', *Medieval Archaeology*, 1: 57–77.

Crawford, S. (1993), 'Children, death and the afterlife in Anglo-Saxon England', *Anglo-Saxon Studies in Archaeology and History*, 6: 83–92.

——(1999), *Childhood in Anglo-Saxon England* (Stroud: Sutton Publishing).

——(2008), 'Special burials, special buildings? An Anglo-Saxon perspective on the interpretation of infant burials in association with rural settlement structures', in K. Bacvarov (ed.), *Babies Reborn: Infant/Child Burials in Pre- and Protohistory*, BAR International Series, 1832 (Oxford: British Archaeological Reports), 197–204.

Crewe, V. (2009), 'The appropriation of prehistoric monuments in early to middle Anglo-Saxon Settlements', *Medieval Settlement Research Group Annual Report* 23: 1–8.

Crowson, A., Lane, T., Penn, K., and Trimble, D. (2005), *Anglo-Saxon Settlement on the Siltland of Eastern England* (Sleaford: Heritage Trust of Lincolnshire).

Cunliffe, B. (1976), *Excavations at Portchester Castle. Volume II: Saxon* (London: Society of Antiquaries).

——and Poole, C. (1995), 'Pits and propitiation', in B. Cunliffe, *Danebury: An Iron Age Hillfort in Hampshire. Vol. 6: A Hillfort Community in Perspective* (London: Council for British Archaeology), 80–6.

————(2000), *The Danebury Environs Programme: The Prehistory of a Wessex Landscape. Houghton Down, Stockbridge, Hants. 1994* (OUCA Monograph No. 49, Oxford: Oxford University Committee for Archaeology).

Damminger, F. (1998), 'Dwellings, settlement and settlement patterns in Merovingian south-west Germany', in I. Wood (ed.), *Franks and Alamanni in the Merovingian Period* (Woodbridge: Boydell Press), 33–88.

Daniels, R. (1989), 'The Anglo-Saxon monastery at Church Close, Hartlepool, Cleveland', *The Archaeological Journal*, 145: 158–210.

Dark, K. (2004), 'The Late Antique landscape of Britain, AD 300–700', in N. Christie (ed.), *Landscapes of Change: Rural Evolutions in Late Antiquity and the Early Middle Ages* (Aldershot: Ashgate), 279–300.

Dark, P. (2000), *The Environment of Britain* (London: Duckworth).

Darrah, R. (2007), 'Identifying the architectural features of the Anglo-Saxon buildings at Flixborough, and understanding their structures', in Loveluck (ed.), *Rural Settlement, Lifestyles and Social Change*, 51–65.

David, A. (1994), 'The role of geophysical survey in early medieval archaeology', *Anglo-Saxon Studies in Archaeology and History*, 7: 1–26.

Davis, S., Stacy, L., and Woodward, P. (1986), 'Excavations at Allington Avenue, Fordington, Dorchester', *Proc. Dorset Natural History and Archaeology Society*, 107: 101–10.

Davison, B. (1977), 'Excavations at Sulgrave, Northamptonshire, 1960–76: an interim report', *The Archaeological Journal*, 134: 105–14.

Dickinson, T., and Richards, A. (2011), 'Early Anglo-Saxon Eastry', *Anglo-Saxon Studies in Archaeology and History*, 17.

Dixon, P. (1982), 'How Saxon is the Saxon house?', in P. Drury (ed.), *Structural Reconstruction: Approaches to the Interpretation of the Excavated Remains of Buildings*, BAR British Series 110 (Oxford: British Archaeological Reports), 275–86.

——(1988), 'Crickley Hill 1969–1987', *Current Archaeology*, 110: 73–8.

——(2002), 'The reconstruction of the buildings', in Losco-Bradley and Kinsley (eds), *Catholme*, 89–99.

Dodwell, N., Lucy, S., and Tipper, J. (2004), 'Anglo-Saxons on the Cambridge Backs: the criminology site settlement and King's Garden Hostel cemetery', *Proc. Cambridgeshire Antiquarian Society*, 93: 95–124.

Dölling, H. (1958), *Haus und Hof in Westgermanischen Volksrechten* (Münster: Aschendorffsche Verlagsbuchhandlung).

Down, A., and Welch, M. (1990), *Apple Down and The Mardens, Chichester Excavations 7* (Chichester: Chichester District Council).

Draper, S. (2004), 'Roman estates to English parishes? Bonney reconsidered', in R. Collins and J. Gerrard (eds), *Debating Late Antiquity*, BAR British Series 365 (Oxford: British Archaeological Reports), 55–64.

——(2008), 'The significance of Old English *burh* in Anglo-Saxon England', *Anglo-Saxon Studies in Archaeology and History*, 15: 240–53.

Dyer, C. (2004), Review of T. Williamson, *Shaping Medieval Landscapes*, in *Landscape History*, 26: 130–2.

Eagles, B. (1994), 'The archaeological evidence for settlement in the fifth to seventh centuries AD', in M. Aston and C. Lewis (eds), *The Medieval Landscape of Wessex* (Oxford: Oxbow), 13–32.

Es, W. A. van (1967), *Wijster: A Native Village Beyond the Imperial Frontier*, Palaeohistoria, 11.

Esmonde Cleary, S. (1989), *The Ending of Roman Britain* (London: Batsford).

——(2011), 'The endings of Roman Britain', in H. Hamerow, D. Hinton, and S. Crawford (eds), *The Oxford Handbook of Anglo-Saxon Archaeology* (Oxford: Oxford University Press), 13–29.

Etté, J. (1993), 'The Late Bronze Age', in A. Clark, *Excavations at Mucking. Volume 1: The Site Atlas* (London: English Heritage), 18–19.

Evans, D., and Loveluck, C. (2009), *Life and Economy at Early Medieval Flixborough, c. AD 600–1000: The Artefact Evidence* (Oxford: Oxbow Books).

Fairbrother, J. (1990), *Faccombe Netherton: Excavations of a Saxon and Medieval Manorial Complex*, 2 vols. (London: The British Museum).

Faith, R. (1997), *The English Peasantry and the Growth of Lordship* (London and New York: Leicester University Press).

—— (1999), '*Feorm*', in M. Lapidge, J. Blair, S. Keynes, and D. Scragg (eds), *The Blackwell Encyclopaedia of Anglo-Saxon England* (Oxford: Blackwell), 181–2.

Fasham, P., and Whinney, R. (1983), *Archaeology and the M3* (Stroud: Alan Sutton).

Fell, C. (1984), *Women in Anglo-Saxon England* (London: British Museum Press).

Fernie, E. (1986), 'Anglo-Saxon lengths: the "Northern" system, the perch and the foot', *The Archaeological Journal*, 142: 246–54.

—— (1991), 'Anglo-Saxon lengths and the evidence of the buildings', *Medieval Archaeology*, 35: 1–5.

Field, N., and Leahy, K. (1993), 'Prehistoric and Anglo-Saxon remains at Nettleton Top, Nettleton', *Lincolnshire History and Archaeology*, 28: 9–38.

Finn, N. (2004), *The Origins of a Leicester Suburb: Roman, Anglo Saxon, Medieval and Post-Medieval Occupation on Bonners Lane*, BAR 372 (Oxford: British Archaeological Reports).

—— (forthcoming), 'The Anglo-Saxon settlement at Eye Kettleby'.

Foot, S. (2007), 'The historical setting of the seventh- to tenth-century settlement within northern Lindsey', in Loveluck (ed.), *Rural Settlement, Lifestyles and Social Change*, 130–5.

Foreman, S., Hiller, J., and Petts, D. (2002), *Gathering the People, Settling the Land: The Archaeology of a Middle Thames Landscape* (Oxford: Oxford Archaeology).

Fowler, P. (1997), 'Farming in early medieval England: some fields for thought', in J. Hines (ed.), *The Anglo-Saxons from the Migration Period to the Eighth Century* (Woodbridge: Boydell), 245–60.

Freeman, E. (1888), *Four Oxford Lectures, 1887: Fifty Years of European History. Teutonic Conquest in Gaul and Britain* (London: Macmillan).

Fulford, M. (2001), 'Links with the past: pervasive "ritual" behaviour in Roman Britain', *Britannia*, 32: 199–218.

Gaimster, M., and O'Conor, K. (2005), 'Medieval Britain and Ireland 2004', *Medieval Archaeology*, 49: 323–474.

Gameson, R. (1992), 'The cost of the Codex Amiatinus', *Notes & Queries* (March), 2–9.

Gardiner, M. (1990), 'An Anglo-Saxon and medieval settlement at Botolphs, Bramber, West Sussex', *The Archaeological Journal*, 147: 216–75.

—— (1993), 'The excavation of a Late Anglo-Saxon settlement at Market Field, Steyning, 1988–89', *Sussex Archaeological Collections*, 131: 21–67.

—— (2004), 'Timber buildings without earth-fast footings in Viking-Age Britain', in Hines (ed.), *Land, Sea and Home*, 345–58.

—— (2006), 'Implements and utensils in *Gerefa* and the organization of seigneurial farmsteads in the High Middle Ages', *Medieval Archaeology*, 50: 260–7.

Gardiner, M. (2007), 'The origins and persistence of manor houses in England', in M. Gardiner and S. Rippon (eds), *Medieval Landscapes in Britain* (Macclesfield: Windgather Press), 170–84.

——(2011), 'Late Saxon settlements', in H. Hamerow, D. Hinton, and S. Crawford (eds), *The Oxford Handbook of Anglo-Saxon Archaeology* (Oxford: Oxford University Press).

——(forthcoming), 'The sophistication of late Saxon timber buildings', in M. Bintley and M. Shapland (eds), *Woodlands, Trees and Timber in the Anglo-Saxon World*.

——and Greatorex, C. (1997), 'Archaeological excavations in Steyning, 1992–95', *Sussex Archaeological Collections*, 135: 143–71.

——and Murray, E. (forthcoming), *Timber Buildings in England in the High Middle Ages, 900–1200*.

Garrow, D., Lucy, S., and Gibson, D. (2006), *Excavations at Kilverstone, Norfolk, East Anglian Archaeology* 113 (Cambridge: Cambridge Archaeological Unit).

Geake, H. (2007), 'The human burials', in C. Loveluck and D. Atkinson, *The Early Medieval Settlement Remains from Flixborough Lincolnshire: The Occupation Sequence, c. AD 600–1000* (Oxford: Oxbow Books), 113–18.

Gelling, M. (1994), *Place-Names in the Landscape: The Geographical Roots of Britain's Place-Names* (London: J. M. Dent & Son).

——(1997), *Signposts to the Past: Place-Names and the History of England*, 3rd edn (Chichester: Phillimore).

Gerrard, C., with Aston, M. (2007), *The Shapwick Project, Somerset: A Rural Landscape Explored* (Leeds: Society for Medieval Archaeology).

Gerritsen, F. (1999), 'To build and to abandon: the cultural biography of late prehistoric houses and farmsteads in the southern Netherlands', *Archaeological Dialogues*, 6/2: 76–97.

Gibson, C., with Murray, J. (2003), 'An Anglo-Saxon settlement at Godmanchester, Cambridgeshire', *Anglo-Saxon Studies in Archaeology and History*, 12: 137–217.

Giffen, A. E. van (1963), 'Het bouwoffer uit de oudste hoeve te Ezinge (Gr.)', *Helinium*, 3: 246–53.

Gilbert, D. (2006), 'An archaeological excavation at St Mary's Church, Black Bourton, Oxfordshire', Unpublished client report, John Moore Heritage Services.

Gilchrist, R. (forthcoming), *Medieval Lives: Archaeology and the Life Course* (Woodbridge: Boydell & Brewer).

Glass, H., Garwood, P., Champion, T., Booth, P., Reynolds, A., and Munby, J. (forthcoming), *Tracks Through Time: The Archaeology of the Channel Tunnel Rail Link* (Oxford: Oxford Archaeology).

Going, C. (1993a), 'Roman pottery from the *Grubenhäuser*', in Hamerow, *Excavations at Mucking*, 71–2.

—— (1993b), 'Middle Saxon, medieval and later', in A. Clark, *Excavations at Mucking Volume 1: the site atlas*, 22 (London: English Heritage).

Grant, A. (1976), 'Animal bones', in Cunliffe, *Excavations at Portchester Castle*, 262–86.

Gray, M. (1974), 'The Saxon settlement at New Wintles, Eynsham', in T. Rowley (ed.), *Anglo-Saxon Settlement and Landscape*, 51–5, BAR British Series 6 (Oxford: British Archaeological Reports).

Green, C., and Davies, S. (1987), *Excavations at Poundbury, Dorchester, Dorset, 1966–1982. Volume 1: The Settlements* (Dorchester: Dorset Natural History and Archaeological Society).

Green, F. (1994), 'Cereals and plant food: a reassessment of the Saxon economic evidence from Wessex', in Rackham (ed.), *Environment and Economy*, 83–8.

Green, H. (1978), 'A village estate at Godmanchester', in M. Todd (ed.), *Studies in the Romano-British Villa* (Leicester: Leicester University Press), 103–16.

Haarnagel, W. (1979), *Die Grabung Feddersen Wierde Bd II: Methode, Hausbau, Siedlungs- und wirtschaftsformen Sowie Sozialstruktur* (Wiesbaden: F. Steiner).

Hadley, D. (2007), 'The garden gives up its secrets: the developing relationship between rural settlements and cemeteries, c. 750–1100', *Anglo-Saxon Studies in Archaeology and History*, 14: 195–203.

Hagen, A. (1992), *A Handbook of Anglo-Saxon Food: Processing and Consumption* (Pinner: Anglo-Saxon Books).

——(1995), *A Second Handbook of Anglo-Saxon Food and Drink: Production and Distribution* (Frithgarth: Anglo-Saxon Books).

Hall-Torrance, M., and Weaver, S. (2003), 'The excavation of a Saxon settlement at Riverdene, Basingstoke, Hants. 1995', *Proc. Hants. Field Club & Archaeological Society*, 58: 63–105.

Halsall, G. (2005), 'The barbarian invasions', in P. Fouracre (ed.), *The New Cambridge Medieval History* (Cambridge: Cambridge University Press), 1: 35–55.

——(2007), *Barbarian Migrations and the Roman West* (Cambridge: Cambridge University Press).

Hamerow, H. (1991), 'Settlement mobility and the "Middle Saxon Shift": rural settlement and settlement patterns in Anglo-Saxon England', *Anglo-Saxon England*, 20: 1–17.

——(1992), 'Settlement on the gravels in the Anglo-Saxon period', in M. Fulford and L. Nichols (eds), *Developing Landscapes of Lowland Britain: The Archaeology of the British Gravels* (London: Society of Antiquaries), 39–46.

——(1993), *Excavations at Mucking. Volume 2: The Anglo-Saxon Settlement* (London: English Heritage).

——(1997), 'Migration theory and the Anglo-Saxon "identity crisis"', in J. Chapman and H. Hamerow (eds), *Migrations and Invasions in Archaeological Explanation* (Oxford: British Archaeological Reports IS 664), 33–44.

——(1999), 'Anglo-Saxon timber buildings: the continental connection', in Sarfatij et al. (eds), *In Discussion with the Past*, 119–28.

——(2002a), *Early Medieval Settlements: The Archaeology of Rural Communities in North-West Europe 400–900* (Oxford: Oxford University Press).

——(2002b), 'Catholme: the development and context of the settlement', in Losco-Bradley and Kinsley, *Catholme*, 123–9.

——(2004), 'The archaeology of Early Anglo-Saxon settlements: past, present and future', in N. Christie (ed.), *Landscapes of Change: Rural Evolution in Late Antiquity and the Early Middle Ages* (London: Ashgate/Scolar), 301–16.

——(2006), '"Special Deposits" in Anglo-Saxon settlements', *Medieval Archaeology*, 50: 1–30.

——(2007), 'Agrarian production and the *emporia* of Mid Saxon England', in J. Henning (ed.), *Post-Roman Towns, Trade and Settlement in Europe and Byzantium*, Volume 1 (Berlin: De Gruyter), 219–32.

——Hayden, C., and Hey, G. (2008), 'Anglo-Saxon and earlier settlement near Drayton Road, Sutton Courtenay, Berkshire', *The Archaeological Journal*, 164: 109–96.

Hansen, I., and Wickham, C. (2000), *The Long Eighth Century. Production, Distribution and Demand* (Leiden: Brill).

Hansen, T. E. (1987), 'Die Eisenzeitliche Siedlung bei Nørre Snede, Mitteljütland', *Acta Archaeologica*, 58: 171–200.

Harding, P., and Andrews, P. (2002), 'Anglo-Saxon and medieval settlement at Chapel Street, Bicester: excavations 1999–2000', *Oxoniensia*, LXVII: 141–79.

Hardy, A., Charles, B., and Williams, R. (2007), *Death and Taxes: The Archaeology of a Middle Saxon Estate Centre at Higham Ferrers, Northamptonshire* (Oxford: Oxford Archaeology).

——Dodd, A., and Keevill, G. (2003), *Aelfric's Abbey: Excavations at Eynsham Abbey, Oxfordshire 1989–92*, Thames Valley Landscapes Monograph 16 (Oxford: Oxford Archaeology).

Härke, H. (1997), 'Early Anglo-Saxon social structure', in J. Hines (ed.), *The Anglo-Saxons from the Migration Period to the Eighth Century* (Woodbridge: Boydell Press), 125–59.

Hart, C. (1999), 'The Bayeux Tapestry and schools of illumination at Canterbury', *Anglo-Norman Studies*, XXII: 117–67.

Hart, E. (2004), *The Practice of Hefting* (Ludlow).

Harvey, P. D. A. (1989), 'Initiative and authority in settlement change', in D. Austin and C. Dyer (eds), *The Rural Settlements of Medieval England* (Oxford: Blackwell), 125–59.

——(1993), 'Rectitudines Singularum Personarum and Gerefa', *English Historical Review*, 126: 1–22.

Haughton, C., and Powlesland, D. (1999), *West Heslerton: The Anglian Cemetery* (Yedingham: Landscape Research Centre).

Hawkes, J., and Mills, S. (eds) (1999), *Northumbria's Golden Age* (Stroud: Sutton).

Hawkes, S. (1986), 'The Early Saxon period', in G. Briggs, J. Cook, and T. Rowley (eds), *The Archaeology of the Oxford Region* (Oxford: Oxford University Department for External Studies), 64–108.

——and Gray, M. (1969), 'A preliminary note on the Early Anglo-Saxon settlement at New Wintles Farm', *Oxoniensia*, XXXIV: 1–4.

——and Matthews, C. (1985), 'Early Saxon settlements and burials on Puddlehill, near Dunstable, Bedfordshire', *Anglo-Saxon Studies in Archaeology and History*, 4: 1–115.

Heaton, M., (1993), 'Two mid-Saxon grain-driers and later medieval features at Chantry Fields, Gillingham, Dorset', *Proc. Dorset Natural History and Archaeology Society*, 114: 97–126.

Heidinga, H. A. (1987), *Medieval Settlement and Economy North of the Lower Rhine* (Assen/Maastricht: Van Gorcum).

——(1990), 'From Kootwijk to Rhenen: in search of the elite in the central Netherlands in the early Middle Ages', in J. Bestemann, J. Bos, and H. Heidinga (eds), *Medieval Archaeology in the Netherlands* (Assen/Maastricht: Van Gorcum), 9–37.

——and Offenberg, A. (1992), *Op Zoek naar de vifde eeuw: de Franken tussen Rijn en Maas* (Amsterdam: De Bataafsche Leeuw).

Herschend, F. (1989), 'Changing houses: early medieval house types in Sweden, 500–1100 A.D.', *TOR* 22: 79–103.

——(1998), *The Idea of the Good* (Uppsala: University of Uppsala).

Hey, G. (2004), *Yarnton Saxon and Medieval Settlement and Landscape* (Oxford: Oxford Archaeological Unit).

Higham, N. (1992), *Rome, Britain and the Anglo-Saxons* (London: Seaby).

——(1994), 'Literary evidence for villas, towns and hillforts in fifth-century Britain', *Britannia*, 25: 229–32.

Hill, J., and Woodger, A. (1999), *Excavations at 72–75 Cheapside/83–93 Queen Street, City of London* (London: Museum of London Archaeology Service).

Hill, J. D. (1995), *Ritual and Rubbish in the Iron Age of Wessex: A Study on the Formation of a Specific Archaeological Record*, BAR British Series 242 (Oxford: British Archaeological Reports).

Hill, P. (1997), *Whithorn and St Ninian: The Excavation of a Monastic Town* (Stroud: Sutton).

Hill, T. (1977), 'The *Aecerbot* charm and its Christian user', *Anglo-Saxon England*, 6: 213–21.

Hills, C., and O'Connell, C. (2009), 'New light on the Anglo-Saxon succession: two cemeteries and their dates', *Antiquity*, 83/322: 1096–102.

Hinchcliffe, J. (1986), 'An early medieval settlement at Cowage Farm, Foxley, near Malmesbury', *The Archaeological Journal*, 143: 240–59.

Hines, J. (2011), 'No place like home? The Anglo-Saxon social landscape from within and without', in H. Sauer and J. Story (eds), *Anglo-Saxon England and the Continent* (Tempe: ACMRS), 21–40.

——Lane, A., and Redknap, M. (eds) (2004). *Land, Sea and Home: Proceedings of a Conference on Viking Period Settlement* (Leeds: Society for Medieval Archaeology).

Hinton, D. (1998), 'Anglo-Saxon smiths and myths', *Bulletin of the John Rylands University Library, Manchester*, 80: 3–21.

Hirst, S., and Clark, D. (2009), *Excavations at Mucking. Volume 3:The Anglo-Saxon Cemeteries* (London: English Heritage).

——and Rahtz, P. (1973), 'Hatton Rock 1970', *Transactions of the Birmingham and Warwickshire Archaeological Society*, 85: 161–77.

Hodder, I. (1994), 'Architecture and meaning: the example of Neolithic houses and tombs', in M. Parker-Pearson and C. Richards (eds), *Architecture and Order: Approaches to Social Space* (London: Routledge), 73–86.

Holden, E. (1976), 'Excavations at Old Erringham, Shoreham, West Sussex', *Sussex Archaeological Collections*, 114: 306–21.

Hooke, D. (1988), *Anglo-Saxon Settlements* (Oxford: Basil Blackwell).

——(1998), *The Landscape of Anglo-Saxon England* (London and Washington: Leicester University Press).

Hope-Taylor, B. (1977), *Yeavering: An Anglo-British Centre of Early Northumbria* (London: HMSO).

Hoskins, W. G. (1955), *The Making of the English Landscape* (London: Hodder & Stoughton).

Huggins, P. (1991), 'Anglo-Saxon timber building measurements: recent results', *Medieval Archaeology*, 35: 6–28.

Hughes, M. (1984), 'Rural settlement and landscape in Late Saxon Hampshire', in M. Faull (ed.), *Studies in Late Anglo-Saxon Settlement* (Oxford: Oxford University Department for External Studies), 65–80.

Huijbers, A. (2007), *Metaforiseringen in beweging: Boeren en hun gebouwde ogeving in de Volle Middeleeuwen in het Maas-Demer-Scheldegebied*, Academisch Proefschrift, University of Amsterdam.

Hull, B., and O'Connell, T. (2011), 'Diet: recent evidence from analytical chemical techniques', in H. Hamerow, D. Hinton, and S. Crawford (eds), *The Oxford Handbook of Anglo-Saxon Archaeology* (Oxford: Oxford University Press), 667–87.

Hvass, S. (1983), 'Vorbasse: the development of a settlement through the first millennium A.D.', *Journal of Danish Archaeology*, 2: 127–36.

Ingold, T. (2000), *The Perception of the Environment* (London: Routledge).

Jackson, D., Harding, D., and Myres, J. N. L. (1969), 'The Iron Age and Anglo-Saxon site at Upton, Northants', *The Antiquaries Journal*, 49: 202–21.

James, S., Marshall, A., and Millett, M. (1985), 'An early medieval building tradition', *The Archaeological Journal*, 141: 182–215.

Johnson, B., and Waddington, C. (2009), 'Prehistoric and Dark Age settlement remains from Cheviot Quarry, Milfield Basin, Northumberland', *The Archaeological Journal*, 165: 107–264.

Jones, M. (1982), 'Crop production in Roman Britain', in D. Miles (ed.), *The Romano-British Countryside* (Oxford: British Archaeological Reports), 97–198.

Jones, R., and Page, M. (2006), *Medieval Villages in an English Landscape: Beginnings and Ends* (Macclesfield: Windgather Press).

Kershaw, J. (2010), 'Culture and gender in the Danelaw: Scandinavian and Anglo-Scandinavian brooches, 850–1050', unpublished D.Phil. thesis, University of Oxford.

King, A. (2004), 'Post-Roman upland architecture in the Craven Dales and the dating evidence', in Hines et al. (eds), *Land, Sea and Home*, 335–44.

Kopytoff, I. (1986), 'The cultural biography of things: commoditization as process', in A. Appadurai (ed.), *The Social Life of Things: Commoditization in Cultural Perspective* (Cambridge: Cambridge University Press), 64–91.

Larsson, L. (2002), 'Uppåkra: research on a central place: recent excavations and results', in B. Hårdh and L. Larsson (eds), *Central Places in the Migration and Merovingian Periods: Papers from the 52nd Sachsensymposium* (Stockholm: Almqvist & Wiksell International), 19–30.

Leahy, K. (2007), *Interrupting the Pots: The Excavation of Cleatham Anglo-Saxon Cemetery* (York: Council for British Archaeology).

Leech, P., and Evans, C. (2001), *Fosse Lane, Shepton Mallet, 1990: Excavation of a Romano-British Roadside Settlement in Somerset* (London: Society for the Promotion of Roman Studies).

Leeds, E. T. (1923), 'A Saxon village near Sutton Courtenay, Berkshire', *Archaeologia*, LXXIII: 147–92.

——(1927), 'A Saxon village near Sutton Courtenay, Berkshire (second report)', *Archaeologia*, LXXVI: 12–80.

——(1947), 'A Saxon village at Sutton Courtenay, Berkshire: a third report', *Archaeologia*, XCII: 73–94.

Lethbridge, T., 'An Anglo-Saxon hut on the Car Dyke at Waterbeach', *Antiquaries Journal*, 7: 141–6.

——and Tebbutt, C. (1933), 'Huts of the Anglo-Saxon period', *Cambridge Antiquarian Society's Communications*, 33: 133–51.

Lewis, C. (2010), 'Exploring black holes: recent investigations in currently occupied rural settlements in eastern England', in N. Higham and M. Ryan (eds), *The Landscape Archaeology of Anglo-Saxon England* (Woodbridge: The Boydell Press), 83–105.

——Mitchell-Fox, P., and Dyer, C. (2001), *Village, Hamlet and Field: Changing Medieval Settlements in Central England* (Macclesfield: Windgather Press).

Lewis, E. (1985), 'Excavations in Bishops Waltham 1967–78', *Proc. Hants. Field Club & Archaeological Society*, 41: 81–126.

Lewit, T. (2003), '"Vanishing villas": what happened to elite rural habitation in the West in the 5th–6th centuries?', *Journal of Roman Archaeology*, 16: 260–74.

Liebermann, E. (1903), *Die Gesetze der Angelsachsen* (Halle: M. Niemeier).

Losco-Bradley, S., and Kinsley, G. (eds) (2002), *Catholme: An Anglo-Saxon Settlement on the Trent Gravels in Staffordshire* (Nottingham: University of Nottingham).

——and Wheeler, H. M. (1984), 'Anglo-Saxon settlement in the Trent Valley: some aspects', in M. Faull (ed.), *Studies in Anglo-Saxon Settlement* (Oxford: Oxford University Department for External Studies), 101–14.

Loveluck, C. (1998), 'A high status Anglo-Saxon settlement at Flixborough, Lincolnshire', *Antiquity*, 72: 146–61.

——(2001), 'Wealth, waste and conspicuous consumption: Flixborough and its importance for Mid and Late Saxon settlement studies', in H. Hamerow and A. MacGregor (eds), *Image and Power in the Archaeology of Early Medieval Britain: Essays in Honour of Rosemary Cramp* (Oxford: Oxbow), 78–130.

——(2007), *Rural Settlement, Lifestyles and Social Change in the Later First Millennium AD: Anglo-Saxon Flixborough in its Wider Context*, Excavations at Flixborough 4 (Oxford: Oxbow).

——and Walton Rogers, P. (2007), 'Craft and technology—non-agrarian activities underpinning everyday life', in Loveluck, *Rural Settlement, Lifestyles and Social Change*, 99–111.

Lowe, C. (2006), *Excavations at Hoddom, Dumfriesshire: An Early Ecclesiastical Site in South-West Scotland* (Edinburgh: Society of Antiquaries of Scotland).

Lucy, S. (2000), *The Anglo-Saxon Way of Death: Burial Rites in Early England* (Stroud: Alan Sutton).

——Tipper, J., and Dickens, A. (2009), *The Anglo-Saxon Settlement and Cemetery at Bloodmoor Hill, Carlton Colville, East Anglian Archaeology* 131.

McCormick, F. (2008), 'The decline of the cow: agricultural and settlement change in early medieval Ireland', *Peritia*, 20: 209–24.

MacGowan, K. (1996), 'Barking Abbey', *Current Archaeology*, 149: 172–8.

McKinley, J. (1994), *The Anglo-Saxon Cemetery at Spong Hill, North Elmham. Part VIII: The Cremations*, East Anglian Archaeology 69 (Dereham: Norfolk Museums Service).

MacKreth, D. (1996), *Orton Hall Farm: A Roman and Early Anglo-Saxon Farmstead* (Manchester: University of Manchester).

Maitland, F. W. (1897), *Domesday Book and Beyond: Three Essays in the Early History of England* (Cambridge: Cambridge University Press).

Manby, T. (1985), *Thwing: Excavation and Field Archaeology in East Yorkshire*, Unpublished interim report.

Manby, T. (1986), *Thwing: Excavation and Field Archaeology in East Yorkshire. The Anglo-Saxon Cemetery*, Unpublished interim report.

——(1987), *Thwing: Excavation and Field Archaeology in East Yorkshire 1985. The Final Season*, Unpublished interim report.

Marshall, A., and Marshall, G. (1991), 'A survey and analysis of the buildings of early and middle Anglo-Saxon England', *Medieval Archaeology*, 35: 29–43.

————(1993), 'Differentiation, change and continuity in Anglo-Saxon buildings', *Archaeological Journal*, 150: 366–402.

Maynard, G. (1952), 'Butley, Neutral Farm', *Proc. of the Suffolk Institute of Archaeology and Natural History*, XXV: 207–8.

Meadows, I. (2002), 'Peterborough Road, Warmington, Northants, excavations 1998', unpublished report of Northamptonshire County Council.

——(forthcoming), 'The excavation of a Late Saxon site at the Castle Cement Quarry, Ketton, Rutland'.

Meaney, A. (1995), 'Pagan English sanctuaries, place-names and hundred meeting-places', *Anglo-Saxon Studies in Archaeology and History*, 8: 29–42.

Metcalf, D. M. (1993–4), *Thrymsas and Sceattas in the Ashmolean Museum*, 3 vols. (London: Royal Numismatic Society and Ashmolean Museum).

——(1996), 'Viking Age numismatics 2: Coinage in the Northern Lands in Merovingian and Caroline times', *The Numismatic Chronicle* 156: 399–428.

——(2003), 'Variations in the composition of the currency at different places in England', in Pestell and Ulmschneider (eds), *Markets in Medieval Europe*, 37–47.

Miles, D. (1986), *Archaeology at Barton Court Farm, Abingdon, Oxon: An investigation of Late Neolithic, Iron Age, Romano-British, and Saxon Settlements* (Oxford: Oxford Archaeological Unit).

Miller, D., and Tilley, C. (eds) (1984), *Ideology, Power and Prehistory* (Cambridge: Cambridge University Press).

Millett, M., with James, S. (1984), 'Excavations at Cowdery's Down, Basingstoke, 1978-1981'. *The Archaeological Journal*, 140: 151–279.

——(1988), 'The question of continuity: Rivenhall reviewed', *The Archaeological Journal*, 144: 434–7.

Mills, S. (1999), '(Re)constructing Northumbrian timber buildings: the Bede's World Experience', in Hawkes and Mills (eds), *Northumbria's Golden Age*, 66–72.

Milne, G., and Richards, J. (1992), *Wharram VII: A Study of Settlement on the Yorkshire Wolds. Two Anglo-Saxon Buildings and Associated Finds* (York: Department of Archaeology, University of York).

Moffett, L. (1994), 'Charred cereals from some ovens/kilns in Late Saxon Stafford and the botanical evidence for the pre-*burh* economy', in Rackham (ed.), *Environment and Economy*, 55–64.

——(2011), 'Food plants on archaeological sites', in H. Hamerow, D. Hinton, and S. Crawford (eds), *The Oxford Handbook of Anglo-Saxon Archaeology* (Oxford: Oxford University Press), 346–60.

MoLAS, *see* Museum of London Archaeological Service.

Monk, M., and Kelleher, E. (2005), 'An assessment of the archaeological evidence for Irish corn-drying kilns in the light of the results of archaeological experiments and archaeobotanical studies', *Journal of Irish Archaeology*, XIV: 77–114.

Moore, J. (1963–6), 'An Anglo-Saxon settlement at Wykeham, North Yorkshire', *Yorkshire Archaeological Journal*, 41: 403–43.

Moreland, J. (2000), 'The significance of production', in I. L. Hansen and C. Wickham (eds), *The Long Eighth Century: Production, Distribution and Demand* (London, Boston, and Cologne: Brill), 1–34.

Morris, J., and Jervis, B. (2011), 'What's so special? A reinterpretation of Anglo-Saxon "special deposits"', *Medieval Archaeology*, 55: 66–81.

Morris, R. (1983), *The Church in British Archaeology*, CBA Res. Report 47 (York: Council for British Archaeology).

Mortimer, R. (2000), 'Village development and ceramic sequence: the Middle to Late Saxon village at Lordship Lane, Cottenham, Cambridgeshire', *Proc. Cambridgeshire Antiquarian Society*, 89: 5–33.

——Regan, R., and Lucy, S. (2005), *The Saxon and Medieval Settlement at West Fen Road, Ely: The Ashwell Site, East Anglian Archaeology* 110.

Mudd, A. (2002), *Excavations at Melford Meadows, Brettenham, 1994: Romano-British and Early Saxon Occupations* (Oxford: Oxford Archaeological Unit).

Mulville, J., and Ayres, K. (2004), 'Animal bone', in Hey (ed.), *Yarnton*, 325–50.

Murphy, P. (1994), 'The Anglo-Saxon landscape and rural economy: some results from sites in East Anglia and Essex', in Rackham (ed.), *Environment and Economy*, 23–39.

——(2010), 'The landscape and economy of the Anglo-Saxon coast: new archaeological evidence', in N. Higham and M. Ryan (eds), *The Landscape Archaeology of Anglo-Saxon England* (Woodbridge: The Boydell Press), 211–22.

Murray, J. with McDonald, T. (2006), 'Excavations at Station Road, Gamlingay, Cambridgeshire', in *Anglo-Saxon Studies in Archaeology and History*, 13.

Museum of London Archaeological Service (2004), *The Prittlewell Prince: The Discovery of a Rich Anglo-Saxon Burial in Essex* (London: Museum of London).

Näsman, U. (1987), 'House, village and settlement', in *Danmarks længste udgravning: arkæologi på naturgassens vej 1979–86* (Herning: Poul Kristensen), 457–65.

Nielson, P. O., Randsborg, K., and Thrane, H. (1993), *The Archaeology of Gudme and Lundeborg* (Copenhagen: University of Copenhagen).

O'Brien, C., and Miket, R. (1991), 'The early medieval settlement of Thirlings, Northumberland', *Durham Archaeological Journal*, 7: 57–92.

O'Neill, H. (1952), 'Report of the excavations undertaken from 1948–1951', *Transactions of the Bristol and Gloucestershire Archaeological Society*, 71: 13–87.

O'Sullivan, A. (2008), 'Early medieval houses in Ireland: social identity and dwelling spaces', *Peritia*, 20: 225–56.

Oliver, T., Howard-Davis, C., and Newman, R. (1996), 'A post-Roman settlement at Fremington, near Brougham', in J. Lambert (ed.), *Transect Through Time* (Lancaster: University of Lancaster), 127–69.

Oosthuizen, S. (2005), 'New light on the origins of open-field farming?', *Medieval Archaeology*, 49: 165–94.

——(2010), 'Medieval field systems and settlement nucleation: common or separate origins?', in N. Higham and M. Ryan (eds), *The Landscape Archaeology of Anglo-Saxon England* (Woodbridge: The Boydell Press), 107–32.

Page, R. (1970), *Life in Anglo-Saxon England* (London and New York: Batsford).

Palmer, B. (2003), 'The hinterlands of three southern English *emporia*: some common themes', in Pestell and Ulmschneider (eds), *Markets in Early Medieval Europe*, 48–60.

Pantos, A., and Semple, S. (eds) (2004), *Assembly Places and Practices in Medieval Europe* (Dublin: Four Courts Press).

Parker-Pearson, M. (2003), *The Archaeology of Death and Burial*, 2nd edn (Stroud: Sutton Publishing).

——and Richards, C. (eds) (1994), *Architecture and Order: Archaeological and Ethnological Studies of Social Space* (London: Routledge).

Parkhouse, J. (1997), 'The distribution and exchange of Mayen lava quernstones in early medieval northwest Europe', *Papers of the 'Medieval Europe Brugge 1997' Conference. Volume 3: Exchange and Trade in Medieval Europe* (Aellik: Instituut voor het Archeologisch Patrimonium), 97–106.

Parry, S. (2006), *Raunds Area Survey. An Archaeological Study of the Landscape of Raunds, Northamptonshire 1985–94* (Oxford: Oxbow Books).

Partridge, C. (1989), *Foxholes Farm: A Multi-Period Gravel Site* (Hertford: Hertfordshire Archaeological Trust).

Pelling, R. (2001), 'Charred plant remains', in Booth et al., *Excavations in the Extramural Settlement of Roman Alchester*, 18–22.

——(2002), 'Charred plant remains', in Harding and Andrews, 'Anglo-Saxon and medieval settlement at Chapel Street, Bicester', 167–70.

Pestell, T., and Ulmschneider, K. (eds) (2003), *Markets in Early Medieval Europe: Trading and 'Productive' Sites, 650–850* (Macclesfield: Windgather Press).

Philp, B. (1973), *Excavations in West Kent 1960–70* (Dover: Kent Archaeological Rescue Unit).

——(1984), *Excavations in the Darenth Valley, Kent* (Dover: Kent Archaeological Rescue Unit).

Pine, J. (2001), 'The excavation of a Saxon settlement at Cadley Road, Collingbourne Ducis, Wiltshire', *Wiltshire Archaeology and Natural History Magazine*, 94: 88–117.

Pitts, M. (2011), 'Kent plough challenges farming history', *British Archaeology* (May/June), 7.

Plunkett, S. (1999), 'The Anglo-Saxon loom at Pakenham, Suffolk', *Proceedings of the Suffolk Institute of Archaeology*, 39: 277–98.

Poole, K. (2010), 'Mammal and bird remains', in G. Thomas, *The Later Anglo-Saxon Settlement at Bishopstone* (York: Council for British Archaeology), 142–56.

Powlesland, D. (1987), 'Excavations at Heslerton, North Yorkshire 1978–82', *The Archaeological Journal*, 143: 53–173.

——(1989), 'West Heslerton: the Anglian settlement', *Medieval Settlement Research Group*, 4: 46.

——(1997), 'Anglo-Saxon settlements, structures, form and layout', in J. Hines (ed.), *The Anglo-Saxons from the Migration Period to the Eighth Century: An Ethnographic Perspective* (Woodbridge: Boydell Press), 101–16.

——(1998), 'The West Heslerton assessment', *Internet Archaeology*, 5.

——(2003), *25 Years of Archaeological Research on the Sands and Gravels of Heslerton* (Colchester: The Landscape Research Centre).

Bibliography

Preston, S. (2004), *Bronze Age Occupation and Saxon Features at the Wolverton Turn Enclosure, Near Stony Stratford, Milton Keynes*, Unpublished report, Thames Valley Archaeological Services.

Price, E. (2000), *Frocester: A Romano-British Settlement, its Antecedents and Successors* (Stonehouse: Gloucester & District Archaeological Research Group).

Price, N. (2002), *The Viking Way: Religion and War in Late Iron Age Scandinavia* (Uppsala: Uppsala University).

Pryor, F. (1996), 'Sheep, stockyards and field systems: Bronze Age livestock populations in the fenlands of eastern England', *Antiquity*, 70: 313–24.

Rackham, J. (1994), 'Economy and environment in Saxon London', in Rackham (ed.), *Environment and Economy*, 126–35.

——(ed.) (1994), *Environment and Economy in Anglo-Saxon England* (York: Council for British Archaeology).

Radford, C. R. (1958), 'The Saxon house: a review and some parallels', *Medieval Archaeology*, 1: 27–38.

Rahtz, P. (1976), 'Buildings and rural settlement', in D. Wilson (ed.), *The Archaeology of Anglo-Saxon England* (Cambridge: Cambridge University Press), 49–98.

——(1979), *The Saxon and Medieval Palaces at Cheddar*, BAR British Series 65 (Oxford: British Archaeological Reports).

——and Meeson, R. (1992), *An Anglo-Saxon Watermill at Tamworth*, CBA Research Report 83 (London: Council for British Archaeology).

——Hirst, S., and Wright, S. (2000), *Cannington Cemetery: Excavations 1962–3 of Prehistoric, Roman, Post-Roman, and Later Features at Cannington Park Quarry, near Bridgwater, Somerset* (London: Society for the Promotion of Roman Studies).

Rees, W. (1963), 'Survivals of ancient Celtic custom in medieval England', in J. R. R. Tolkien et al., *Angles and Britons* (Cardiff: University of Wales Press), 148–68.

Reichmann, C. (1982), 'Ländliche Siedlungen der Eisenzeit und des Mittelalters in Westfalen', *Offa*, 39: 163–82.

Reynolds, A. (1999), *Later Anglo-Saxon England: Life and Landscape* (Stroud: Tempus).

——(2003), 'Boundaries and settlements in later sixth- to eleventh-century England', *Anglo-Saxon Studies in Archaeology and History*, 12: 98–136.

——(2005), 'From *pagus* to parish: territory and settlement in the Avebury region from the Late Roman period to the Domesday survey', in G. Brown, D. Field, and D. McOmish (eds), *The Avebury Landscape: Aspects of the Field Archaeology of the Marlborough Downs* (Oxford: Oxbow), 164–80.

——(2006), 'The early medieval period', in N. Holbrook and J. Jurica (eds), *Twenty-Five Years of Archaeology in Gloucestershire: A Review of New Discoveries and New Thinking* (Bristol & Gloucestershire Archaeological Society), 133–60.

——(2009), *Anglo-Saxon Deviant Burial Customs* (Oxford: Oxford University Press).

——(2009), 'Meaningful landscapes: an early medieval perspective', in R. Gilchrist and A. Reynolds (eds), *Reflections: 50 Years of Medieval Archaeology, 1957–2007* (London: Society for Medieval Archaeology), 409–34.

Richards, J. (1999), 'Cottam: an Anglo-Scandinavian settlement on the Yorkshire Wolds', *The Archaeological Journal*, 156: 1–111.

Richards, J. (2000), 'Identifying Anglo-Scandinavian settlements', in D. Hadley and J. Richards (eds), *Cultures in Contact: Scandinavian Settlement in England in the Ninth and Tenth Centuries* (Turnhout: Brepols), 295–310.

Rickett, R. (1995), *The Anglo-Saxon Cemetery at Spong Hill, North Elmham. Part VII: The Iron Age, Roman and Early Saxon Settlement*, East Anglian Archaeology 73 (Gressenhall: Norfolk Museums Service).

Rippon, S. (2008), *Beyond the Medieval Village. The Diversification of Landscape Character in Southern Britain* (Oxford: Oxford University Press).

——(2009), 'Understanding the medieval landscape', in R. Gilchrist and A. Reynolds (eds), *Reflections: 50 Years of Medieval Archaeology, 1957–2007* (London: Society for Medieval Archaeology), 227–54.

——(2010), 'Landscape change during the "long eighth century" in southern England', in N. Higham and M. Ryan (eds), *The Landscape Archaeology of Anglo-Saxon England* (Woodbridge: The Boydell Press), 39–64.

Roberts, B. (2008), *Landscapes, Documents and Maps: Villages in Northern England and Beyond, AD 900–1250* (Oxford: Oxbow Books).

Robertson, D. A. (2003), 'A Neolithic enclosure and Early Saxon settlement: excavations at Yarmouth Road, Broome, 2001', *Norfolk Archaeology*, XLIV/II: 222–50.

Robinson, M. (1991), 'Environment, archaeology and alluvium on the river gravels of the South Midlands', in S. Needham and M. Macklin (eds), *Alluvial Archaeology in Britain: Proceedings of a Conference Sponsored by the RMC Group plc, 3–5 January 1991, British Museum* (Oxford: Oxbow Books), 197–208.

——(2007), 'The Thames and changing environments in the river valley', in P. Booth, A. Dodd, M. Robinson, and A. Smith (eds), *The Thames Through Time: The Early Historic Period* (Oxford: Oxford Archaeology).

——(unpublished), 'Overview of the Saxon and medieval environmental archaeology of the West Cotton Area', Unpublished draft report.

Rodwell, W., and Rodwell, K. (1985), *Rivenhall: Investigations of a Villa, Church, and Village, 1950–1977* (London: Chelmsford Archaeological Trust and the Council for British Archaeology).

Rogerson, A. (1995), *A Late Neolithic, Saxon and Medieval Site at Middle Harling, Norfolk*, East Anglian Archaeology 74 (London: The British Museum).

Rowley, T. (ed.) (1974), *Anglo-Saxon Settlement and Landscape*, BAR British Series 6 (Oxford: British Archaeological Reports).

Sarfatij, H., Verwers, W., and Woltering, P. (eds) (1999), *In Discussion with the Past: Archaeological Studies Presented to W. A. van Es* (Zwolle: Stichting Promotie Archeologie).

Saunders, T. (2000), 'Class, space and "feudal" identities', in William O. Frazer and Andrew Tyrrell (eds), *Social Identity in Early Medieval Britain* (London: Leicester University Press), 209–32.

Sawyer, P. (1985), 'The Anglo-Norman village', in D. Hooke (ed.), *Medieval Villages: A Review of Current Work* (Oxford: Oxford University Committee for Archaeology), 3–6.

Scott, E. (1991), 'Animal and infant burials in Romano-British villas: a revitalization movement', in P. Garwood, D. Jennings, et al. (eds), *Sacred and Profane: Proceedings of a Conference on Archaeology, Ritual and Religion: Oxford 1989* (Oxford: Oxford University Committee for Archaeology), 115–21.

Scull, C. (1991), 'Post-Roman Phase I at Yeavering: a re-consideration', *Medieval Archaeology*, 35: 51–63.
—— (1993), 'Archaeology, early Anglo-Saxon society and the origins of Anglo-Saxon kingdoms', *Anglo-Saxon Studies in Archaeology and History*, 6: 65–82.
—— (1997), 'Urban centres in pre-Viking England?', in J. Hines (ed.), *The Anglo-Saxons from the Migration Period to the Eighth Century* (Woodbridge: Boydell Press), 269–97.
—— (2009), 'The human burials', in Lucy et al., *The Anglo-Saxon Settlement and Cemetery at Bloodmoor Hill*, 385–424.
—— and Harding, A. (1990), 'Two early medieval cemeteries at Milfield, Northumberland', *Durham Archaeological Journal*, 6: 1–29.
Seebohm, F. (1883), *The English Village Community* (London: Longmans, Green).
Semple, S. (2004), 'Locations of assembly in early Anglo-Saxon England', in Pantos and Semple (eds), *Assembly Places*, 135–54.
—— (2007), 'Defining OE *hearg*: a preliminary archaeological and topographic examination of *hearg* place-names and their hinterlands', *Early Medieval Europe*, 15/4: 364–85.
Shapland, M. (2009), 'St Mary's Church, Broughton, Lincolnshire: a thegnly tower-nave in the Late Anglo-Saxon landscape', *The Archaeological Journal*, 165: 471–519.
—— (forthcoming), 'Timber as the secular building material of Anglo-Saxon society', in M. Bintley and M. Shapland (eds), *Woodlands, Trees and Timber in the Anglo-Saxon World*.
Sherlock, S., and Simmons, M. (2008), 'The lost royal cult of Street House, Yorkshire', *British Archaeology* (May/June), 30–7.
Simmonds, A., Anderson-Whymark, H., and Norton, A. (2011), 'Excavations at Tubney Wood Quarry, Oxfordshire, 2001–9', *Oxoniensia*, 76: 105–72.
Smith, I. (1984), 'Patterns of settlement and land use of the Late Anglian period in the Tweed basin', in M. Faull (ed.), *Studies in Late Anglo-Saxon Settlement* (Oxford: Oxford University Department for External Studies), 177–96.
Snape, M. (2003), 'A horizontal-wheeled watermill of the Anglo-Saxon period at Corbridge, Northumberland, and its river environment', *Archaeologia Aeliana*, 32: 37–72.
Sofield, C. (2012), 'Placed deposits in Anglo-Saxon England', D.Phil. thesis, Oxford University.
Stamper, P., and Croft, R. (2000), *The South Manor Area: Wharram: A Study of Settlement on the Yorkshire Wolds VIII* (York: University of York).
Stansbie, D. (2008), *Brooklands, Milton Keynes: Post-Excavation Assessment and Update Project Design*, Unpublished report, Oxford Archaeology.
Steedman, K. (1995), 'Excavation of a Saxon site at Riby Cross Roads, Lincolnshire', *The Archaeological Journal*, 151: 212–306.
Stenton, F. (1971), *Anglo-Saxon England*, 3rd edn (Oxford: Clarendon Press).
Stevens, C. (2004), 'Yarnton: charred plant remains', in Hey, *Yarnton*, 351–64.
Stoertz, C. (1997), *Ancient Landscapes of the Yorkshire Wolds* (London: RCHME).
Swanton, M., ed. and transl. (1975), *Anglo-Saxon Prose* (London: Dent).
Sykes, N. (2004), 'The dynamics of status symbols: wildfowl exploitation in England AD 410–1550', *The Archaeological Journal*, 161: 82–105.

Sykes, N. (2006), 'From *Cu* and *Sceap* to *Beffe* and *Motton*', in C. Woolgar, D. Serjeantson, and T. Waldron (eds), *Food in Medieval England: Diet and Nutrition* (Oxford: Oxford University Press), 56–71.

——(2007), *The Norman Conquest: A Zoological Perspective* (Oxford: Archaeopress).

——(2010), 'Deer, land, knives and halls: social change in early medieval England', *The Antiquaries Journal*, 90: 175–93.

Taylor, C. (1983), *Village and Farmstead: A History of Rural Settlement in England* (London: George Philip).

Taylor, G. (2003a), 'Hall Farm, Baston', *Lincolnshire History & Archaeology*, 38: 5–15.

——(2003b), 'An early to middle Saxon settlement at Quarrington, Lincolnshire', *The Antiquaries Journal*, 83: 231–80.

Taylor, J. (2007). *An Atlas of Roman Rural Settlement in England* (York: Council for British Archaeology).

Theuws, T. (1991), 'Landed property and manorial organisation in northern Austrasia', in N. Roymans and F. Theuws (eds), *Images of the Past: Studies on Ancient Societies in Northwest Europe* (Amsterdam: Instituut voor Pre- en Protohistorische Archeologie), 299–407.

Thomas, G. (2003), 'Bishopstone, East Sussex', www.sussexpast.co.uk/research.

——(2004). 'Excavation and survey in Bishopstone, East Sussex, 2003', *Society for Medieval Archaeology Newsletter*, 30: 6–7.

——(2005), 'Bishopstone, East Sussex', www.sussexpast.co.uk/research.

——(2009), 'The symbolic lives of Late Anglo-Saxon settlements: new evidence', *The Archaeological Journal*, 165: 334–98.

——(2010), *The Later Anglo-Saxon Settlement at Bishopstone: A Downland Manor in the Making*, CBA Research Report No. 163 (York: Council for British Archaeology).

——(2011a), 'Overview: craft production and technology', in H. Hamerow, D. A. Hinton, and S. Crawford (eds), *The Oxford Handbook of Anglo-Saxon Archaeology* (Oxford: Oxford University Press), 405–22.

——(2011b), 'Bishopstone and Lyminge', *British Archaeology* (July/August), 43–7.

Thomas, J. (2007), 'Cossington: Saxon cemetery and settlement in a barrow context', *Medieval Archaeology*, 51: 264–7.

——(2008), *Monument, Memory and Myth: Use and Re-use of Three Bronze Age Round Barrows at Cossington, Leicestershire*, Leicester Archaeology Monograph 14 (Leicester: University of Leicester).

Tilley, C. (1999), *Metaphor and Material Culture* (Oxford: Blackwell).

Timby, J., Brown, R., Hardy, A., Leech, S., Poole, C., and Webley, L. (2007), *Settlement on the Bedfordshire Claylands: Archaeology along the A421 Great Barford Bypass*, Bedfordshire Archaeology Monograph 8 (Oxford: Oxford Archaeology and Bedfordshire Archaeological Council).

Tipper, J. (2004), *The* Grubenhaus *in Anglo-Saxon England* (Yedingham: Landscape Research Centre).

Tummusscheit, A. (1995), 'Ländliche Siedlungen des 5.-7. Jh. in England und ihre kontinentalen Vorgänger', Unpublished MA thesis, Christian-Albrechts University, Kiel.

Tyler, S., and Major, H. (2005), *The Early Saxon Cemetery and Later Settlement at Springfield Lyons, Essex*, East Anglian Archaeology 111 (Chelmsford: Essex County Council).

Upex, S. (2002), (2003a), (2004) (2005), *A Migration Period Site at Polebrook, Northamptonshire: Survey and Excavation*, Unpublished interim reports.

——(2003b). 'Landscape continuity and the fossilization of Roman fields', *The Archaeological Journal*, 159: 77–108.

van der Veen, M. (1989), 'Charred grain assemblages from Roman-period corn driers in Britain', *The Archaeological Journal*, 146: 302–19.

——(2010), 'Agricultural innovation: invention and adoption or change and adaptation?', *World Archaeology*, 42/1: 1–12

Waddington, C. (2005), 'Yeavering in its Stone Age landscape', in P. Frodsham and C. O'Brien (eds), *Yeavering: People, Place and Power* (Stroud: Tempus), 84–97.

——(forthcoming), 'Maelmin West', in *Landscape, Settlement and Society: Ancient Northumberland and its Wider Context*.

Wade, K. (1980), 'A settlement site at Bonhunt Farm, Wicken Bonhunt, Essex', in D. Buckley (ed.), *Archaeology in Essex* (York: Council for British Archaeology), 96–102.

——(1988), 'Ipswich', in R. Hodges and B. Hobley (eds), *The Rebirth of Towns in the West* (London: Council for British Archaeology), 93–100.

Wade-Martins, P. (1980), *Excavations in North Elmham Park*, 2 vols, East Anglian Archaeology 9 (Gressenhall: Norfolk Museums Service).

Walker, J. (1999), 'Late 12th and early 13th century aisled buildings: a comparison', *Vernacular Architecture*, 30: 21–53.

Ward-Perkins, B. (2005), *The Fall of Rome and the End of Civilization* (Oxford: Oxford University Press).

Waterbolk, H. T. (1982), 'Mobilität von Dorf, Ackerflur und Gräberfeld in Drenthe seit der La Tènezeit', *Offa*, 39: 97–137.

——(1991), 'Das mittelalterliche Siedlungswesen in Drenthe: Versuch einer Synthese aus archäologischer Sicht', in Böhme (ed.), *Siedlungen und Landesausbau*, 47–108.

——(1999), 'From Wijster to Dorestad and beyond', in Sarfatij et al. (eds), *In Discussion with the Past*, 107–18.

Watts, M. (2002), *The Archaeology of Mills and Milling* (Stroud: Tempus).

Welch, M. (1992), *Anglo-Saxon England* (London: English Heritage).

——(2008), 'Report on excavations of the Anglo-Saxon cemetery at Updown, Eastry, Kent', *Anglo-Saxon Studies in Archaeology and History*, 15: 1–146.

West, S. (1969), 'The Anglo-Saxon village of West Stow: an interim report of the excavations, 1965–8', *Medieval Archaeology*, XIII: 1–20.

——(1986), *West Stow: The Anglo-Saxon Village*, 2 vols, East Anglian Archaeology 24 (Ipswich: Suffolk County Planning Department).

Whitelock, D. (1955), *English Historical Documents*. Volume I: *c. 500–1042* (London: Eyre & Spottiswoode).

Wickham, C. (2005), *Framing the Early Middle Ages: Europe and the Mediterranean 400–800* (Oxford: Oxford University Press).

Williams, A. (1992), 'A bell house and a *burh-geat*: lordly residences in England before the Norman Conquest', in C. Harper-Bill and R. Harvey (eds), *Medieval Knighthood IV: Papers from the Fifth Strawberry Hill Conference 1990* (Woodbridge: Boydell), 221–40.

Williams, D., and Vince, A. (1997), 'The characterization and interpretation of Early to Middle Saxon granitic tempered pottery in England', *Medieval Archaeology*, 41: 214–19.

Williams, H. (1997), 'Ancient landscapes and the dead: the reuse of prehistoric and Roman monuments as early Anglo-Saxon burial sites', *Medieval Archaeology*, 41:1–32.

——(2006), *Death and Memory in Early Medieval Britain* (Cambridge: Cambridge University Press).

Williams, P., and Newman, R. (2006), *Market Lavington, Wiltshire: An Anglo-Saxon Cemetery and Settlement* (Salisbury: Wessex Archaeology).

Williams, R. (1993), *Pennyland and Hartigans: Two Iron Age and Saxon Sites in Milton Keynes* (Aylesbury: Buckinghamshire Archaeological Society).

Williamson, T. (2003), *Shaping Medieval Landscapes: Settlement, Society, Environment* (Macclesfield: Windgather Press).

Wilson, D. M., and Hurst, J. G. (1958), 'Medieval Britain in 1957', *Medieval Archaeology*, 2: 183–214.

Windell, D., Chapman, A., and Woodiwiss, J. (1990), *From Barrows to Bypass: Excavations at West Cotton, Raunds, Northants. 1985–1989* (Northampton: Northamptonshire County Council/English Heritage).

Winkelmann, W. (1958), 'Die Ausgrabungen in der frühmittelalterlichen Siedlung bei Warendorf', in *Neue Ausgrabungen in Deutschland* (Berlin: Römisch-Germanische Kommission), 492–517.

Wright, J. (2006), 'An Anglo-Saxon settlement at Cherry Orton Road, Orton Waterville, Peterborough', *Proc. Cambridgeshire Antiquarian Society*, 95: 115–20.

Wulf, F.-W. (1991), 'Karolingische und Ottonische Zeit', in H.-J. Häßler (ed.), *Ur- und Frühgeschichte in Niedersachsen* (Stuttgart: Theiss), 321–68.

Zimmermann, W. H. (1982), 'Archäologische Befunde frühmittelalterliche Webhäuser', *Jahrbuch der Männer von Morgenstern*, 61: 111–44.

——(1988), 'Regelhafte Innengliederung prähistorische Langhäuser in den Nordseeanrainerstaten: Ein Zeugnis enger, langandauender kultureller Kontakte', *Germania*, 66/2: 465–89.

——(1992), *Die Siedlungen des 1. bis 6. Jh. n. Christus von Flögeln-Eekhöltjen, Niedersachsen: Die Bauformen und ihre Funktionen. Probleme der Küstenforschung im Südlichen Nordseegebiet*, Bd. 19 (Hildesheim: Verlag August Lax).

Index

Bold numbers denote references to illustrations

Abbots Worthy (Hants) 2
Æcerbot charm 139
Aerial photography 3, 16, 70, 105
Alchester (Oxon) 146–7
Animal bones, *see* faunal remains
Animal husbandry 99, 129, 155–61, 163, 166

Barking (Essex) 4, 5, 153
Barley 146, 149–50, 152; *see also* crop husbandry, plant remains
Barns 23 n., 37, 46, 50–1, 73, 84, 114–15, 152, 155
Barrow Hills, Radley, *see* Barton Court Farm (Oxon)
Barton Court Farm (Oxon) 4, 5, 12, 61, 143, 145
Baston, Hall Farm (Lincs) 4, 5, 84, 88, 95
Bayeux Tapestry 45
Bede, the Venerable 7, 21, 43, 53, 102, 105, 139, 141, 149
'Beowulf' 34, 102
Bicester (Oxon) 4, 5, 26 n., 41–2, 46, **47**–8, 50
Bishopstone (Sussex) 4, 5, 28, 36, 45, 52, 87, 95, 100 n., 137, 157, 162
Black Bourton (Oxon) 4, 5, 142
Bloodmoor Hill, *see* Carlton Colville (Suffolk)
Boldon Book 47
Botolphs (Sussex) 57, 61
Bramford (Suffolk) **113**, 127
Brandon (Suffolk) 4, 5, 9, 133, 157–8, 161–2
Brandon Road, *see* Thetford
Bread wheat 149–51, 154; *see also* spelt, wheat
Brooklands (Bucks) 136
Broome (Norfolk) 4, 5, 34
Building techniques 22, 27–32, 48
Buildings
    Cellared buildings 137, 140
    Grubenhäuser 7, 8, 11, 12, 15, 21, 31, 44, 50, 53–66, 69, 70, 71 n., 73, 78, 80, 83, 94, 95, 98, 101 n., 117, 119, 124, 130, 131, 135, 136, 138, 141, 143, 146 n., 148, 159, 167
        Dimensions of 54, 64
        Entrances to 58
        Fills of 60
        Floors in 56–7, 58, 59
        Functions of 56, 59, 60–4, 85 n., 121, 137, 140, 158
        Reconstructions of 55–60
        Relationship to earth-fast buildings 59, 64–6
        Stakeholes in the base of 57, 58
    'Hybrid' buildings 65–6, 141
    Stone buildings 48
    Timber buildings, earth-fast 17–53, 55, 56, 67, 70, 73, 83, 98, 99, 100, 111, 114, 117, 119, 124, 137, 141
        Annexed 21, 22, **23**, 35, 39, 40, 41, 141
        Chronological development of 22–**4**, 26–7
        Entrances to 20 n., 25, 40–3, 48, 105, 107
        Floor surfaces in 43, 44, 48, 50, 106
        Functions of 46–53, 63, 127
        Ground plans of 25–7
        'life cycles' of 32, 33–7, 48, 67, 165
        Regional variation 31–3
        Relationship to *Grubenhäuser* 59, 64–6
    Roundhouses/other circular structures 53, 142
    see also barns, churches, halls, kitchens, latrines
Burhs 109–10
Burials 39, 43 n., 50, 91, 106–7, 109, 121–9, 132–3, 139, 141, 165; *see also* cemeteries, 'deviant' burials
Butley (Suffolk) 130 n.

Cadbury-Congresbury (Som) 4, 5, 33
Canterbury 59
Car Dyke (Cambs) 138
Carlton Colville, Bloodmoor Hill (Suffolk) 4, 5, 6, 57, 85 n. 9, 124–6, 127, 165
Cassington (Oxon) 95
Catholme (Staffs) 4, 5, 6, 27, 35, 89, 91, **93**, 94, 116 n., **134**
Cattle 89–90, 107, 131, 133, 135, 139, 140, 148, 155, 157, 159–61, 162 n.;
    see also animal husbandry, faunal remains
Cemeteries
    Anglo-Saxon xi, 71, 81, 100 n., 113, 117, 120–9, 141–3; *see also* burials
    Romano-British 10–11
Cesspits 52, 84, 94, 111; *see also* latrines
Chalton (Hants) 3, 4, 5, 39, 40, 41 n., 64 n., 102, **104**, 105, 117 n., 141 n., 151
Cheddar (Som) 4, 5, 8, 26 n., 41–2, 45, 46, 48, 52, 111, 133, 135–6
Churches, churchyards 27, 39, 53, 80 n., 107, 110, 126–9, 133, 142, 154
Coinage 3, 99–100, 107, 137, 166–7

Collingbourne Ducis, Cadley Road (Wilts) 4, 5, 83, 156 n.
Corbridge (Northumb) 4, 5, 152, 154
Corn dryers 146–7, 151, 155; *see also* malting ovens
Corrals 71, 115; *see also* enclosures, paddocks
Cossington (Leics) 4, 5, 143
Cottam (Yorks) 4, 5, 32, 88 n., 135
Cottenham (Cambs) 4, 5, 6, 73, **74–5**, 83, 88, 90, 91, 160, 164–5
Cowdery's Down (Hants) 3, 8, 20 n., **23**, 29, **30**, 34, 39, 40, 44, 46, 48, 102, **103**, **104**, 105, 107, 117 n., 133, 138, 140, 141
Craft production 95, 99, 100; *see also* metalworking, textile production
Crofts 84, 85
Crop husbandry 129, 146–55, 163, 166; *see also* barley, fields, manuring, oats, ploughs, rye, wheat

Dalem (Germany) 63
'deviant' burials 129, 135; *see also* burials
Domesday Book 1, 7, 152
Dorchester-on-Thames (Oxon) 145
Dorney, Lake End Road (Berks) 3 n., 4, 5, 95
Drayton (Oxon), *see* Sutton Courtenay
Droveways 71 n., 73, 78, 80, 89–90, 98, 128, 145, 149, 163–4; *see also* trackways

Eastry (Kent) 122 n.
Ebbsfleet (Kent) 4, 5, 151–2, **154**
Edwin, king of Northumbria 7, 102
Ely, West Fen Road (Cambs) 4, 5, 75–**6**, 85, 88, 90, 91, 159, 164–5, 167
Emporia 1, 87, 96, 156, 159–61, 166, 168; *see also* towns
Enclosed settlements 73, 109–19
Enclosures **23**, 40, 71, 72, 73–4, 75, 78, 80, 81, 83, 85, 88–90, 91–4, 98, 101 n., 105, 109–14, 117, 119, 126, 128, 133, 141–2, 163–4, 166; *see also* paddocks, corrals
Estate centres 100, 117, 126, 153–4, 159; *see also* high status settlements
Eye Kettleby (Leics) 4, 5, 34, 44, 64 n., 65, 71, 94, 136
Eynsham (Oxon) 4, 5,
  Eynsham Abbey 52, 135–6, 161
  New Wintles Farm 39, 83, 141

Faccombe Netherton (Hants) 4, 5, 43, 44, 48 n., **49**, 52, 110 n., 117 n.
Farming, *see* animal husbandry, crop husbandry, fields/field systems
Faunal remains 50, 99, 106, 107, 130–3, 135–6, 155–62
Feasting, evidence for 50, 100, 106, 135, 139; *see also* faunal remains

Feltham (Middlesex) 151
Fields / field systems xii, 78, 83, 85, 90, 91, 94, 111, 144–9, 151, 164–6; *see also* crop husbandry, ploughs
Field surveys/ fieldwalking 3, 145, 165
Flixborough (Lincs) 4, 5, 9, 27, 32, 34–5, 44, 85 n., 99–101, 126, 129, 157, 159, 161, 165
Flixton Park Quarry (Suffolk) 4, 5, 65, 122, 141, 143
Foxley (Wilts) **104**, 105
Fremington (Cumbria) 4, 5, 31
Friars Oak (Sussex) 4, 5, 131, 136
Frocester Court villa (Glocs) 14

Gamlingay (Cambs) 4, 5, 71 n., 80–3, 126–7, 129, 155, 165
Gates 52, 80, 100 n., 110–11, 113, 114, **117**
Gerefa 46, 110 n., 154
Geþyncdo (the 'promotion law') 52, 110
Gillingham (Dorset) 152 n.
Godmanchester (Cambs) 4, 5, 71 n., 73, **76**, 90, 98 n., 137, 145–6
Goltho (Lincs) 4, 5, 26 n., 27 n., 28 n., 36, 41, **42**, 46, 48, 49, 50, 52, 115, 117, 157
Grain storage 61–2, 140, 151–2; *see also* granaries
Granaries 12, 46, 50, 80, 81, 83, 98, 152; *see also* grain storage
Gravesend (Kent) 95
'Great halls', *see* halls
Grubenhäuser, *see* Buildings
Gudme (Denmark) 107, 138

Halls 9, 17 n., 34, 46–**9**, 102–4, 105, 106–9, 111, 117, 140; *see also* buildings, 'Long halls', 'narrow-aisled' halls
Hamwic 26, 87, 95, 156
Hartlepool (Co. Durham) 4, 5, 32, 41, 100
Hatton Rock (Warwickshire) 104 n.
Hay meadows 90, 129, 148, 149, 161, 164
Hearths 43–5, 46, 48, 50, **51**, 52, 55, 57–8, 64 n., 83, 106, 115, 135, 151
Hefting 89
Hereford 151
High status settlements 1, 52, 100–9, 116, 117, 135, 143, 157, 161–2, 164; *see also* estate centres, settlement status
Higham Ferrers (Northants) 4, 5 28, 35, 51, 113–15, **116**, 152, **153** 164
Hoddom (Dumfriesshire) 4, 5, 152
Horses 131, 133, 138, 161 n.; *see also* faunal remains
Horticulture 150, 164
Households, size of 122–3; *see also* population size
Hunting 100, 162
Hurst Park, East Molsey (Surrey) 58 n.

Index

Ipswich 4, 5
Ipswich Ware 71 n., 78, 80, 99, 142, 166

Jarrow (Co. Durham) 4, 5, 100, 105, 161

Ketton (Rutland) 4, 5, **49**, **118**, 142
Kilns 78; *see also* ovens
Kilverstone (Norfolk) 71, **72**, 94
Kitchens 44, 46, 48–50, 53, 106, 110, 111

Lakenheath (Suffolk) 4, 5, 15, 121
Latrines 46, 52–3, 94, 95; *see also* cesspits
Law codes, Anglo-Saxon 45, 139
  of Ine, king of Wessex 43, 89, 109
Lechlade, Sherborne House (Glocs) 57 n.
Leicester, Bonners Lane 66
Linford (Essex) 8; *see also* Mucking
Little Paxton (Hunts) 111
London 26, 45, 151, 160
'Long halls' 26 n., 41, **42**, 45, 46–7, 48, 50, 116; *see also* halls
Longhouses, Continental 17, 19, 20, 21, 26, 43 n., 140
'long ranges' 104 n., 116, 117 n.
Looms/ loomweights 59, 63; *see also* textile production
Lyminge (Kent) 61 n., 85 n., 95, 148

Malting ovens 50, 64 n., 115, 152, **153**, 164; *see also* corn dryers
Manuring 150; *see also* crop husbandry
Market Lavington (Wilts) 4, 5, 130 n., 148, 150
Markets 3 n., 150, 156, 159, 166; *see also* trade
Mawgan Porth (Cornwall) 4, 5, 33
Maxey Ware 71 n.
Measurements, used in buildings and settlements 25, 91
Melford Meadows (Suffolk) 4, 5, 155
Metal-detector use 3
Metalworking, evidence for 61, 64 n., 84, 85 n., 100 n., 108–9, 115, 119
Middens 1, 50, 60, 61, 69, 95, 99, 119, 124, 150
Migrations, Anglo-Saxon 16, 19
Milfield (Northumb) 4, 5, 105–6
Monasteries 1, 100, 101, 105, 135, 148, 159, 161, 163, 164 n., 166
Monkwearmouth (Co. Durham) 100, 161
Mucking (Essex) 4, 5, 6, 8, 9, 14, 15, 17, 18, 25, 34, 54, 61 n., 67, **68**, 69, 71, 78, 121, 122, 126 n., 136, 143; *see also* Linford

'Narrow-aisled' halls 48, 116, 117; *see also* halls
Nettleton Top (Lincs) 94
New Wintles Farm, *see* Eynsham
Northampton 4, 5, 48
North Elmham (Norfolk) 4, 5, 24, 35, 40, 41, 43, 44, 48, 52, **86**, 87
Nucleated settlements 94, 149, 150–1, 165, 167

Oats 150, 152, 154, 161; *see also* crop husbandry, plant remains
Old Erringham (West Sussex) 158–9
Old Windsor 4, 5, 153
Orton Hall Farm (Northants) 4, 5, 12, 14, 50
Orton Waterville (Northants) 77
Ovens 46, 48, 49, 50, 63, 94, 115, 119, 151–2; *see also* kilns, malting ovens
Oxen, *see* cattle

Paddocks 71, 73, 77, 80, 85, 89, 91, 98, 149–50; *see also* enclosures, corrals
Pakenham (Suffolk) 158–9
Pasture 89, 148; *see also* animal husbandry
Paulinus, St., bishop of Northumbra 102
Peasants 52
Pennyland (Bucks) 4, 5, 9, 50, 78, **81**, 98 n., 159
Pigs 131, 157, 160–2; *see also* animal husbandry, faunal remains
Pits 3, 50, 83, 94–5, 98, 106, 107, 111, 121, 124, 130, 131, 135, 142, 167; *see also* cesspits
Place-names 6, 83 n., 152
'Placed' deposits 43, 106–8, 120, 129–40, 160 n.
Planning in settlements 69, 70, 91, 94, 102
Plant remains 50, 115, 146, 149, 151–2, 155
Ploughs/ ploughing 90, 148, 150, 164; *see also* crop husbandry, fields
Polebrook (Northants) 4, 5, 28 n., 44, 106 n.
Pollen analysis 144, 147–8, 150
Population size, estimates of 71; *see also* households
Portchester (Hants) 4, 5, 30, 40, 41, 44, 45, 48 n., 49, 110
Poundbury, Dorchester (Dorset) 4, 5, 11, 33
Prehistoric monuments, re-use of 50, 105–6, 120, 141–3
Prittlewell (Essex), princely burial 40 n.
'productive sites' 3 n.
Puddlehill (Beds) 136 n.

Quarrington (Lincs) 4, 5, 31, 53, 91, **92**, 159
Queenford Farm, Romano-British cemetery (Oxon) 11

Radiocarbon dates 58 n., 83, 124, 127, 129, 135, 148, 152–3
Raunds, Furnells (Northants) 4, 5, 46 n., **49**, 88, 105 n., 117, **119**, 147
Raunds, West Cotton (Northants) 4, 5, 148
Rectilinear settlements 72–8, 88, 90–4, 151 n.
Rectitudines Singularum Personarum 98
Renhold, Water End West (Beds) 4, 5, 35, **36**, 40, 43, 46, 151
Ribblehead, Gauber High Pasture (Yorks) 4, 5, 9, 32
Riby Cross Roads (Lincs) 4, 5, 9, 90, 101 n.
Ritual structures 39, 50, 106, 120, 131, 140–2

Rivenhall (Essex) 4, 5, 13
Riverdene (Hants) 71
Romano-British buildings and settlements 10–15, 16, 19, 20, 144, 146–7, 168; *see also* villas
Ryall Quarry (Worcs) 4, 5, 15, 58 n., 65
Rye 149–50; *see also* crop husbandry

St Albans (Herts) 161 n.
Saltwood (Kent) 122
Sceattas, *see* Coinage
Scole (Essex) 150
Settlement hierarchy, *see* settlement status
Settlement patterns xii, 2–3, 10
Settlement shift 67–70, 95 n.
Settlement status 52, 72, 98–101, 109–10, 119; *see also* high status settlements
Shakenoak (Oxon) 4, 5, 11, 14
Sheep 89, 131–2, 155–7, 160, 162 n.; *see also* animal husbandry, textile production, wool
Shrines, *see* ritual structures
Simy Folds (Co. Durham) 4, 5, 32
Spelt 146, 149, 151; *see also* crop husbandry, wheat
Spong Hill (Norfolk) 4, 5, 122, 137
Springfield Lyons (Essex) 4, 5, 28, 35, 40, 41, 44, 45, 50, 95, 111, **112**, 143, 151
Sprouston (Roxboroughshire) 4, 5
Stafford 148, 151
Steyning (Sussex) 4, 5, 27, 28, **29**, 85–6, 95, 110, 111, 167
Streethouse (Yorks) 121
Sulgrave (Northants) 4, 5, 26 n., **42**, 46–8, 50, 117 n.
Sutton Courtenay (Oxon) 4, 5, 7, 17, 102, **103**, 105, 108–9, 131 n., 133

Tamworth (Staffs) 2 n., 4, 5, 28 n., 153
Textile production 63–4, 99, 137–8, 156–9; *see also* looms/loomweights, sheep, wool
Thetford (Norfolk) 4, 5, 61, 70, 117
Thirlings (Northumb) 4, 5, 21, 31, 39
Thwing (Yorks) 4, 5, 143
Tissø (Denmark) 107
Tofts 73, 88
Tools 100, 119, 137
Towers 45, 53, 111, 137

Towns 1, 85–7, 159; *see also emporia*
Trackways 73, 80, 83, 85, 89, 91, 101 n., 116, 126; *see also* droveways
Trade 95, 99, 101 n.; *see also* markets

Uppäkra (Sweden) 107, 138
Upton (Northants) 4, 5, 59, 137, 158–9

Villas, Romano-British 1, 2, 9, 10–15, 16, 144–5
Viticulture 150, 164

Walpole St Andrews (Norfolk) 149 n.
Wareham (Dorset) 153
Warmington (Northants) 4, 5, **79**, 164 n., 165
Wasperton (Warwicks) 11
Watermills 2 n., 117, 152–5, 163, 164
Wellington (Worcs) 4, 5, 153
Wells 80, 87, 94, 95, 98, 111
West Cotton (Northants) 117, 153
West Heslerton (Yorks) 4, 5, 6, 9, 14, 15–16, 31, 33, 54, 65, 69, 71, 122–3, 138
West Stow (Suffolk) 4, 5, 18, 19, 34, 44, 54, 55, 58, 60, 67, 70 n., 71, 78, **80**, 131 n., 133, 155–7
Wharram Percy (Yorks) 4, 5, 58 n., 61, 64 n., 88 n., 132
Wheat 90, 146, 149–50, 152; *see also* bread wheat, spelt
Whithorn (Dumfries and Galloway) 4, 5, 32
Wicken Bonhunt (Essex) 4, 5, 50, 87, 88, 161
Wics, see *emporia*
Wijster (Netherlands) 19, 20 n.
Wolverton (Bucks) 4, 5, 77, 90, 152, 156, 161 n., 164 n.
Wool 156–7; *see also* sheep, textile production
Wykeham (Yorks) 4, 5, 8, 130 n.

Yarnton (Oxon) 4, 5, 6, 35, 50, **51**, 83, **84**, 90, 93, 95, **96**, **97**, 124, 127, 129, 148, 150, 157, 161 n., 165
Yeavering (Northumb) 4, 5, 8, 17 n., 25, 28 n., 34, 39, 43, 44, 46, 48, 50, 53, 59, 65, 99, 102, **103**, 104–8, 117, 133, 135, 138–41, 143 n., 160–1
York 45

Zones within settlements 64, 70, 94–8, 99, 111

Printed and bound by CPI Group (UK) Ltd, Croydon, CR0 4YY